Manual Communication
Implications for Education

Harry Bornstein, Editor

Gallaudet University Press
Washington, D.C.

Gallaudet University Press, Washington, D.C. 20002
© 1990 by Gallaudet University. All rights reserved
Published 1990
Printed in the United States of America

Library of Congress Cataloging-in-Publication Data

Manual communication: implications for education / Harry Bornstein, editor.
    p.   cm.
   Includes bibliographical references and index.
   Contents: Manual codes on English and American sign language / Joseph D. Stedt, Donald F. Moores—A manual communication overview / Harry Bornstein—Communication in classrooms for deaf students / Thomas E. Allen, Michael A. Karchmer—Sign English in the education of deaf students / James Woodward—ASL and its implications for education / Robert J. Hoffmeister—Signing exact English / Gerilee Gustason—Signed English / Harry Bornstein—Cued speech / Elizabeth L. Kipila, Barbara Williams-Scott—Manual communication with those who can hear / George R. Karlan—Some afterwords / Harry Bornstein.
   ISBN 0-930323-57-2: $34.95
   1. Deaf—United States—Mean of communication. 2. Sign language. 3. Deaf—Education—United States. I. Bornstein, Harry.
HV2471.M36 1990
419—dc20

90-40934
CIP

Contents

Contributors

Thomas E. Allen, Ph.D.
Office of Assessment and
  Demographic Studies
Gallaudet University
Washington, D.C.

Harry Bornstein, Ph.D.
610 Teresita Boulevard
San Francisco, California

Gerilee Gustason, Ph.D.
Department of Special Education
San Jose State University
San Jose, California

Robert J. Hoffmeister, Ph.D.
School of Education
Boston University
Boston, Massachusetts

Michael A. Karchmer, Ph.D.
Graduate Studies and Research
Gallaudet University
Washington, D.C.

George R. Karlan, Ph.D.
Department of Educational
  Studies
Purdue University
West Lafayette, Indiana

Elizabeth L. Kipila, M.A.
Department of Audiology
Gallaudet University
Washington, D.C.

Donald F. Moores, Ph.D.
Center for Studies in Education
  and Human Development
Gallaudet University
Washington, D.C.

Joseph D. Stedt, Ph.D.
Department of Psychology
Cameron State University
Lawton, Oklahoma

Barbara Williams-Scott, M.A.
Department of Audiology
Gallaudet University
Washington, D.C.

James Woodward, Ph.D.
Culture and Communication
  Studies Program
Gallaudet University
Washington, D.C.

Preface

About twelve years ago, the editor prepared a chapter called "Systems of Sign" for inclusion in a comprehensive text entitled *Hearing and Hearing Impairment* (Bradford and Hardy, eds., New York: Grune and Stratton, 1979). In that chapter I attempted to present an overview of the varieties of manual communication that might be used with deaf students in educational settings. Those who have devised manual systems have continued to refine these tools. Additional research has been done on American Sign Language (ASL) and other manual language varieties. Also, much has happened to the social status of ASL that is worth reporting, not the least of which has been the change in image of signing from stigmata to prideful cultural symbol, as epitomized in the recent selection of a deaf president of Gallaudet University. It has also become clear that there are a number of variables that markedly affect using hands and eyes in communicating with other human beings that were not adequately covered earlier. In short, it is time for a much more comprehensive work on this very complex topic.

This text attempts to offer an authoritative description of manual communication as it is used in the United States. It is designed for professionals who work with deaf and language-delayed children and adolescents (including some who may hear). It should also be useful for teachers-in-training and interested parents. It begins with a history and overview of the logic and nature of manual communication in schools in the United States. These chapters are designed to enable the reader to better understand and evaluate the information that follows. Next, descriptions of usage, present and past, are offered by scholars who have much experience and special research expertise.

Each of the remaining chapters has been prepared by (a) a recognized student of a language variety, such as ASL or Pidgin Sign English, (PSE) or (b) a major designer or administrator of Manual English systems, such as Signing Exact English, Signed English, and Cued Speech. Far too often, professionals and students learn about these communication systems or techniques from secondary sources, many of which are incomplete and/or contain serious errors and biases.

Here, in somewhat more detail, is how the book is organized:

The opening chapter by Stedt and Moores provides a history of manual communication in United States education. It describes both native and foreign influences. Most readers will be surprised at the persistence of the differing viewpoints and how contemporary the arguments appear.

Next, I offer an overview of factors that affect manual communication. These include learner characteristics, the basic logic and physical characteristics of some varieties of manual communication, and the research evidence that bears on their effectiveness.

Allen and Karchmer analyze the responses of the teachers of a nationwide sample of students and report patterns of communicative use that vary by educational setting, degree of deafness, teacher characteristics, etc. Using the same sample, Woodward reports on teacher-stated use of manual systems. He also offers a description of PSE usage and its salient features.

Hoffmeister, from a bilingual's perspective, describes ASL and makes recommendations for its best use in school settings.

Two manual English systems in current use, Signing Exact English and Signed English, are separately described by their chief designers, Gustason and me. Kipila and Williams-Scott, who administer the Cued Speech office, give a description of this supplement to speech.

All these chapters are directed at the education of deaf children. In recent decades, signs have also come to be more widely used in the education of language-delayed children who are able to hear but suffer from mental retardation, cerebral palsy, etc. Karlan offers a description of the work being done in this important area. He pays special attention to the selection and teaching of a child's initial vocabulary.

In the closing chapter, I offer a subjective explanation of why people behave as they do in this highly controversial field. Different points of view are persistent and strong. The reader may be sure that many others believe they have explanations that are much more accurate and plausible.

Some early words about nomenclature should be useful because different writers use different names for the same type of manual communication. Manual systems that have been specifically designed to represent English are variously called English, Manual English, contrived manual systems, manual codes, or methodical signs. The two Manual English systems most widely used in the United States are *Signing Exact English* and *Signed English*.

Signing that is used simultaneously with spoken or voiced English can be called *Sign English*, *Pidgin Sign English*, or *Siglish*. Signing that is used without intent to represent English or to communicate with an English-speaking person is termed *Sign* or *American Sign Language*.

Outside of the chapter that deals with the history of manual communication, the terms you will most frequently see in this book are ASL, PSE, and Manual English.

I would like to thank Mrs. Karen L. Saulnier for her comments on early drafts of my three chapters and also Mr. Arthur N. Schildroth for CADS data and his comments on the use of the same data.

I would also like to thank Grune and Stratton for permission to use Table 3 in chapter 2 and the American Annals of the Deaf for Table 1 in chapter 7.

CHAPTER 1

Manual Codes on English and American Sign Language: Historical Perspectives and Current Realities

Joseph D. Stedt, Donald F. Moores

What experience and history teach is this—that people and governments never have learned anything from history, or acted on principles developed from it.

Georg Wilhelm Friedrich Hegel, 1832

The development of English-based sign systems and their rapid spread throughout the 1970s have introduced almost revolutionary changes in the modes of communication used with deaf children in classroom settings. The acceptance and adoption of these pedagogical systems after decades of adherence to oral-only programs of instruction has led some educators of the deaf to believe that English-based signs— or signs based on a spoken national language—are recent developments in themselves. Such a belief demonstrates a total lack of historical perspective.

The almost inevitable resultant conflict between proponents of English-based signs and American Sign Language (ASL) in contemporary America also has been perceived as *sui generis*, whereas the nineteenth century in the United States and the eighteenth and nineteenth centuries in France are replete with cycles of conflict between "natural" and "methodical" signs. Because American educators of the deaf have been preoccupied with the oral-manual controversy, there is little awareness of the fact that the ASL/Signed English— to use contemporary terms—debate in the

1

United States precedes the oral-manual controversy and at times has been even more acrimonious. The authors of this chapter, in 1983, made the argument that such controversy is misplaced and that both ASL and some form of English-based signing will continue to exist because they fulfill distinct needs. It is hoped that an explication of previous developments can help us build on the work of our predecessors while avoiding at least some of their mistakes.

HISTORICAL PERSPECTIVE

It comes as a surprise to most educators of the deaf to learn that there is much more historical information on English-based sign systems in the United States than there is on natural sign languages. That is because the first instructional system for the deaf introduced to this country was based on the French system of "methodical" signs, a system consciously developed to illustrate the syntax and vocabulary of French. In order to understand the principles of methodical signs, it is necessary to consider the development of education of the deaf in France by the Abbé Charles Michel de l'Epée and subsequent modifications by his successor, Abbé Roch Ambroise Cucurron Sicard.

Methodical Signs and Education of the Deaf in France

The Abbé de l'Epée does not hold the distinction of being the first teacher of the deaf in France, or even the first teacher to use signs in instruction (Moores 1987). His contribution lay more in his efforts to integrate two apparently disparate forms of communication into an instructional medium that could express the full range of French syntax and vocabulary. Epée's original efforts involved the analysis and modification of signs used by deaf people in Paris in such a way as to develop a visual analog to written French.

Through a serendipitous introduction to the first manuscript ever written on education of the deaf, Bonet's (1620) *The Reduction of Letters and the Art of Teaching the Mute to Speak*, Epée became acquainted with the Spanish Manual Alphabet. He had the insight to understand that the manual alphabet and signs could be synthesized to develop a new system of communication that could be used in the instruction of deaf children.

Epée, then, invented what might be considered a manual code on French, if not a full-fledged language. The signs used by Epée were ordered in the methodical syntax of French, hence the name "methodical signs."

In the development of individual signs, Epée frequently invented "initialized" signs; that is, he would add a handshape from the manual alphabet to an existing sign. For example, the sign *good* (which is identical to the present-day ASL sign) was initiated with fingerspelled *B*'s to represent the French *bon*. Similarly, days of the week were differentiated through handshape, as were colors and other categories.

Epée also developed signs for all French bound morphemes and function words. An example of his impact on ASL is the fact that his invented gender signs for the French articles *le* (male) and *la* (female) are used by current signers as root morphemes for ASL nouns (*man, brother, boy, woman, sister, girl*, etc.).

In Epée's system each verb had signs for mood and tense and each noun had indicators of number and gender. In addition, his approach was analytical. According to Bebian ([1817], Lane 1984a) he sought signs in the "physical decomposition" of French words rather than from nature (ibid. 140). Because Epée had an orientation toward classical languages, many of the signs he invented were based on Latin or Greek etymology. For example, he developed root and bound morpheme signs for the work *comprendre* (to understand) as follows:

comprendre = prende + avec
(Latin cum) = take with

Instead of using one sign for a word, he would break it down into two or more morphemes that together did not adequately reflect the meaning of the word. Other examples include:

French	Latin Base	English Equivalent
satisfaire	facere + statis	to do enough
introduire	ducere + intro	to lead into

In English it would be similar, without going back to Latin roots, to sign *understand* using two signs:

understand = under + stand

Thus, using two signed morphemes, *under + stand*, instead of the commonly accepted sign for *understand*, may dimly reflect the etymology of the English word used, but it does not contribute to speed or fluency. This is especially true when a word might require five or more signs to represent it grammatically. Lane (1984b) cited Epée on the development of the signs for the French equivalent of the English word, *unintelligibility*: The two base signs came from the Latin *legere + intus* (to read + within). Added to these would be signs of negation, possibility, and abstract quality. As might be expected, the system was slow, artificial, and cumbersome, although Epée claimed the signs could be made "in the twinkling of an eye" (Bender 1970, 84).

Despite the claim that methodical signs could be quickly produced, they were found to take too long for fluent communication. The original signs of Epée were soon produced in shortened versions called "signes raccourcis," or shortened signs. The entire system that was developed for teaching deaf children was explained in Epée's book, *The Instruction of the Deaf and Dumb by Means of Methodical Signs*, published in 1776. Eight years later, an expanded version of this work was published, titled *The True Manner of Instructing the Deaf and Dumb Confirmed by a Long Experience*. It finally appeared in English translation 200 years later.

The curriculum in the Paris institution under Epée concentrated almost completely on French for most of the four or five years of a typical student's attendance. The primary goal was literacy. Initial instruction began with the manual alphabet, leading to the reading, writing, and signing of French nouns. The second level concentrated on formal instruction in French verbs, adverbs, prepositions, and pronouns, to be followed by attention to French syntax. It wasn't until near the end of a student's education that subjects such as history and geography received attention.

When Abbé de l'Epée died, his work was continued by Roch Ambroise Cucurron Sicard (1741–1822). In 1818 Sicard published *The Theory of Signs* (Theorie des Signes), which was an elaborate, two-volume dictionary of signs. Volume 1 consisted of nouns and adjectives and Volume 2 had verbs and grammatical signs. The signs were arranged in classes, with each group of signs having a mimetic root sign. For example, with the root sign of *house* the appropriate initializations and additions produced signs to indicate *village, city, hamlet, palace, church*, and *hotel*.

Sicard was critical of some of the extremes of Epée's system and his method of instruction. He claimed ([1800], Lane 1984a) that pupils could translate from French to sign under Epée but they didn't understand what they did. According to Sicard, the deaf students were not taught to compose sentences themselves but were merely trained as automatons would be to translate what was presented. He also emphasized that the sign language used in instruction was given to the students by Epée. It should be stressed, however, that Sicard modified Epée's methodical signs and made them more efficient, but did not introduce any new sign system or language to instruction. Clerc, in commenting on Sicard's modifications of Epée's system (1818, 3), noted that "every invention or discovery, however, ingenious and laudable it may be, is never quite right in its beginning."

Clerc's Instructional Sign System

The early French system of methodical signs may be described as "prescriptive." The system was developed to teach a rather formal, "correct," literate French and was based on the prevalent classical orientation of the time. Educators of the deaf at this time were not particularly concerned with dialects or everyday communication. The system, although reflecting a narrow and rigid view of language and communication, was developed to a high degree of sophistication by brilliant scholars such as Epée and Sicard. It was at this point of development that the American, Thomas Hopkins Gallaudet, visited Paris in 1816 to investigate the efficacy of the French system of teaching the deaf and its potential application in the United States. After studying with Sicard at the Paris institution for several months, Gallaudet returned to the United States in August 1816 with Laurent Clerc, a brilliant deaf teacher who had been educated by Sicard. On April 15, 1817, the Connecticut Asylum for the Education of the Deaf and Dumb (now the American School for the Deaf) was opened in Hartford, Connecticut, with Gallaudet serving as the first principal and Laurent Clerc as the first teacher for the original seven students.

Clerc was a remarkable individual who had an awesome responsibility. According to a diary of his voyage to America (1817), Clerc's duties were agreed upon as: (1) being the first teacher of the deaf in the United States, (2) instructing Gallaudet and new teachers in methods of teaching the deaf, and (3) instructing Gallaudet and new teachers in the use of methodical signs. All of this was to be conducted in a language he did not know—English. Before leaving Paris, Gallaudet began teaching Clerc English while Clerc taught Gallaudet signs. This continued on an intensive basis

during the fifty-two-day trip from France to America. Less than a year later, Clerc had developed an English-based methodical sign system established on the same principles as Epée's French methodical signs.

Clerc used the Spanish/French manual alphabet as a basic component of his American methodical sign system. This enabled him to continue the process of initialization, which Epée and Sicard had employed extensively. In some cases, he simply changed the handshape to represent English rather than French spelling, as in days of the week (*M* for *Monday*, instead of *L* for *lundi*), or colors (*G* for *green* instead of *V* for *vert*). The influence of French signs in American sign systems is clear to this day, and there are numerous American signs that reflect French spelling through the handshapes of the manual alphabet. These include the *A* handshape for *other* (*autre*), *B* for *good* (*bon*), *C* for *hundred* (*cent*), *M* for *thousand* (*mille*), and *C* for *search* (*chercher*). We have been unable to find any explanation of why Clerc didn't change all the initialized signs to reflect English spelling. Possibly there were functional constraints on sign constitution. For example, signing *good* with *G* handshapes might be confused with the sign for *correct*; the movement involved in the sign for *other* may be more comfortable with an *A* handshape, etc. Quite possibly Clerc himself might have been unaware of the representation of French in some of the signs.

Indigenous Sign Languages

Clerc's methodical sign system, in addition to having an English-based sign vocabulary, also followed English word order. This system, then, provided the base for the later development of what is known as American Sign Language (ASL), although ASL has a syntax that is different from that of English. Given the significant differences between ASL and English, there has been speculation that Clerc's methodical sign system may have merged with one or more sign languages existing in America prior to the establishment of the American School for the Deaf. Special interest has been focused on the community of Martha's Vineyard, an island off the coast of Massachusetts that had a large deaf population due to generations of inbreeding among a homogeneous population with a pool of recessive genes for deafness (Groce 1981, 1985). According to Groce, the first deaf inhabitant of Martha's Vineyard was Jonathan Lambert, who moved to the island in 1694. Lambert and his hearing wife were parents of seven children, two of whom were deaf. The numbers of deaf people on the island increased over a period of 150 years, especially in a few isolated communities settled by populations of Kentish stock moving from Massachusetts. The population of deaf islanders peaked around the middle of the nineteenth century and then rapidly declined, due to an influx of "mainlanders" and Portuguese fishermen and an out-migration of the island population to the mainland. The dramatic effects of intermarriage on genetic deafness are attested to by the fact that only fifteen deaf individuals remained on the island by 1900, four by 1925, and one by 1945 (Groce 1981, 234).

When Groce conducted her research in the late 1970s, there were no deaf people remaining on the island. Most of her information was gathered through oral histories by means of interviews with elderly hearing natives of the island, who recollected experiences from their early lives with the few remaining deaf islanders. From her work, Groce concluded that the hearing population of Martha's Vineyard, at least those in communities with large numbers of deaf people, maintained bilingual communication, based on spoken English and a sign language. She concluded that the deaf had no communication barriers to overcome and participated in all aspects of the community, sometimes as leaders.

No description of the sign language exists and Groce (ibid., 154) concluded that it may be impossible to reconstruct it. Groce noted that the island sign language appeared to have acquired many aspects of ASL during the nineteenth century and that the last deaf island inhabitant, a very elderly woman, used the manual alphabet.

The dearth of information about the sign language itself during the peak of the deaf population, in the 1840s, prevents us from ascertaining to what extent, if any, Martha's Vineyard's sign influenced the development of ASL. Of approximately eighty deaf individuals on the island over a period of 250 years, more than half, apparently, were alive in the middle of the nineteenth century. Groce (ibid., 123) reported that there was a significant deaf population in the 1840s in five of the six island communities (the exception was Gay Head, an Indian community). One out of every twenty people in Chilmark, the most isolated community on the island, was deaf at this time, with one of four people in one neighborhood of sixty people and seven families, identified as deaf. Since the 1850 Census count for Chilmark was 846 (ibid., 116), a rate of one deaf person per twenty-five residents leads to an estimated thirty-four deaf people in Chilmark alone. It is from this time that information is needed about the lives of the members of the Deaf community in Martha's Vineyard and the ways in which they communicated.

Through the help of the Alexander Graham Bell Association, Groce gained access to materials compiled by Bell in his research in the nineteenth century on the deaf population of Martha's Vineyard (ibid., 53–58). Bell compiled a list of all islanders known to be deaf, which Groce was able to utilize in her research. He also talked (whether he used signs is not clear) with several deaf residents of Chilmark and obtained "oral" histories.

According to Groce (ibid., 57), Bell confined himself solely to genealogical materials and made no comment on linguistic or social aspects of life for deaf residents of Chilmark. Bell did not mention the use of signs on the island, either of a local variety or of ones in general use throughout the United States. Perhaps this is not surprising, given Bell's well-known antipathy to signs (Moores 1987), but he certainly expressed his opposition in other environments. It should be noted that the relatively large numbers of deaf people on Martha's Vineyard was a contributing factor to Bell's later publications, *Memoir on the Formation of a Deaf Variety of the Human Race* (1883), and "Fallacies Concerning the Deaf" (1884). Bell proposed, among other things, that marriages among the congenitally deaf should be prevented and that a practical step might even include forbidding the marriage of anyone—hearing or deaf—"belonging to families containing more than one deaf mute" (ibid., 45).

Groce (1981) reported that deaf residents of Martha's Vineyard were sent to the American School for the Deaf in the 1820s and 1830s. Interestingly enough, she reported that the deaf of Martha's Vineyard, during the last half of the nineteenth century, were better educated than the hearing population of the island. The deaf members of the community could read and write at a time when literacy on the island was not widespread. Perhaps the favorable position of deaf islanders was due as much to their educational attainments at the American School as to a sign system.

Since islanders were sent to the American School at Hartford, it is here that any evidence of the influence of indigenous signs on the development of ASL should be found. However, it wasn't until the tenth Annual Report of the American School for the Deaf (T. Gallaudet 1826) that the enrollment of three students from Chilmark was noted. They were two sisters, Sally and Mary Smith, and Lovely Mayhew, who was joined by her brother, Alfred, the following year. According to the twenty-seventh annual report of the American School for the Deaf (Weld 1843), which listed all students enrolled from 1817 to 1843 and their home towns, only two additional students from the island were enrolled in the 1830s, one in 1832 and one in 1834. Only six of 619 individuals who had attended the school during the twenty-seven years were identified as being from Martha's Vineyard, and all of them were from Chilmark. It is unlikely that a sign system used by 1 percent of the school's students would have a major impact on the signing behavior of the student body as a whole.

The 1843 report also found that of the 629 students who had attended the school, only one had two deaf parents. This suggests that marriages of the deaf in America were extremely rare before the establishment of educational programs.

Prior to the establishment of the *American Annals of the Deaf* in 1848, there was no general resource on the education of deaf children that could address the existence of indigenous sign languages. The authors of this chapter examined the annual reports of the American School for the Deaf for a thirty-year period, from 1817 to 1846, in hopes of finding references to existing sign languages. The annual reports address an impressive range of subjects, including causes of deafness, knowledge of the deaf child before instruction, optimum ages of instruction, articulation, general health of deaf individuals, and acquisition of written language. In these reports, however, no mention is made of a sign language in existence in America independent of the schools. There are references to the "natural language of signs," which was viewed as a universal gesture system that existed in all parts of the world. This was viewed as a limited and ungrammatical system of communication that in no way could be compared to ASL.

In the 1838 annual report, in a discussion of prior knowledge, there is mention of the case of one student who had been taught by a judge, who himself was the father of five deaf children. The use of signs prior to instruction was quite unusual and it was stated that cases such as the instruction of the deaf child by the judge were "exceedingly rare" (Weld 1838, 21).

The Spread of Clerc's System of Instruction

The system of instruction formulated by Clerc contained four modes of communication: (1) the natural language of signs of the deaf, (2) the natural language of signs as methodized by Epée and Sicard, (3) the manual alphabet, and (4) writing.

As with education in the Paris institution, the major emphasis was on the acquisition of literacy. In many cases, instruction could lead from one mode of communication to another. For example, a subject might be introduced and discussed in "natural" signs, then followed by a presentation by means of "methodical" signs, ending in a lesson with the manual alphabet and drill and practice in writing.

Clerc instructed all teachers in the American School in his system of instruction, as well as in the use of methodical signs. Many of these teachers went on to found and teach in other schools for deaf children. In addition, several men (education of the deaf at this time was done by men only) were trained by Clerc before establishing schools by themselves. As a result, the system of instruction developed at the American School extended throughout the country by 1828 (T. Gallaudet 1828).

The American School still used the original system of instruction in 1835, employing the "systematic language of signs," which had been "methodized and enlarged by the admirable genius of the Abbé de l'Epée and the still more ingenious improvements of his venerable successor, the Abbé Sicard, so as to accommodate it to the structures and idioms of written language and thus render it in itself a perspicuous, complete, and copious medium of thought" (Weld 1833, 18–19).

Natural versus Methodical Signs

The passage by Weld, the principal of the American School for the Deaf, is in conflict with a statement by Lane (1984) that by the 1830s methodical signs had disappeared on both sides of the Atlantic. Lane (1984a, 127) claimed that Roch Ambroise Bebian (1789–1834), more than any other man, "was responsible for ending the world-wide practice of teaching the deaf in a manual version of the natural language rather than in their own sign language." Bebian ([1817], Lane 1984a) considered the language of gesture to be the native language of human beings, and he believed that sign language had an absence of grammatical forms (ibid., 145). Bebian criticized the French system of methodical signs of Epée and Sicard as follows:

> Signs were considered only in relation to French, and great efforts were made to bend them to that language. But as sign language is quite different from all other languages, it had to be distorted to conform to French usage, and was sometimes so disfigured as to become unintelligible. ([1817], Lane 1984a)

Berthier ([1817], Lane 1984a) also was highly critical of the use of the methodical sign system as developed by Epée and Sicard and opposed the use of the manual alphabet. Berthier reported that Bebian was opposed to resorting to initialization and using handshapes of the manual alphabet to distinguish words such as T for *temps* (time), P for *pendant* (while), and D for *durant* (during).

The first school for the deaf in the United States to move away from reliance on methodical signs was apparently the New York Institution for the Instruction of the Deaf and Dumb. In the institution's sixteenth annual report (Peet 1834), two approaches to instruction were considered. The first involved adapting the "colloquial" signs of the deaf in the classroom (i.e., signs used in everyday communication). The second entailed the use of Epée, Sicard, and Clerc's methodical system of affixing a definite sign to every word in spoken language. The report was highly critical of the second approach and claimed that methodical signs were never used by deaf students on a daily basis outside the classroom and that the system conveyed no idea to the mind of the student. In other words, the emphasis was on the structure of English and not on content. Finally, it claimed that methodical signs were not learned by deaf students but had to be taught to them.

The 1834 report noted that methodical signs had been abandoned the previous year and that colloquial signs had been adapted. The overall curricular methods, interestingly enough, were not significantly changed. According to this report, the first step was to teach the students to write (p. 14), and later the manual alphabet could be introduced (p. 16). The emphasis on written English, then, was continued as the essential part of the curriculum. The difference was that only colloquial (natural) signs were used in conjunction with written and fingerspelled English, as opposed to Clerc's employment of English-based methodical signs to mediate or bridge the gap between natural signs and English. Peet did acknowledge some difficulties in adapting the syntax of the existing colloquial sign system. It was pointed out that, instead of writing "Cat eats meat," a student might follow the order of the language of signs and write "Meat eats cat." It was stated that the responsibility of remedying "this error" rested with the teacher (p. 16), but no indication was given as to how the remediation should take place.

The annual reports of various institutions for deaf children suggest a diversity of usage of sign systems from 1830 to 1850. However, annual reports do not provide a forum for discussion or for consideration of alternative viewpoints. They are written in such a way as to present an institution in the best possible light and usually avoid controversial subjects. Because of this, conflict within a school over methodology would tend to be unreported.

Information regarding sign usage in classrooms became much more prevalent

from 1848 on, with the publication of the *American Annals of the Deaf*. Between 1850 and 1880, vehement debate raged regarding the best method of educating deaf children. The consensus among educators circa 1850 was that deaf students must be educated using some form of sign language or sign system. The form of the sign language was hotly debated, however. One group supported the use of methodical signs (i.e., signs presented in English morphology and syntax), while the other group thought that natural or colloquial signs (i.e., the forerunner of ASL) were superior.

Some idea of the prevalence of methodical (or English-based) signs during the first half of the nineteenth century can be seen in Burnet's statement (1854, 1–2), that "in this country . . . their [methodical signs] use was once universal or nearly so, they have been discussed wholly in some schools, partially in others, and in some cases, after being denounced, again taken in partial favor. . . . The prevailing opinion among the more experienced American teachers is that these signs are useful, at least to some extent and in the earlier lessons." The previous quote clearly indicates that methodical signs were widely accepted in the first half of the eighteenth century. It also suggests that in the period from 1830 to 1850 the situation was highly volatile and in a state of flux. It should also be pointed out that, even in the nineteenth century, methodical signs were highly refined. For example, signs had been invented for even the functor words such as *the* and *to be* (Jacobs 1856).

Among his colleagues, Burnet alone seemed to have a sensitivity toward the benefits and limitations of both methodical and natural sign systems. In 1854 he wrote,

> If . . . the pupils of our institutions could be induced to use habitually methodic signs among themselves, it cannot be doubted that the advantage would be considerable. In this case, they would become familiarized with the syntax of our language, in the same way in which speaking children are, by daily use; and the younger pupils might be expected

to learn much of the correct forms of the language from the elder: thus reducing their instruction to little more than the cultivation of the memory. . . . But since the best masters of methodic signs have never been able to bring them into colloquial use among their pupils, there must be some principal of repugnance, some antagonism in the mental habits of the deaf and dumb and in the genius of their native language, which opposes this attempt to make a language of one set of elements conform in syntax to a language of a totally diverse set of elements. The ideas of the deaf and dumb will not follow the order of methodical signs more readily than they will follow directly the order of words, and I seriously doubt if the very composition of methodical signs, found on signs taken from the pupils' colloquial language, but mixed with others which are useless and unintelligible in that language, and then placed in an unnatural order, (for so it is to him) will not tend to induce a confusion of ideas and to make any complex sentence more unintelligible to the deaf mute than if he had been taught to look only to the written words themselves, aided by a paraphrase, when necessary, in natural, (i.e., colloquial) signs. (pp. 5–6)

Burnet also was aware that the prescriptive methodical signs would not supplement the natural sign language used by the deaf in everyday use. Rather than suppress any type of communication, he urged utilization of both.

Since, in an institution, we cannot prevent the deaf-mute pupils from communicating with each other by gestures in preference to all other modes of communication, it is the wisdom to avail ourselves of whatever advantages this colloquial language of gestures may present for the imparting of knowledge, the definition of words, and the interpretation of phrases, and especially for giving life and interest to the otherwise dull and formal lessons of the school-room. (pp. 140–141)

To sum up: the main difference between a teacher who uses only "colloquial signs," and one who depends on "general signs following the order of the words," that is, on methodical signs, is that the former is content to translate words in colloquial signs,

phrase for phrase; the latter thinks himself obliged to manufacture a new dialect of signs into which to translate written sentences, word by word. (p. 152)

For some reason, the extent of the popularity and use of English-based signs in the nineteenth century has received little attention from modern-day educators of the deaf. Ignorance of this historical reality led some inventors of recent English-based systems to believe and claim that their developments were without precedent where, in reality, the techniques can be traced back over two centuries to Clerc, Sicard, and Epée.

John Carlin, a deaf educator, was a particularly strong advocate of the manual alphabet and methodical signs and an opponent of natural or colloquial signs. In discussing relative merits of the different systems, Carlin wrote

That the American system, adapted after the Abbés de l'Epée and Sicard's, has proved itself superior to any already known, except the French, none can have reason to deny; nor can he ever disagree with me that the manual alphabet, being the principal branch of our system, is the best and surest channel of knowledge and communication for the deaf and dumb; nor can he offer any dissent to the fact that the language of signs, properly used is indispensable to their mental improvement in the school-room and chapel. (1851, 51)

The natural signs, by their beauty, grace and impressiveness, have a tendency to encourage his predilection for them and excessive indulgence in their use, and, by their being mostly superfluous, to retard his intellectual progress. (p. 55)

In a response to Harvey Peet, principal of the New York Institution, Carlin condemned "the excessive use of colloquial signs in the classroom" (1859, 12). He also said that he

Would respectfully suggest that, for the one-year, two-year and three-year classes, easy and familiar words should be taught by appropriate signs, on the fingers, and by writing; and that the simple rules of grammar should be explained in the signs in the order of words. As the pupil needs but one systematic course of study, I would . . . employ signs in the orders of the words which . . . I would call systematic signs, in relating all examples, illustrations, sentences, and stories, the colloquial signs being altogether dispensed with. . . .

Colloquial signs are often accompanied by grimaces, and laryngean creakings, extremely disagreeable to the ears; but in the exercise of systematic signs, these accompaniments are impossibilities, for a systematized mind regulates all things.

I confess I do not understand why Dr. Peet should labor to prove that the colloquial signs are the soul of our system of instruction, whereas I consider the English grammar really at its soul, vitalizing the deaf-mute's intellect, regulating this language and facilitating his expressions. I myself would certainly keep the grammar constantly in view before my pupils, throughout their term of pupilage. (pp. 15–16)

Jacobs was another strong proponent, at that time, of the use of methodical signs, by which he meant "the natural signs of deaf mutes extended, systematized and conformed to the arrangement of idiom of written language" (1853, 102). He wrote

That deaf mutes should acquire the use of written language with facility and correctness, it would seem to be desirable, if not indeed necessary, that they should learn to think, when they are using it, in the order of its expression, and to disuse, as far as it is possible to lead them to do so, the order and method of thought natural to them. If the natural sign language be still used in the school-room as the instrument of instruction, is a complete counteraction to the acquirement of a habit of thinking in written language or rather in its forms. . . . If we wished to teach a foreigner to speak and write our language, we should surely, as soon as possible, require him to continue himself to its idiom, and would not first communicate every sentence taught, in that of his own language and then in ours. This would be to teach him to continue to think in the arrangement and idiom of his vernacular tongue, and of course,

to write and speak ours after idioms of his own. We would endeavor, as soon as possible, to lead him to discontinue thinking of his own, and to think in our language. He would then speak and write with comparatively little difficulty. As long as he should continue to think in his native tongue, so long would he continue to use ours in its peculiar idiom. (pp. 96–97)

Jacobs was as strong an opponent of colloquial signs as was Carlin. His position is expressed as follows:

Now what my theory proposes is, to discontinue the instrumentality, as far as possible, of this class or order of signs, and by signs following the order of words, and by language either alphabetical or written, to accustom them to think, as far as possible, in the order of spoken language. That they will do this faster and easier by disusing their colloquial sequence of signs, both "theory" and years of practice abundantly convince me. If, in the course of time, they can learn to attach their ideas to the written symbols of speech, it does not affect, but confirms the propriety of my theory. (1855, 71)

Not infrequently I find it easier to communicate the ideas of a complicated sentence by dactylology and signs in the order of the words, than by colloquial signs. These last, as is well known, cannot communicate the ideas and facts of a long sentence with involved members and complicated language; it is necessary by colloquial signs to take the sentence to pieces, and present the ideas or facts, in successive, disconnected sentences. The use of these signs cherishes the sequence and manner of thought natural to the mute, and leads him, of course to a corresponding expression in endeavoring to put down his ideas in language. No wonder, so long as natural signs are employed in instruction, that he should find it so difficult to learn the idiom of written language; no wonder that his composition should so frequently be a mere "jargon" of words,—no jargon in his own mind. His ideas are clear enough; but when they assume a written form, they may be understood, but are found to be arranged in the order of his vernacular. (p. 73)

Porter, the editor of the *American Annals*

of the Deaf, arguing that the most important acquisition for the deaf student is the knowledge of written language, stated, in 1852, that, "a too abundant and too constant use of dactylology, to the neglect of spoken and written language, is the grand practical error of the American institutions for the deaf and dumb" (p. 24). He emphasized the distinction between natural signs and written language by arguing that, "a deaf-mute may reach the highest excellence in the language of signs, without advancing in the knowledge of written language for the sufficient reason that the two languages are totally different from each other in construction and general character" (p. 26).

The evidence suggests that there was as much variation in methodology in schools for the deaf in Europe as there was in the United States. In fact, given the interest in teaching articulation in the European schools (Peet 1861b), there was probably more diversity. A report by the Reverend George Day (1861) on his observations of schools for the deaf in the Netherlands provides an interesting insight into what probably was a unique approach at that time at the St. Michielsgestel School for the Deaf.

> The method of instruction pursued in this Institution is peculiar. Writing and the manual alphabet are employed but in addition to these, a system of signs, conformed entirely to the grammatical construction of the Dutch language, is made a prominent medium of communication and instruction. Each word is expressed by one or more signs which indicate both the word in its absolute state and the changes which it has undergone in construction. These signs follow each other in exactly the order prescribed by the rules of Dutch syntax. In place, therefore, of the natural language of signs, in which thoughts are expressed in their logical form, an artificial or conventional sign language is substituted, which represents the words and follows the order of this Dutch language.
>
> The disadvantages of this method of sign making, are, in my judgement, the following: 1st. It is artificial and in no sense natural to the deaf and dumb, and must therefore be learned by a distinct effort, while at the same time their own natural sign language must be disused. 2d. The tension of the mind required in this system is much more severe than is necessary in the use of natural signs. This is evident, especially in the lower classes, from their appearance under instruction. 3d. It is not so well adapted to deaf mutes of limited mental capacity. Hence, the large number of pupils at St. Michielsgestel, who never reach the highest class and make but little progress. 4th. It is stiff, and not nearly so agreeable as the natural language of signs.
>
> The advantage, on the other hand, of this method of instruction is that the pupils have thus but one syntax, which is the same for signs as for words, while in the natural sign language, the syntax is different from that of written or spoken discourse, and sometimes in conflict with it. And since the latter mode of sign making is the one most natural and convenient for the deaf and dumb, he is very apt to connect its peculiarities here and there with the use of words, and this tendency can only be remedied by repeated written or oral exercises.
>
> The employment of natural signs in instruction produces, in my opinion, a more symmetrical and complete development; the use of this artificial sign-language on the other hand, given to a higher degree the power of reading and correct expression by words. (pp. 17–18)

At first glance, it is not clear why the Reverend Day would describe the St. Michielsgestel method of instruction as "peculiar." From the present perspective it would appear to follow the very same procedures as do English-based sign systems that are based on English morphology and syntax. If lessons had been taught in conjunction with speech, the approach might be considered as part of a Total Communication system.

Superficially, this approach could be equated with the methodical sign approach used on both sides of the Atlantic, but Day obviously did not think so. He probably regarded the method as peculiar because it had no place in the classroom for natural sign language, unlike the

Epée/Sicard/Clerc system. Whether or not any other schools in Europe used a similar method is not known. Still, by 1860, there were at least three systems of instruction, using different modes of communication.

Methodical System	Natural System	St. Michiels-gestel System
writing	writing	writing
manual alphabet	manual alphabet	manual alphabet
methodical signs	natural signs	methodical signs
natural signs		

In short, the commonalities among the three systems were writing and the manual alphabet. The natural system did not employ methodical signs and the St. Michielsgestel system did not employ natural signs. The methodical system is somewhat misnamed because it employed both natural and methodical signs. The agreement over writing and the manual alphabet is understandable given the attention devoted to what Harvey Peet described as "the great and peculiar difficulties of written language for the deaf" (1861a, 24). Peet also differentiated between means and ends, stating, "the language of signs is a *means* of instruction while written language is the *end* of instruction [original emphasis]." To this end, it is of benefit to mention the course of instruction at the New York Institution for the Instruction of the Deaf and Dumb in 1861, when Peet was principal (1861a). The subjects studied in the Intellectual Department were vegetable physiology, grammar, algebra, bookkeeping, French, geography and history, Japan, moral science, and composition.

Given Peet's concerns over the problems American deaf students faced in learning English, it is somewhat unsettling to note French on the curriculum. However, the report claims that the students knew the leading principles of French "sufficiently well already to trace the etymologies of words which we have derived from the Latin through the French

and perceive that the principles of general grammar which they have been taught are applicable to the English and the French alike" (Peet 1861b, 42).

The use of initialization received new attention in the middle of the nineteenth century as the pendulum swung somewhat back to the use of the methodical system. Jacob Peet, who taught under his brother Harvey at the New York Institution, believed that natural signs were generally deficient and inferior to methodical signs because they were inadequate for conveying abstract ideas and were not precise enough to express synonyms. The best way to handle synonyms, argued Peet, was through initialization of a basic sign, called a radical. For example, the radical sign, *clean*, was signed with an *H* handshape to produce *holy*, a *P* handshape for *pure*, and with an *N* handshape for *neat*. This, of course, follows Sicard's use of *T* for *temps*, *P* for *pendent* and *D* for *durant*, which Berthier criticized so strongly.

Cochrane (1871) stated that methodical signs should be used during the first years of instruction. Later, more fingerspelling could be used. He thought that the main job of the teacher was to be a facilitator of language (English), not a facilitator of knowledge, and the best way to facilitate language was through methodical signs. Similarly, Valentine (1872) said that natural signs must be discouraged so that deaf children would learn the syntax of English, a position in accord with the Dutch-based system employed at St. Michielsgestel (Day 1861).

The support for methodical signs was by no means unanimous. There were numerous educators of the deaf who had a strong antipathy toward the use of methodical signs, which they viewed as stilted and unnatural. Stone (1851, 189) argued that "methodical signs are too artificial and stiff to be used in conversations and they are never used for this purpose. The only use to which they are applied is to teach language by means of dictation." Rae, in one of the strongest condemnations on record, claimed "Sicard's system of methodical signs (are) charlatanry, from beginning to end . . . time will come and at not distant day, when all our American schools . . . will discard methodical signs" (1852, 167). T. Gallaudet thought that methodical signs "tend toward degeneration. If we are to assist the deaf mute mind, by methodical arrangement, let us use grammatical symbols, but let us keep our noble sign language free from the fetters and shackles of the arbitrary rules of those languages which have been started and perfected using different principles" (1858, 189). If this is an accurate reflection of Gallaudet's philosophy, it seems to run counter to the system of instruction introduced by Clerc at the American School for the Deaf, where Gallaudet was principal until 1830.

Keep (1871) believed that natural signs were better for describing events that are difficult to describe using methodical signs. Seeming to be an advocate of both systems, Boothe (1893) stated that natural signs were useful for communication outside of the classroom but could not be used to teach English because they constituted a picture language.

The confusion over the most appropriate methods of instructing deaf children and the conflicting claims of proponents of different approaches probably mask deep frustrations of educators of the deaf of a century ago in the face of the enormous difficulties in helping deaf children acquire mastery of the language of the dominant community. These difficulties remain with us today. E. A. Fay best summed up the dilemma as follows:

We are none of us satisfied in the attainments in language ordinarily made by the deaf and dumb. The great majority of pupils born deaf graduate from our institutions without the ability to express their ideas in correct idiomatic language, or to understand readily the language of books. . . . Even the students who enter college and who represent the greatest intelligence and highest attainments of the deaf and dumb of this country encounter no little difficulty in the concise and often technical phraseology of college textbooks. In all the writer's acquaintance with deaf mutes, which includes many of the most accomplished graduates of the high classes at Hartford and White Plains, and the students of the College at Washington, he does not know one deaf person who uses language with the freedom and accuracy of an educated hearing and speaking man. (1869, 194)

Fay's comments reflect the difficulties faced by educators of the deaf over the generations, and they were consonant with the opinions of many of his contemporaries. For example, the following year, in a treatment of language and deafness, Gillett reported a general dissatisfaction with the rate of progress of deaf students in the schools at that time. The testimony of Fay and Gillett documents that the acquisition of English—which is what they meant by the term "language"—has always presented severe obstacles for deaf American children.

Educators of the deaf in the middle third of the nineteenth century were bitterly divided on the issue of what kind of signs to use, despite the fact that neither side had any type of data to support their arguments, a situation uncomfortably like that of today. In fact, we have resorted to extensive direct quotes to demonstrate that the arguments of a century ago are being repeated by educators today, who are unaware that they are refighting ancient battles.

It is ironic that present-day educators of the deaf are unaware of the fact that the first long-lasting methods controversy in America was over methodical versus natural signs. This "manual-manual" conflict has been obscured over the past century by the "oral-manual controversy," but has resurfaced since the reemergence of manual communication in the classroom.

In the late nineteenth century, the disputes over the use of natural and methodical signs in the classroom were resolved by the defeat of both systems and their banishment from the classrooms, at least with preadolescent children. The rise of oralism, which opposed manual communication in any form, rendered the arguments of the contending schools irrelevant. As oralism, with its promise of intelligible speech for all deaf children, tightened its grip on education of the deaf, the controversies regarding sign language slowly died. The revolutionary nature of the changes toward signs and their place in education of the deaf are highlighted by the titles of three articles written by E. H. Gallaudet over the last third of the nineteenth century. In 1878[1] he wrote, "Is the Sign Language Used to Excess in Teaching Deaf Mutes?" In 1887, in a more defensive frame of mind, he published "The Values of Sign language for the Deaf." In 1899, in clear retreat, he asked, "Must the Sign Language Go?" In a period of fewer than thirty years, Gallaudet went from treating the possible overuse of sign language to facing the possibility of its demise.

Just before the turn of the century, even the supporters of some kind of sign system made very limited claims as to classroom application. For example, Boothe (1893) believed that sign language was an unquestionably useful mode of communication, but only *outside* of the classroom. He did not believe that sign language could be used to teach English, and it was his position that sign language was nothing more than a concrete picture language.

Dudley was a firm advocate of the use of signs in instruction at a time when this was not a popular position. He was convinced that signs would endure even in the face of attempts to stomp them out. He stated (1894, 39), "If anybody thinks this method (the use of signs) is dead or dying, as he passes among the institutions (even some of the pure oral ones), he will find it a very lively corpse, indeed." Dudley, of course, was right. Signing went underground, passed on from deaf child to deaf child, only to resurface in the schools when educators of the deaf became less punitive toward it.

From the beginning of the twentieth century to the 1960s, information on sign language and sign systems, and their application in the classroom, is sparse. It is possible that the dominance of oralism, with its simple answers, was facilitated by the internecine strife of the two manual groups.

THE RETURN TO ENGLISH-BASED SIGNING

During the first half of the twentieth century, little attention was paid to the use of sign language or to English-based signing systems. All schools for the deaf taught by oral-only instruction through the elementary grades, and the "pure" oral schools continued this process through the secondary years. Some schools would employ what was known as the "combined" system, in which older students would be tracked into "manual" and "oral" departments. The manual departments typically served children who would be classified as "oral failures."

In 1948, Coats advocated an English-based system that he termed Manual English. He proposed signing in the word order of English, with heavy dependence on fingerspelling for function words and bound morphemes. This was in opposition to eighteenth- and nineteenth-century methodical systems that depended more heavily on invented signs.

A decade after Coats' work, Stokoe published the seminal linguistic study of ASL, demonstrating that the structure of ASL could be analyzed using linguistic methods. Following the appearance of Stokoe's analysis, a variety of researchers became interested in ASL, giving sign language and sign systems new hope. With researchers using subjects ranging from chimpanzees to humans, sign communication began to gather more attention than at any previous time in history. With these changes came the dramatic return of Manually Coded English systems.

Bornstein claimed that "the first gesture system designed to approximate English was the Systematic Sign Language developed by Richard Page in 1951" (1973, 457). This, of course, referred to the first gesture system designed during the twentieth century. Paget, working in Great Britain, was a physical scientist who based his Systematic Sign Language on the assumptions that: (1) signs should represent a single word or part of a word, (2) the syntax should approximate English, (3) the signs should have the same morphology as English, and (4) signs should be adapted or invented to form a basic vocabulary. The core lexicon of Paget's system was the Ogden Basic English Test, which gives the majority (850) of words encountered in written English. Paget's system received, at best, a modicum of support and attention. The system was used for approximately a decade in England but was never related to the sign language used by deaf adults (Bornstein 1979).

In 1966 David Anthony, working with deaf retarded children, came up with an insight that seemed novel at the time. That idea was to use signs in a structure that replicated English. Anthony's idea grew out of a master's thesis to become an educational philosophy. Anthony and his associates explained their system in the following statement:

> The major drawback of the American Sign Language has been that it has followed its own syntax and developed its own idioms. Recently a group of people—led by Mr. David Anthony—developed a new approach to the language of signs. Using the American Sign Language as a base, Mr. Anthony added verb tenses and appropriate endings, noun, adjective, and adverb suffixes and prefixes; and signs for words such as articles for which there have been no signs before. Mr. Anthony gives praise and credit to the members of his group—all of whom are born deaf people ranging in age from 15 to 67 who met at least once a week to discuss, devise and decide on signs. The exciting development in a system of signs now permits us to have one sign for each word, and—of the utmost importance—allows us to use the language of signs in the correct patterns of English

syntax. Mr. Anthony calls the new sign system SEEING ESSENTIAL ENGLISH. (Anthony et al. 1971, v)

Perhaps the most surprising aspect of this introduction to Seeing Essential English is its complete lack of historical perspective. There was a mistaken assumption among these sign creators that they were doing something that had never been done before. In order to form a philosophical basis for Seeing Essential English (henceforth, SEE I), a series of assumptions, all untested and some without logical support, were made. One of these was the assumption that ASL is basically a concept-oriented language where signs do the work of words, although there is not a direct word-to-sign correspondence. Anthony used a total of twelve sources, including Ogden's Basic English, on which to base the core lexicon of SEE I.

In order to handle words that sound alike and are spelled alike, the Anthony group adopted the "two-out-of-three" rule. Each sign considered three aspects of a word, its sound, its meaning, and its spelling. If two of these three aspects were the same, the word would be signed the same. For example, the word pair *so/sew* would be signed differently because only the sound is the same and the meanings and spellings are different. The words *right* (direction) and *right* (correct) would be signed the same because the spelling and sound are the same even though the meanings are different. According to Moores (1977), the outcome of this procedure is to give sound and spelling some precedence over meaning. There are numerous English words, particularly one-syllable words with three or four letters (e.g., *run, can, may, will*), that sound and are spelled the same but have different meanings. There apparently are no words that mean and sound the same but are spelled differently or mean and are spelled the same but sound different.

The SEE I method used word roots that were either words or morphemes. Compound words were made merely by putting two words together. The sign for *understand* was made by joining the signs *under* and *stand*. Similarly, even when a word was composed of two unrelated words, it was signed as two separate signs. For example, the signs *for* and *get* were combined to form the sign *forget*. As previously noted, this technique was employed two centuries ago by Epée.

Due to differences concerning methods for dividing and inventing words, part of the original SEE I group decided to create their own signing system. The resultant method was Signing Exact English (henceforth, SEE II), created by Gustason, Pfetzing, and Zawolkow (1972). SEE II was much more conservative in breaking words down to multiple signs. The developers contended that SEE II was easier to use than SEE I and more understandable. Gustason, Pfetzing, and Zawolkow explained their approach to dividing words as follows:

> Compound words are signed as the component words if the meaning of the compound word is related to the meanings of the separate words: COWBOY, UNDER-COOK, CHALKBOARD, for example, would be signed COW-BOY, UNDER-COOK, CHALK-BOARD. If the meaning is not so related, as in UNDERSTAND, FORGET, BUTTERFLY, the word is treated as a single basic word rather than a compound of two separate words. (p. 5)

A somewhat different orientation is represented in the Signed English system (Bornstein, Hamilton, and Saulnier 1980, 1983). This system is based on the argument that an alternative to ASL is necessary because: (1) ASL is not used in 97 percent (or more) of the homes of deaf children who are enrolled in programs for the deaf, (2) it is not possible to simultaneously speak English and sign ASL, (3) ASL has no orthography, and (4) people in the United States do not readily learn second languages.

The Signed English authors contend that

their system is the easiest of all the signing English systems to use. It does not incorporate the two-out-of-three rule that guided SEE I and SEE II. Instead of representing sounds or syllables, the Signed English signs were designed to represent words. There are fourteen sign markers, thirteen of which go after the word. *The Comprehensive Signed English Dictionary* (Bornstein, Hamilton, and Saulnier 1983) has more than 3000 entries, of which 1700 could be represented using ASL signs. The rest of the signs were invented or taken from other systems.

The three major systems have a number of characteristics in common. They borrow liberally from ASL vocabulary. They have been developed for use by hearing parents of deaf children as well as by teachers. Conscious attempts have been made to generate new signs for elements that in the past would have been fingerspelled or omitted, such as pronouns (he, she, it), affixes (-*ly*, -*ness*, -*ment*), verb tenses, and articles (as, an, the). The systems also differ in significant ways. SEE I and SEE II have different rules for establishing sign boundaries. Signed English renounces the two-out-of-three rule and is limited to only fourteen sign markers to indicate plurality, etc., arguing that the manual alphabet is a convenient tool for infrequently used words and relatively infrequent changes in word form (Bornstein, Hamilton, and Saulnier 1983).

In addition to Signed English, SEE I, and SEE II, there are other pedagogical systems in use. For example, the Texas system of Preferred Signs (Statewide Project for the Deaf 1977) and Washington's Manual English (Washington State School for the Deaf 1972) represent two statewide attempts at Manually Coded English (MCE). The proliferation of MCE systems has upset a number of educators and deaf people alike. In fact, McClure (1979) warned that if there was no standardization of MCE systems, the result could be a "Tower of Babel," where different systems are mutually unintelligible. While this warning seems logical, the same warning was made more than a century before. In 1872, Talbot was upset because many institutional schools for the deaf had idiosyncratic signs that could not be understood by deaf students in different educational programs. Talbot explained,

> I have observed with some astonishment that pupils from different institutions do not always understand each other when talking by signs. This arises from the fact that different signs are made in different institutions for the same thing. And should variations in the sign-language go on for the next hundred years to the same extent that they have in the last forty, the glorious, universal, natural language, of which the pioneers of the profession used to speak so proudly, will have settled down into a score or two of provincial dialects. (p. 156)

More than a hundred years have passed, but Talbot's prediction did not come to pass. Despite fears that too many versions of sign language would result in a degeneration, this obviously has not happened. There seems to be something about sign language that helps it endure. The fact that sign language has survived, relatively intact, despite its use being outlawed by schools for many decades, is remarkable.

ASL and Signed English Systems

The relationship between ASL on one hand and spoken or written English on the other is many-faceted and complex, a complexity compounded by the intensity of emotion exhibited by educators, linguists, and psychologists who are concerned with it. It is undeniable, however, that a fundamental root of ASL is the English-based methodical sign system developed by Clerc. Its influence, and even that of its French-based predecessor, are readily apparent in the signs of ASL. It is also apparent that the borrowing has gone both ways. Current English-based sign systems borrow heavily from ASL. In fact, most of the vocabularies for the major English-based signing systems come from ASL. At times

the line between ASL and a manual code of English may become blurred. In some cases, this may involve the borrowing of English-based signs by ASL. However, vocabulary borrowing is common across all known languages and by itself is of relatively little importance.

Of more interest is the evidence that the English-based sign systems tend to be modified with use. Again, this is not surprising. Language evolves over centuries. No one would expect any individual or team to come up with a flawless system of communication that would require no modification. As has been noted, Epée's original sign system was modified in Paris, and colleagues modified many awkward elements of the instructional system developed by Clerc. Kluwin (1981a, 1981b) reported that the invented systems included some inefficient elements that detracted from the communication of content because they were more concerned with English structure than with ease of communication. He found that deaf teachers and experienced hearing teachers modified the system by using three-dimensional space in their communication.

The intriguing thing about research findings and observations, at least on a superficial level, is the suggestion that teachers and students using English-based systems seem to modify them in such a way as to make them more ASL-like. They tend to use three-dimensional space, as in incorporating subject-verb indirect object into one sign or setting up pronominal references in space. The hands may be used to sign the equivalent of two spoken words at one time (e.g., *six months, two weeks*), negative incorporation is employed so that *don't know* or *don't like* are made in one sign.

However, all these changes do not necessarily reflect a trend to ASL. To some extent, they may reflect the different constraints placed on a linear spoken system and a multidimensional signed system. In other words, changes in the everyday use of English-based signs may reflect physical and linguistic constraints.

The complexity of the interrelationship of ASL and English can be illustrated by the study of the etymology of an esoteric sign by Stedt and Moores (1980). Over a period of years, a sign that could be glossed as "excuse me" underwent systemic modification while being adopted by a growing body of signers. Originally used by a small group of children of similar ages in a residential school for the deaf, the sign first involved the positioning of both hands above the head and extensive body movement and facial expression. Following linguistic principles of ASL— and perhaps general principles for all sign languages— the evolution of the sign transformed it to a position in front of the body, a neutral signing space, which would seem to conform to a principle of least effort. Within a short period of time, reliance on both hands was dropped and it became a one-handed sign, again a predictable development. As a final development, the signing hand assumed the *E* handshape, apparently following a principle of initialization to reflect English spelling. By the time of our report, the sign for "excuse me" had gone from an esoteric to a "school" sign, with ASL and English both apparently influencing the evolution of its formational characteristics. The authors have since been informed that it has grown to become a "state" or "regional" sign and is used in day school programs and in a postsecondary program for the deaf in the state. The complexities of the interaction of ASL and English make it difficult to isolate the specific contributions of each to the development of specific new signs.

A fundamental problem is the fact that, despite decades of interest in ASL by American linguists, disappointingly little is known about the underlying mechanisms of ASL in particular and sign communication in general. The basic reference work, after 30 years, is still that of Stokoe, with its treatment of *cheremes*, which are not analagous to phonemes, but certainly are submorphemic in form and function. For whatever reason, it appears that more advances were made in the study of ASL in the 1960s than in the ensuing two decades. In spite of undeniable advances, the fact remains that only limited progress has been made in developing a grammar of ASL. In fact, the authors know of no serious attempt to establish a generative-transformational grammar of ASL along a Chomskyan model. It appears that leadership in the study of sign languages has passed to European linguists, especially in Scandinavia, Italy, and Great Britain. It is perhaps from these efforts that major breakthroughs and new developments will come.

CONCLUSION

The brief review presented in this chapter should establish the fact that present issues regarding the relationship of ASL to English-based sign systems do not represent unique developments but, rather, have been presaged by similar controversies in the eighteenth and nineteenth centuries in Europe and the United States. The issues have been obscured because of the obsession of the field with the oral-manual controversy. Because of a lack of perspective regarding historical realities, and because the English-ASL controversy touches raw emotional nerves, there is a lack of factual information on the nature of ASL and an unwillingness or inability to address important questions in an objective manner. Because of this we are still unable to specifically identify the differences between ASL and English that may be attributed to purely linguistic consideration and those that reflect the constraints of visual-motor versus auditory-vocal channels. Since both ASL and English-based sign systems (or natural and methodical signs) have existed for over a century and a half in the United States, it is clear that they serve essential functions. It is safe to assume that they will continue to coexist for the foreseeable future, no matter how much mental anguish this may cause some educators and linguists. It is incumbent upon educators of the deaf, among whom the authors count themselves, to explore the issues as thoroughly as possible.

REFERENCES

Anthony, D. A. 1966. Signing Essential English. Master's thesis, Eastern Michigan University, Ypsilanti.

Anthony, D. A., and Associates. 1971. *Seeing Essential English*. Anaheim, CA: Educational Services Division, Anaheim Union High School District.

Bebian, R. A. [1817] 1984. Essay on the deaf and natural language. In *The deaf experience: Classics in language and education*, ed. H. Lane, trans. F. Philip., Cambridge, MA: Harvard University Press.

Bell, A. 1883. *Memoir upon the formation of a deaf variety of the human race*. Washington, DC: National Academy of Sciences.

Bell, A. 1884. Fallacies concerning the deaf. *American Annals of the Deaf* 28(2):124–139.

Bender, R. 1970. *The conquest of deafness*. Cleveland, OH: The Case Western University Press.

Berthier, F. [1817] 1984. The deaf before and since the Abbé de l'Epée. In *The deaf experience: Classics in language and education*, ed. H. Lane, trans. F. Philip. Cambridge, MA: Harvard University Press.

Bonet, J. 1620. *Reduction de las letras y arte para ensenara hablar los mudos*. Madrid: Par Francisco Arbaco de Angelo.

Boothe, F. W. 1893. The sign language: Its use and abuse in the classroom. *Convention of American Instructors of the Deaf* 13:58–63.

Bornstein, H. 1973. A description of some current sign systems designed to represent English. *American Annals of the Deaf* 118:454–463.

Bornstein, H. 1979. Systems of sign. In *Hearing and hearing impairment*, ed. L. Bradford and W. Hardy, 333–361. New York: Academic Press.

Bornstein, H., Hamilton, L., and Saulnier, K. 1980. Signed English: A first evaluation. *American Annals of the Deaf* 125:467–481.

———. 1983. *The comprehensive Signed English dictionary*. Washington, DC: Gallaudet University Press.

Burnet, J. 1854. The necessity of methodical signs considered. *American Annals of the Deaf* 7:1–15.

———. 1855. Colloquial versus methodical signs. *American Annals of the Deaf* 8:1–15.

Carlin, J. 1851. Advantages and disadvantages of the use of signs. *American Annals of the Deaf* 4:49–57.

———. 1859. Words regarded as units. *American Annals of the Deaf* 11:12–17.

Clerc, L. 1817. *The diary of Laurent Clerc's voyage from France to America in 1816*. West Hartford, CT: American School for the Deaf.

———. 1818. *An address before the Governor and both houses of the Legislature*. Hartford, CT: Hudson and Co.

Coats, G. 1948. Manual English. *American Annals of the Deaf* 93:174–177.

Cochrane, W. A. 1871. Methodical signs instead of colloquial. *American Annals of the Deaf* 16:11–17.

Day, G. 1861. Report on the institutions for the deaf and dumb in Holland. In *Forty-Second Annual Report on the New York Institution for the Instruction of the Deaf and Dumb*. Albany, NY: Charles Van Benthussen.

Dudley, D. 1894. Signs in oral schools. *American Annals of the Deaf* 39:37–40.

Epée, Abbé de l' C. [1784] 1984. The true method of educating the deaf, confirmed by a long experience. In *The deaf experience: Classics in language and education*, ed. H. Lane, trans. F. Philip. Cambridge, MA: Harvard University Press.

Fay, E. 1869. Acquisition of language. *American Annals of the Deaf* 14:193–204.

Gallaudet, E. 1871. Is the sign language used to excess in teaching deaf mutes? *American Annals of the Deaf* 16:26–33.

———. 1887. The values of sign language for the deaf. *American Annals of the Deaf* 32:141–147.

———. 1899. Must the sign language go? *American Annals of the Deaf* 44:225–229.

Gallaudet, T. 1826. *Tenth annual report of the American Asylum at Hartford for the Education of the Deaf and Dumb*. Hartford, CT.

———. 1828. *Twelth annual report of the American Asylum at Hartford for the Education of the Deaf and Dumb*. Hartford, CT.

———. 1858. Methods of perfecting the sign-language. *Convention of American instructors of the deaf* 5:180–192.

Gillet, H. 1870. Language. *American Annals of the Deaf* 15:232–244.

Groce, N. 1981. Hereditary deafness on the island of Martha's Vineyard: An ethnohistory of a genetic disorder. Doctoral dissertation, Brown University, Providence, RI.

———. 1985. *Everyone here spoke sign language: Hereditary deafness on Martha's Vineyard*. Cambridge, MA: Harvard University Press.

Gustason, G., Pfetzing, D., and Zawolkow, E. 1972. *Signing Exact English*. Silver Spring, MD: National Association of the Deaf.

Jacobs, J. A. 1853. On the disuse of natural signs in the instruction of deaf mutes. *American Annals of the Deaf* 5:95–110.

———. 1855. Philosophy of signs. *American Annals of the Deaf* 7:197–228.

————. 1856. The methodical signs for AND and the verb TO BE. *American Annals of the Deaf* 8:185–186.

Keep, J. 1871. Natural signs. *American Annals of the Deaf* 16:17–25.

Kluwin, T. 1981a. The grammaticality of manual representations of English. *American Annals of the Deaf* 126:417–421.

————. 1981b. A rationale for modifying classroom signing systems. *Sign Language Studies* 31:179–187.

————. 1984a. *The deaf experience: Classics in language and education.* Cambridge, MA: Harvard University Press.

Lane, H. 1984b. *When the mind hears.* New York: Random House.

McClure, W. 1979. Comment: The widespread acceptance of total communication. *American Annals of the Deaf* 124:336.

Moores, D. 1977. Issues in the utilization of manual communication. *Proceedings of National Symposium on Sign Language Research and Teaching.* Silver Spring, MD: National Association of the Deaf.

————. 1987. *Educating the deaf: Psychology, principles and practices.* 3rd ed. Boston: Houghton Mifflin.

Peet, H. 1834. *Sixteenth annual report of the New York Institution for the Instruction of the Deaf and Dumb.* New York: Mahlon and Day.

————. 1861a. *Forty-third annual report of the New York Institution for the Instruction of the Deaf and Dumb.* New York.

————. 1861b. Initial signs. *American Annals of the Deaf* 5:21–31.

Porter, S. 1852. Editorial comment. *American Annals of the Deaf* 4:24–26.

Rae, L. 1852. On the proper use of signs. *American Annals of the Deaf* 5:21–31.

————. 1853. Philosophical basics of language. *American Annals of the Deaf* 3:155–167.

Sicard, R. A. [1800] 1984. Course of instruction for a congenitally deaf person. In *The deaf experience: Classics in language and education,* ed. Harlan Lane, trans. F. Philip. Cambridge, MA: Harvard University Press.

————. 1818. *Theorie des signes pour l'instruction des sourds-muets.* Paris: Institution des Sourds-Muets.

Statewide Project for the Deaf. 1977. *Preferred signs for instructional purposes.* Austin, TX.

Stedt, J., and Moores, D. 1980. The etymology of a sign. *Sign Language Studies* 29:371–376.

————. 1983. American Sign Language and Signed English systems: Contemporary issues. In *Focus on infusion: Volume II. Proceedings of the 50th biennial meeting of the Convention of American Instructors of the Deaf,* eds. F. Solano, J. Egelston-Dodd, and E. Costello. Silver Spring, MD: CAID.

Stokoe, W. C. 1958. Sign language structure. *Studies in Linguistics* 8.

Stone, C. 1851. On the use of methodical signs. *American Annals of the Deaf* 4:187–192.

Talbot, C. H. 1872. The Kentucky Institution and methodical signs. *American Annals of the Deaf* 9:158–165.

Valentine, R. G. 1872. Shall we abandon the English order? *American Annals of the Deaf* 17:21–33.

Washington State School for the Deaf. 1972. *An introduction to Manual English.* Vancouver, WA.

Weld, L. 1833. *Seventeenth annual report of the American Asylum at Hartford for the Education of the Deaf and Dumb.* Hartford, CT.

————. 1838. *Twenty-second annual report of the American Asylum at Hartford for the Education of the Deaf and Dumb.* Hartford, CT.

————. 1844. *Twenty-eighth annual report of the American Asylum at Hartford for the Education of the Deaf and Dumb.* Hartford, CT.

CHAPTER 2

A Manual Communication Overview

Harry Bornstein

The purpose of this chapter is to provide sufficient objective information to enable the reader to better evaluate the often conflicting claims presented in succeeding chapters. Where possible, this information will be research-based. Hence, the reader will often be given a description of how data were obtained when such is available. Be forewarned! It is in the nature of this field of human endeavor that there will be some who will regard the information given here as biased in commission and/or omission. Ultimately, the reader will have to be the judge of that.

To be truly meaningful, a discussion of manual communication in American education should begin with a description of some important basic characteristics of the students, their parents, and their teachers that bear directly on students' needs and learning circumstances. For example, the amount of hearing loss a child has and at what age that loss occurred are central to the child's communication needs. It affects the type and quality of the language input

that he or she will receive. Further, the skills, attitudes, and opportunities of those parents and teachers who serve as language models for the child are, in large part, a function of their circumstances. As will become clear, these are inseparable from and integral to the use of manual communication.

The best source of nationwide information comes from the Annual Survey of Hearing-Impaired Children and Youth conducted by the Center for Assessment and Demographic Studies (CADS) at Gallaudet University. Although CADS tries to obtain data for every student in special education programs for the deaf in the United States, it is not completely successful. It receives information from more full-time programs (seven out of ten) than it does from part-time programs (only five out of ten). Since full-time programs serve a larger proportion of profoundly deaf students than do part-time programs, the probable effect of this type of bias on the variables described in the following section will be noted (Ries, 1986). In addition to the basic information it seeks annually, CADS often explores different problems in a given year. Therefore, when cross-comparisons between years or samples are made, they may involve a comparison of percentages rather than the actual numerical data, which change annually.

The data in table 1 indicate that about 40 percent of the students have an *unaided* profound hearing loss. Sixty percent of the students have less than a profound loss. If Ries's proportions were used to "correct" the numbers in table 1, the percentage of students with profound losses would be reduced to 33. Thus, one out of three students has a profound loss. Put another way, this means that at least two thirds of these children are able to acquire some information from sound. How much information they can acquire and how usable it will be varies with the specific circumstances of a given child. It is known, however, that nearly one in four children (23.5 percent) with a profound loss is judged by a teacher to have intelligible speech. Fully 55.8 percent of those children with severe losses are judged to have intelligible speech by their teachers (See chap. 3, table 6).

Almost as important as the extent of the hearing loss is the age at which the loss occurred. CADS files do not include data on this variable for 39.2 percent of the students. Therefore, the percentages listed in table 2 are those of known cases (N = 28,573).

The results are striking. More than 91 percent of these students have lost their hearing by the time they are one year old. Almost 99 percent have suffered their hearing loss before they are of school age. Clearly, it is imperative that special attention be given to their communication needs at the earliest opportunity.

A third important variable is whether manual communication is natural to the home (i.e., used fluently and as a matter of course before the child was born or introduced into the home after it was determined that the child had a hearing impairment). An upper-limit estimate of the number of homes of natural users can be inferred from the number of parents who are themselves deaf. The following should be viewed as an upper-limit estimate because of the aforementioned nature of the sample and the fact that not all deaf people use manual communication. For example, 38.2 percent of the students in the 1987–1988 survey continue to be taught by only the auditory/oral method. It is not known how many of these children have two deaf parents or how many of them might use manual communication.

Only 1,750 children (3.7 percent of the total 1987–1988 group) have two deaf parents. About two-thirds (63.9 percent) of these children have profound losses. Slightly more than one in five (21.3 percent) have severe losses. Only about 14.9 percent have lesser losses. Parenthetically, these percentages are higher than those reported for previous years, when the effects of the maternal rubella epidemic were more evident in the school population. An additional 1,392, or 3 percent, of the stu-

Table 1. Degree of Hearing Loss for Students in Programs for the Deaf 1987–1988
(In terms of Unaided Better-Ear-Average; N = 45,844)

Degree of Loss	Number	Percent
Normal: <27 dB	3,290	7.2
Mild: 27–40 dB	3,996	8.7
Moderate: 41–55 dB	5,274	11.5
Moderate-Severe: 56–70 dB	5,792	12.6
Severe: 71–90 dB	8,743	19.1
Profound: 91+ dB	18,749	40.9

Note. 1,181 cases blank or not estimated.

Table 2. Age at Onset of Hearing Loss

Age	Number	Percent
At Birth to 1 year old	26,087	91.3
2 years old	1,152	4.0
3 to 5 years old	952	3.3
6 to 21 years old & over	382	1.4

dents have either a mother or a father who is reported as deaf. However, past research on families of deaf children indicates that families with one deaf parent are *least* likely to use manual communication. They largely prefer auditory/aural communication (Jensema and Trybus 1978).

By comparing 3.7 percent with the percentage obtained from other data (35 percent), one can infer that families with two deaf parents constitute about 10 percent of the families who use manual communication in the home. The other data come from the 1984–1985 survey, which asked, "Is sign language used by the student's family in the home?" Of the known, 35 percent checked *yes* and 65 percent checked *no*. Most probably, "sign language," in this context, is equivalent to manual communication. Thus, of the parents who use manual communication at home, about 10 percent may be termed natural signers, while fully 90 percent probably began to learn manual communication as a consequence of their children's hearing impairment. There are no good estimates of how soon, after discovering their children's hearing loss, they began to learn manual communication, how many became fluent, and, if that happened, how quickly they became fluent. Finally, if the 35 percent of homes using sign language are compared with the 62 percent of the 1987–1988 group who are not in auditory/oral programs, there is a suggestion that perhaps one-half of those students who are exposed to signs at school may not see them at home. It is not clear what effect this may have on language development.

Here, again, the findings are striking. Almost all parents (97 percent) are not natural users of manual communication. Of the families that do use manual communication in the home (35 percent of the total), 90 percent of the parents are, themselves, learners, either at the same time or after they serve as language models for their children.

Another important factor in the development of effective manual communica-

tion is the opportunity to use it with others. It is difficult to believe that skill can be achieved and maintained without this opportunity. The 1987–1988 survey data cover 47,025 children from 8,310 reporting schools. Remember again that this database overrepresents students who come from full-time special education programs and have profound losses. Slightly more than half the reporting schools enrolled only a single student each, some of whom have extensive impairment (i.e., 11 percent severe and 9 percent profound). It does not seem likely that all or most of the teachers and parents of these children will have effective opportunities to develop and maintain manual skills in such settings. The residential schools in the United States that reported to the Annual Survey served 10,624 students, about 23 percent of the total. As an aside, this is a sharp decrease from the previous high of 17,000 students served in 1982–1983. Subtracting the single-student schools and the residential schools leaves 32,246 students, who are served by about 4,100 schools. It would be surprising, indeed, if differences in manual communication usage and fluency were not the rule rather than the exception, and that is exactly what the thorough analysis in chapter 3 of correlates of school settings reveals.

The information from the annual surveys can be summarized as follows:

1. For all practical purposes, almost all children who attend special programs for the deaf have lost their hearing before school age. Indeed, more than 90 percent have lost their hearing by one year of age.
2. Conservatively estimated, two-thirds or more of the students can receive some information from sound.
3. The 47,000 students in the 1987–1988 Annual Survey are taught in 8,300 schools, ranging from a single student in each of about half of these schools to the 23 percent (10,624) who attend residential schools.
4. Perhaps 3 percent of the children have

parents who used manual communication in the home before they had knowledge of the children's hearing impairment.

5. The remaining parents using manual communication, a group about nine times as large, probably learned it to deal with their children's hearing problems. How quickly and how well they learned manual communication is largely unknown.

6. Possibly half of the children who participate in programs that may use manual communication may not be exposed to it in the home. The consequences of this situation are not known.

Still other variables, most notably socioeconomic status, undoubtedly have significant influence on the securing of audiological services, private schooling, day care, etc. They will not be described here, but they clearly relate to the language achievement of deaf students in the United States (Jensema and Trybus 1978).

SOME RELEVANT FEATURES OF LANGUAGE

Language and communication usually depend on the transmission and reception of sound or, more specifically, speech. Information transfer, however, is not limited to the sound of speech. Information is acquired, as a matter of course, from sight, touch, smell, and proprioceptive stimuli. Since a severe or profound hearing impairment often results in severe speech problems, it is natural to explore the possibilities inherent in alternate modalities of information transfer. Furthermore, since this kind of impairment sometimes drastically interferes with the learning of language, information must be cast into a language-like form so that it can serve an important role in language acquisition. For most practical purposes, the sensory organ used for reception is the eye, and the mechanisms used for transmission are the hands, fingers, arms, face, and body. This

is not to say that tactual and kinesthetic information is not useful. It does play a role in the teaching of speech and conceivably could become a viable alternative to the methods described below.

Two major difficulties exist with using vision as a means for perceiving spoken, language-like information. First, the eye is not nearly as effective a temporal processor as is the ear, which is why motion pictures actually consist of a series of still photos. Spoken language is, of course, transferred on a time basis. Second, the eye resolves only that part of space that is directly imaged on the retina. By turning the head and body, a person can cover all parts of space. This requires effort and attention, however. The ear, on the other hand, is less space-bound. A person can receive information from any direction without involving other musculature or attending to the transmitting source beforehand.

Similarly, the hands, arms, face, and body mechanisms for transmitting manual parallels to spoken language also present some difficulties. First, the rate of information transmission (number of bits) that the large musculature of the body is capable of producing per unit of time appears to be slower than that of the vocal mechanisms. Second, the number of discernible bits of information that can be conveyed by the body mechanisms may be smaller than that conveyed by the vocal mechanisms, although this has not by any means been established as fact.

The language-like information transmitted by the hands, fingers, arms, and face can (a) parallel English, (b) interact with or supplement other means of transmitting English, or (c) be an alternative to English.

Manual English Parallels

Aside from visual expression and body posture, people who parallel their spoken English with simultaneous manual communication transmit three largely redundant forms of information: (1) the sounds of their words, (2) the lip shapes and movements that are required to make those sounds, and (3) one or another specific manual communication system. By redundant, I mean that it is the same information signaled in three different ways, one through sound and two by sight. In fact, lip movements and shapes do not perfectly mirror sounds, nor is there any practical manual system that can completely parallel speech. Because of this, the choice of the most effective manual system has been and still is a matter of considerable contention. At this writing, the three manual parallels reportedly most widely used by teachers are Sign English, or Pidgin Sign English (PSE), a naturally evolved "system," Signed English, and Signing Exact English (SEE II), contrived for educational use. Seeing Essential English (SEE I) is now largely used in one geographical region, and fingerspelling, as a separate system, has almost disappeared.

Manual Supplements to English

Manual systems devised to interact with or supplement spoken English are essentially directed at augmenting the movement of the lips to provide a complete and clear visual parallel to spoken words. In effect, the combination of hand and lip movement becomes the second information source in a two-channel sound and visual system. In the United States today, Cued Speech is the best-known manual supplement. However, the number of children who use it in educational settings appears to be quite small. The 1987–1988 Annual Survey reports only 179 such children.

Manual Alternatives to English

The last approach uses American Sign Language (ASL) in place of spoken English. It is a visual, single information source system with no redundancy except that which is intrinsic to ASL itself. ASL users do not speak while signing and, hence, sound is not used as an information source. Woodward (see chap. 4) found only a handful of teachers who use ASL with their students. However, ASL figures into educational communication in other important ways—it is a source language for the most widely used manual parallels to English; some of its intrinsic characteristics impinge upon and influence the use of manual parallels; and it appears in educational settings regardless of the desires of those who teach deaf students.

It would be useful for the reader to note some features of spoken English that almost inevitably come into play when manual parallels are used.

SOME RELEVANT FEATURES OF ENGLISH

English is a language replete with redundancies. The same information can be conveyed within and between sentences in many ways. An understanding of the interplay between the signal (information source) redundancy already noted and the redundancy inherent in spoken English is crucial to an understanding of how sign systems actually work within three information source systems (i.e., the sounds of speech, speechreading of the lips, and one or another form of manual communication).

Intrasentence Redundancy

Intrasentence redundancy can be illustrated with a few simple examples of the redundancy that is an integral part of spoken English. Consider these two sentences: The men walk to work, and The man walks to work. With one exception, the two sentences are identical in meaning. The subject of the first sentence, *men*, is plural, whereas the subject of the second sentence, *man*, is singular. The verb form is also different due to the redundant feature added to the singularity of the second sentence, namely the *s* on the verb *walk*.

The *s* adds no new information, and if it were deleted, the meaning of the second sentence would be unchanged. But it would not be a standard English sentence, and there is some likelihood that the second sentence in isolation might be misunderstood because we are accustomed to the presence of the *s*.

More to the point, what is most unclear is what loss in comprehension, if any, might occur if the *s* were deleted from the manual signal only, especially since *s* would still be present in the two other information sources (i.e., the sound of the speaker's voice and the movement of his or her lips). Other things being equal, a manual *s* should have principal utility as a model for those who have not yet learned to internalize *s* as part of their normal language pattern or for those who cannot utilize the other two information sources. It would undoubtedly be easier on the signer if the *s* were deleted from the manual signal. It would require one less sign and movement.

Now consider what happens when verbs are changed to the past tense: The men walked to work; The man walked to work.

Exactly the same difference in meaning exists, but now the redundant feature *s* has disappeared. Only the subjects differ. There are no verb form differences, and this time both are standard English sentences. A person who knows the language would have no problem fully comprehending the second sentence.

Intersentence Redundancy

If either or both of the sentences just discussed were included in a passage or discussion about events, feelings, etc., that took place in the past, it is probable that all or almost all verbs in the passage would contain past-tense markers. In effect, redundancy would be found between sentences as well as within each of them. If it were a lengthy passage or story, this would amount to a great deal of redundancy. What purpose would this serve in

the third information source, manual communication? And are the purposes the same regardless of communication direction, that is, from parent or teacher to child, from child to parent or teacher, or from child to child?

WORD MEANING

It should be noted that not all words in English carry the same amount of information. Thus, if either sentence were embedded in a paragraph of description or a story, the article *the* might or might not add information to the rest of the sentence. If not, it too might be deleted from the manual information source. Similarly, depending on context, the *to* might also be deleted from the manual signal without loss of comprehension. Context or intersentence information easily might allow a fluent speaker of English to presume its inclusion. A user who speaks and signs simultaneously might consciously or unconsciously delete these words from the manual signal with, possibly, little loss of information, depending on whether he or she wished to model English manually and/or communicate clearly.

Still another way of looking at the communication problem is to note that the words *man*, *walk*, and *work* carry most of the burden of meaning within the sentence. Other sentence elements and function words might be deleted from the manual signal with relatively little loss of information.

It is a reasonable hypothesis that the effect of deletions in the manual parallel will vary depending on (a) the information received from the two parallel signals (i.e., sound and lip movements), and (b) the amount of English learned and internalized by the student, which might enable him or her to comprehend the message regardless of missing or redundant English features.

BASIC SOURCE INFORMATION

A truly accurate description of the three manual possibilities for communicating can only be derived from a representative sample of actual usage. Since this does not presently exist, some basic quantitative information developed in a pilot study of the time synchrony of spoken and signed English (Bornstein and Pickett 1976) is presented in table 3. One moderately skilled hearing subject simultaneously signed and spoke eight brief sentences, twenty-eight words in all, taken from a book, *Tommy's Day* (Bornstein, Saulnier, and Hamilton 1973), which was designed as a first book for parents. The passage went as follows: "Good morning, Tommy. Time to get up. Let's get dressed. Put on your shirt. Where are your shoes? Here they are. Let's comb your hair. Stand still, please."

The subject spoke and signed the sentences for video recording. The recording was then played back for video and acoustic analysis to determine the time location of the boundaries of sign gestures, pauses, and spoken words. The video and acoustic analyses were carried out separately and then time-aligned by noting the time of occurrence of a highly visible speech event, such as the closing and opening of the lips for the labial consonants *p*, *m*, or *w*. Elapsed time for sign could be counted in terms of picture raster patterns of the video signal. The boundaries of the spoken words were taken from complete spectrograms of the speech.

Subsequent to that study, projections were made of how these same sentences would be transmitted by four other manual systems. Cued Speech was the supplemental or interactive system. There were two additional manual parallels: fingerspelling and one version of PSE. The alternative system included was ASL. These projections are based on known characteristics of the individual systems rather than on the performance of individual persons. In addition, the sentences were read again without manual accompaniment several months after the initial sign and speechreading taping. The entire set of data, as limited as it is, provides a description of some of the characteristics of each system against which we can make some tentative comparisons. The most important things to note are: (a) on the average, it takes about twice as long to sign a word as to speak it, and (b) as one moves from Signed English to PSE to ASL, fewer signs are required to communicate substantially the same ideas.

It is not difficult to foresee some probable consequences of these facts in "real world" usage of manual communication. Look for adjustments, conscious or unconscious, in the manual information source. These are likely to be, on one hand, the deletion of redundant features of spoken English, and, on the other, the inclusion or substitution of the more parsimonious features of ASL (e.g., the use of one sign to express an English phrase).

It is also possible that a speaker will simultaneously modify and/or edit information in spoken English. For example, one might use shorter sentences, employ a more restricted vocabulary, or keep to the active voice, so that it would be easier to sign and speak simultaneously. There is no objective evidence available to support this contention, but I believe that it happens very regularly, especially at secondary and postsecondary levels of education.

The data in table 3 came from a situation in which the speaker was not given the opportunity to change what had to be said, but his speech rate was not paced or restricted. When the speaker paralleled his speech with Signed English, it took an average of 344 msec to speak the words. This was 27 msec or about 8 percent slower than when speaking without any manual accompaniment. The variability in time required for the words in the corpus was about the same on both occasions, 168 and 171 msec, respectively. Yet the correlation between the times required to speak the twenty-eight words on the two occasions

Table 3. Signal and Time Duration Characteristics of Several Manual Systems That Interact with, Parallel, or Serve as an Alternate to Spoken English

Words	Number of Letters	Phonemes Visible on Lips	Changes in Hand Configurations	Changes in Hand Position	Clusters of Signals	Speech Alone	With Sign	Signed English Word	Signed English Markers	Pidgin Sign English	Sign (ASL)†
		Cued Speech*				Time Duration (in msec) Spoken Word					
Good	4	2	2	2	3,3	200	190	870		good	TAP
morning	7	5	4	4	4,3,4,2	540	460	550		morning	good-
Tommy.	5	4	1	2	4,3	440	270	370		(Tommy)	morning
Time	4	4	1	3	4,2,2	300	390	670		Time	now
to	2	2	0	1	3	70	130	400		to (spell)	time
get	3	2	2	1	2.3	150	200	250		get-	get-
up.	2	2	1	0	1.2	300	240	210		up	up
Let's	4	4	3	2	4,3,2	330	460	700	+	Now	Now
get	3	2	2	2	3,3	280	240	250		you	dress
dressed.	7	5	3	2	2,4,2,2	500	630	960	+	dress	
Put	3	3	2	2	4,3	100	190	150		put-	shirt
on	2	2	1	0	1,2	220	300	150		on	put-on
your	4	2	1	1	4	140	270	470		your	(shirt)
shirt.	5	3	2	1	3,3	520	410	1050		shirt	shirt
Where	5	3	2	2	4,3	250	230	800		where	shoes+
are	3	2	2	0	2,2	175	180	360		be	where?
your	4	2	1	1	4	280	310	500		your	
shoes?	5	3	2	2	4,3	700	650	680	+	shoes?+	
Here	4	2	1	2	3,2	180	330	580		shoes+	index(point)
they	4	3	2	2	4,3	150	320	600		be	facial
are.	3	2	1	1	2,2	200	400	390		index(point)	surprise
Let's	4	4	3	2	4,3,2	270	600	1670	+	we	now
comb	4	2	2	0	2,2	375	310	620		comb	comb
your	4	2	1	1	4	225	240	250		your	
hair.	4	2	1	2	3,2	280	700	700		hair	
Stand	5	5	4	3	3,4,3,2	575	570	1180		stay	quiet
still	5	4	3	2	2,4,3	700	620	870		quiet	stop
please.	6	4	3	3	2,4,3	475	630	870		please	
Mean	4.11	2.93	1.89	1.64	2.25‡	317	344	642			
SD	1.25	1.09	.99	.99	.84	171	168	321			
				M	2.86§						
				SD	.86						

4

Note. Reprinted by permission of the publisher, from H. Bornstein, "Systems of Sign," in L. J. Bradford and W. G. Hardy, eds., *Hearing and Hearing Impairment* (1979):155–172. New York: Grune and Stratton.
  * Analysis by Karen L. Saulnier.

† Analysis by James R. Woodward, Jr.
‡ Number of clusters.
§ Size of clusters.
( ) Optional.
+ Repeated (marked).

was .71. Without knowing the normal relationship between speech times over different occasions, it is difficult to say whether or not this normal speech timing was significantly distorted when the speaker spoke and signed simultaneously.

INTERACTIVE SYSTEMS

Although not the first such system devised. Cued Speech is the most sophisticated interactive system in current use (Cornett 1967, 1969). It provides a visible phonetic analogue of speech in the form of lip movements supplemented by hand cues. It also provides both vowel and consonant cues. Vowel cues are place-represented. The hand (either one) is held at a comfortable angle, with the palm toward the speaker. Consonant cues are represented by hand and finger configurations similar to those of the manual alphabet. Each consonant cue represents three or four different consonants. The position in which the consonant cue is made depends on which vowel, if any, follows it. Diphthongs are represented by a sequence of vowel places, and consonant blends by a sequence of configurations. By design, the cues have no meaning independent of the movement of the lips. This is why the system is termed interactive. The consequences of this interaction or interdependence are important, especially when language learning is considered.

The data in table 3 illustrate how Cued Speech functions. The eight simple sentences contain twenty-eight words with an average of about four letters per word. The speech dialect employed in this analysis is that of a midwestern woman. The average number of phonemes visible on the lips per word is about three; the mean number of changes in hand configuration is nearly two; and the mean number of different places is about one and a half. Since many of these signals occur almost simultaneously, it is probably more useful to view them as a sequence of two clusters per word with three elements to a cluster. Ob-

viously, as the number of syllables in a word increases, the number of clusters will also increase. The maximum size of a cluster is fixed at four. (Although only three elements, visible phonemes, and changes in hand configuration and place are represented, some phoneme pairs occur so closely in time as to blend into a unit.)

It takes slightly more than one-third of a second, on the average, to speak a word from this corpus of simple language. Therefore, each of the two clusters of the three elements will be expressed and must be perceived at intervals of one sixth of a second. This rate obtains, more or less, regardless of the number of words expressed per minute, because the cues are linked to the movement of the lips. Generally speaking, variation in speech rate is primarily dependent on the length of pauses between words (Goldman-Eisler 1968). The hands and fingers in all other manual systems can begin before a word is spoken and/or continue (lag) after the word has been finished. It is conceivable, therefore, that silent pauses between words can be both stretched and filled to enhance the probability of correct perception and accurate execution of a manual sign. There does not appear to be nearly as much leeway for the Cued Speech system except when discrete words are dragged or lag for training purposes. The cues must be synchronized with the speech.

From the foregoing, it is possible to conclude that Cued Speech places exacting demands on a one- to five-year-old child's ability to attend, to visually process information, and to develop motor control and stamina. I believe that a thorough empirical analysis of the interactions of these variables and the demands of the systems may be an important means of determining the ultimate value of Cued Speech. The other problems with such a system include:

1. While the system logic is simple, parents and teachers must learn to translate or transform words phonetically. Since this kind of cognitive activity is

unusual and rather demanding, it is not known how many adults will be able and willing to do this. Furthermore, many people do not articulate well. It is not clear what effect this will have on system use. Some adults may learn to articulate better. Others may simply transmit fewer and/or inaccurate and inconsistent cues.

2. There is no sizable group of adults who presently use the technique, as a matter of course, in communicating with one another. This greatly limits the number of language models in the child's environment.

3. Since the child's speech-monitoring mechanism is impaired, there is reason to suppose that the child's lip movements may be tentative, erratic, or inappropriate if his or her speech lags far behind language development. Since cues cannot be interpreted accurately unless paired with the appropriate lip movements, inaccuracies in lip movements could cause adults, as well as other children, to experience difficulty reading the child's productive language. To the extent that such problems could not be overcome (as by having the child practice monitoring his or her lip movements with a mirror and imitating teacher or parent), this would impede language interaction between the child and others.

4. If both cues and lip movements are required for unambiguous interpretation of speech, unaided speech reading should be facilitated better through the use of Cued Speech than any of the other manual systems, since it is a focus of the system. Comprehensive empirical evidence on this point would be most desirable.

SYSTEMS THAT PARALLEL ENGLISH

The Manual Alphabet

Fingerspelling may be the best example of a manual system limited primarily by physical and perceptual constraints. As this is the only place it will be described in this volume, it will be treated in somewhat more detail here than the other manual systems. Relatively little research has been directed at the technique since the early 1970s.

Since the hand configurations in the manual alphabet are associated with familiar alphabetic symbols, the twenty-six letters of the manual alphabet are easily learned by adults. Most adults can form and recognize individual letters in a matter of a few hours. Transmitting and reading connected messages, especially the latter, is, however, quite another matter.

Letters are spelled by the preferred hand at a fixed location in front of the upper part of the chest or the lower part of the neck. Nineteen letters, including all the vowels, are formed with the wrist still and the palm out, facing the reader. The wrist rotates to a different position for four letters—*g*, *h*, *p*, and *q*. One letter, *J*, is formed with a moving finger and a rotating wrist. The letter *z* is formed by a moving finger. What a person sees when reading fingerspelling is a sequence of letters, following one after another, in a fixed position with some wrist movement. Adults are usually instructed to try to remember a pattern of letters, for example, common syllables, and to guess which letters might be coming next. The perceptual process involved in reading the manual alphabet is not the same as that involved in perceiving words, phrases, and sentences on the printed page.

For the simple language included in the sample corpus used for table 3, the mean number of letters per word is 4.11. For a person to transmit at a rate parallel to the average speech measurement in table 3, it would require that one letter be formed every 84 msec, or about twelve letters every second, if there were no pauses between words. In fact, fingerspelling can be neither transmitted nor read at that rate by even the most experienced adults. A comfortable rate of speed for adults transmitting to experienced readers is about 300 letters per minute or, using five letters to an average word, sixty words a minute (Bornstein 1965). Moreover, it is doubtful that this rate would be comfortable for much more than fifteen minutes. Using 150 words per minute as an average rate of speech, this fingerspelling rate is about 40 percent of the rate of speech, or a 1:2 1/2 ratio. Interestingly, the same absolute rates and ratio have been reported for spoken and fingerspelled Russian (Solovjev et al. 1971).

Given the above, it can be predicted with certainty that hearing teachers who attempt to parallel their speech with fingerspelling would omit letters and/or make a sizable number of errors. This is precisely what has been found by Reich and Bick (1976). When analyzing recordings of eleven teachers functioning in two schools using Visible English (fingerspelling), they found that 18 percent of the functor morphemes expressed orally were not present in the spelling. Furthermore, of the functor morphemes that were present, only 36 percent were correct. It also may be expected, therefore, that some adults will slow or rephrase their speech in order to coordinate the two signals better.

What, then, is the value of fingerspelling? Before answering this question, it is important to address two others—Exactly what do the letters of the manual alphabet mean to a child who has not yet learned to read, and What do the letters mean to an even younger child who has not acquired a significant amount of language? In all probability, the letters are perceived as part of patterned movements, which, when presented in sequence, blend into a patterned sign. The letters may not be perceived as integral parts of the spelled word. For example, Battison (1976), in his study of the phonology of ASL, demonstrated that there are some signs presently used by deaf adults that are smoothed sequences of letters; for example, the sign for *no* is a smooth blend of the manual letters *n* and *o*. To me, it appears that children may learn to associate segments of these patterned signs sometime after they have begun to become involved in the

reading process. It is doubtful that the simple association of print to manual letter is sufficient to make a child cognitively aware of the connection among the several letters in any given word.

The traditional view that a knowledge of the manual alphabet will facilitate learning to read may be the reverse of what actually happens to young children. More likely, it may be the process of learning to read that facilitates awareness and comprehension of the elements (letters) in frequently used words (patterned signs), and thus, possibly, permits the child to recombine these elements into new signs that represent new English words. The nature of this interaction is probably very complex and is not reflected at all in instructional strategies that depend on the manual alphabet. Parenthetically, the nature of the Cued Speech signal is not all that unequivocal either. There are anecdotal reports that some young children, at very early stages of language development, perceive and react to some of the cues as if they were signs; for example, one of the cues for *toilet* becomes or takes on the meaning of a sign for *toilet*.

Moreover, this pattern of English language acquisition is still not free of other constraints in the manual mode. The length of a word should relate directly to the complexity of the patterned sign, especially if the child has not seen or understood the spatial presentation of the word on paper. Perhaps using signs that appear to be combinations of the first and last manual letters of certain English words is a way of dealing with word length. Battison (1976) notes that only those finger combinations that ease and speed up sign formation appear to evolve into such signs, and the hand need not be held in the normal spelling positions. If such signs evolve as natural responses to the perception and transmission of complex patterned signs (long words), this would further suggest a practical limit to the length of words that might be profitably used educationally or socially with young deaf children. Perhaps it may be possible to mathematically derive a statement of word acquisition as a function of word length when fingerspelling is used as the principal means of communicating language.

The development of sufficient manual dexterity to transmit at a reasonable rate of speed does not come quickly to a young child. Children, through preschool and the early school years, form letters rather slowly. Moreover, the order of development of control over all the fingers is probably not consistent with the frequency with which manual letters occur in English words. Although attempts to construct and validate a developmental model of finger configurations (dezes) have not been successfully validated (Boyes-Braem 1973; McIntire 1974), the developmental stages of the model bear little relation to the frequency with which certain fingers must be shaped and moved.

It has been established that seventeen-year-old students exposed to fingerspelling perform about one-half grade better than their peers in reading comprehension. (Both kinds of students, however, still perform badly [Quigley 1969]. They read at fourth- to fifth-grade levels). If the foregoing analysis is correct, this "superior" performance may reflect the advantage gained from the use of a difficult sign system rather than the presumed advantageous association between manual and print alphabets. Here, as with Cued Speech, it should be possible to chart the development of motor control and visual processing capability of children to determine how and when this technique can be used optimally.

There is one further clear value to fingerspelling. It can serve as a useful supplement to a sign system to represent words that have a low frequency of use. Such representation will not, of course, be at a comparable rate to speech, but, by definition, this will obtain only a small proportion of the time if the signs truly represent all high-frequency-of-use English words. It is not likely, however, that this supplement will be used to any degree unless and until the child has acquired a well-developed English language system and the requisite perceptual and motor capabilities.

Pidgin Sign English

Apart from fingerspelling, those systems that parallel English are either ones specifically contrived to represent English or those that have evolved naturally either as parallels to English or as a means of communication between hearing and deaf persons. Those that have evolved naturally are properly termed Pidgin Sign English (PSE).

Many, if not most, deaf adults live in a diglossic language situation, with English being the dominant and culturally preferred language and ASL serving as the socially acceptable means of communication (Stokoe 1970; Moores 1972). Because very few hearing adults learn ASL well, most deaf and hearing persons use one or another variety of PSE when communicating with one another. Woodward (1973) hypothesized that there is a continuum bounded with dialects of ASL at one end and an array of contrived systems, called Manual English and designed to represent English, on the other. Between these extremes is PSE a mixture of structures and forms of the two languages. The closer the language variety is to Manual English, the fewer structures of ASL are to be found. The converse is true at the ASL end. Not everyone can move freely over this continuum. Many prelingually deaf people have varying amounts of difficulty at the Manual English end, while most hearing people have difficulty at the ASL end. Woodward has supported part of this hypothesis empirically by providing evidence that different syntactic rules can be ordered linearly in dialects used by different people.

Depending on where on the continuum a particular version of PSE falls, it will generally contain few, if any, of the function words of English, no copula (or one sign to represent all variants of the copula), no determiners, and no English affixes. Furthermore, signs may be used to represent larger or smaller classes of English synonyms. Invariably, sign idioms will be included, as well as some ASL syntactic structures, for example, negative incorporation or agent-beneficiary directionality. Since these pidgin variants and ASL dialects are rarely recorded on paper, it is likely that there is considerable variability from place to place. Sign vocabulary is particularly prone to variations.

CONTRIVED SYSTEMS

A feature common to all contrived Manual English systems is the attempt by system makers to supply a specific sign for a given English word. Where possible, they select an existing sign. Such selections are often arbitrary, since a great many signs can be freely translated to several English words. When no acceptable signs exist, new signs are devised following three basic patterns—(1) a compound of two existing signs; (2) an incorporation of the first English letter into the basic shape and movement of an existing sign (for example, *try*, *effort*, and *attempt* differ by grafting the letters *T*, *E*, and *A* on the basic movement); and (3) an entirely new sign that is somehow suggestive of the concept.

Experienced signers are able to evaluate such "invented" signs for clarity and attractiveness. Of equal importance, deaf college students were able to recognize about 80 percent of the English equivalents on initial presentation. They further showed that such signs were easily learned and retained (Bornstein and Kannapell 1969). Without question, therefore, sign vocabulary can be expanded for educational and other purposes. Certain cautions should be observed in sign invention, however. Compound signs usually take longer to execute. Also, some letters may be more difficult for a child to form. Finally, all new signs should be sympathetic to or conso-

nant with the phonology of signing (e.g., when both hands move they generally have the same shape). The writer prefers to depend on the judgments of native users of the language rather than to follow a set of rules that is really nothing more than a statement of regularities. Irregularities are common to natural languages.

The two most widely used contrived systems in the United States are Signing Exact English (SEE II) and Signed English. Since these will be discussed in some detail elsewhere in this volume, only a general description will be provided here. Further, since they are competing systems and I am the principal designer of Signed English, they will be presented with a minimum of evaluative comments, although I may tend to overemphasize the number of signs that are used to represent a given English word.

Signing Exact English

A key feature of the logic of Signing Exact English (SEE II) is the definition and treatment of words and word parts. The developers reasoned that a word, or word part, could vary by its sound, meaning, or the way it is spelled. Since two entirely different words could sound or be spelled alike, they decided they would accept (or invent) a sign as a separate entity if it were the same in at least two of the three characteristics (sound, spelling, or meaning). In effect, this means that different signs or parts of signs may represent a different pair from the set of three characteristics. Two of these characteristics normally do not relate to sign gestures. ASL signs only parallel or approximate the meaning of some English words, not their spelling and certainly not their sound. Furthermore, English words are not the product of logic but of complicated and often inconsistent historical processes.

Here is an example of SEE II treatment of word parts for such compound and complex words as *today*, *tomorrow*, and *yesterday*. ASL uses a compound of NOW and

DAY for *today* and has separate, individual signs for *tomorrow* and *yesterday*. Because ASL and SEE II also have signs for *to* (the ASL sign means direction) and for *day*, SEE II changes *today* into TO + DAY. *Yesterday* is changed to *Yester* + DAY, and *tomorrow* is changed to TO + MORROW. The ASL signs for *yesterday* and *tomorrow* now stand, respectively, for YESTER and MORROW. There are no modern uses for these words as separate entities. Moreover, one compound and two simple signs (four signs) have been changed into three compound signs (six signs). This increase in the number of signs surely increases the amount of time required to transmit these words. It should be noted, however, that in spite of the attention given to this logic in the introduction to the system, SEE II has a relatively small number of such sign words, perhaps two dozen.

A major characteristic of both SEE II and Signed English is their employment of signs to represent English affixes, which, of course, increases the number of gestures required to represent a word. Although a few affix signs are borrowed from ASL, the vast majority of these signs are arbitrary inventions. SEE II includes forty-nine affixes in an affix section and an additional fourteen throughout the rest of the manual. Both prefixes and suffixes are represented. As Stokoe (1975b) has noted, there is some inconsistency in the meaning and usage of some of these affixes. I believe, however, that these inconsistencies represent only minor flaws in the fidelity of the system to English. This loss in fidelity is less of a problem than the consequences that may flow from the number of affix signs that exist, their design, and how they are used in the system.

Users of SEE II express English words by combining, with a limit, signs for words with signs for affixes; for example, a prefix sign, a sign word, and a suffix sign. Such strings obviously take longer to transmit and should be more difficult to read. Since almost all affix signs are contrived or invented and add to time of transmission,

such signs should be designed so that they can be executed in the minimum amount of time. SEE II sign affixes show no such design. They are formed or executed over the full range of the signing space rather than in the natural space centering where the largest number of signs are formed.

Signed English

The Signed English system was originally designed for preschool children. It has since been extended over the full range of the school years by adding more vocabulary, developing new tools of use, and expanding its rationale for use with older students. Each of the approximately 3,500 sign words in the Signed English system parallels the meaning of a separate word entry in a standard English dictionary. Simple, complex, and compound English words are paralleled by the appropriate ASL sign, where possible, without recombining or reforming the borrowed ASL signs. Fourteen sign markers are used to indicate the meaning of the most frequent word-form changes. Five markers are adapted from ASL. The remaining nine are formed by the preferred hand in the neutral space on the appropriate side of the body. The fourteen markers represent the regular and irregular plurals and past, third person singular, *-ing* verb form, participle, adverbial, adjectival, possessive, comparative, superlative, agent, and "opposite of" prefix. It was arbitrarily determined that only one sign marker be permitted to be added to a sign word. Affixes that cannot be represented by this system are fingerspelled because the system designers believed it would be easier for adults to learn the more frequently used set of twenty-six letters than the much larger set of less frequently used affixes. Almost from the beginning, it was recognized that there would be many adults who could not or would not be able to learn the full set of fourteen markers. Accordingly, a smaller set of seven markers was recommended as a substitute. For children who might have additional handicaps or other problems, no markers might be most appropriate and more effective.

PROBLEMS WITH MANUAL ENGLISH SYSTEMS

Since the problems associated with Signed English are of the same general character as those of other contrived systems, its limitations can be taken as representative of the group. The reader can, once again, refer to the data presented in table 3 in support of this discussion.

Signed English is designed to semantically approximate a complex, natural, spoken language. Any sophisticated user of English can easily find flaws in the approximation for children, and, especially, for adult users. However, the system is designed for children who have massive and often crippling English language problems. Its limitations in fidelity are more properly compared to the limitations in English manifested by deaf children who have been using other communication techniques. For example, it has often been noted that deaf children have difficulty using English determiners, yet determiners are accurately included in all contrived systems. The value of such a system is the elimination or reduction of such difficulties rather than the development of "perfect" English.

Stokoe (1975a) and others have correctly pointed out that an ASL sign, when used in contrived systems, may cause some confusion for the child. Although the same point has been made about ASL dialects and PSE variants, it is worth further discussion. It is logically impossible to borrow wholesale elements (signs) from one language, ALS, and use them to represent elements (words) in a second, different language, English, and still maintain a fixed meaning for the elements. The logic of contrived systems can be described as follows: The borrowed elements (signs) are only features of ASL. For illustrative purposes, they can be likened to the present singular form of English words. When affixes are added that are appropriate only for a second language, it is comparable to adding French tense and gender markers to the present singular form of English words. The resulting constructions would certainly be odd sounds to speakers of English and French. However, there is already an existing pidgin sign language situation, and the hearing mother who wishes her child to learn English is not aware of any oddity or incongruity. Furthermore, there is some evidence that children are capable of code-switching between PSE and ASL (Schlesinger and Meadow 1972; Collins-Ahlgren 1974).

To me, the major problem with all manual communication systems is that they must be learned by hearing adults, ideally when they find out that their child has a hearing impairment. Regardless of what advocates of manual communication claim, this is no small task. Learning Signed English, the simplest contrived system, which comes with the most comprehensive and age-level-designed set of teaching aids, represents a huge investment of time and energy on the part of the family—an investment that many are often unwilling and/or unable to make. To cite some results found with the Parent Counseling Program of the Maryland School for the Deaf, after six months of weekly visits, about half the mothers were able to handle simple sentences in Signed English. Another 40 percent managed separate words. About 10 percent did not sign at all. Half the fathers did not sign at all, with the remainder split between separate words and simple sentences. While this situation improves considerably with more time and contact with the school, it does not happen quickly, and it still does not happen to a sizeable number of parents (Hall 1977). It does matter, however. Crandall (1976) found a significant relationship between the mother's and the child's use of sign affixes. I also found a correlation of .60+ between the father's skill in Signed English and the child's vocabulary development (Bornstein 1976).

In contrast to Cued Speech and the manual alphabet, the number of different symbols (i.e., sign words) in Signed English is very large. To learn all or most of this vocabulary calls for sustained effort with ample opportunity to use the full range of that vocabulary with some frequency. It may well be that one reason PSE is attractive to some people is that one sign often serves as the equivalent of a group of English words meaning approximately the same thing.

Since the number of cues in Cued Speech and the number of letters in the manual alphabet are much fewer than the number of signs contained in sign systems (natural or contrived) and thus permit an adult to express a lot after only a short period of learning, why are these systems used by so few institutions? A partial answer may be found by turning again to the data in the last three columns in table 3. More specifically, the Signed English version of the twenty-eight word corpus contains twenty-eight sign words plus four sign markers, or thirty-two gestures in all. One possible PSE version by a hypothetical hearing user requires twenty-four sign words, two markers, one optional name sign, and one short spelled word, *to*. In all, there are twenty-seven gestures plus an optional name. The final ASL version consists of seventeen gestures and one marker, plus an optional sign for emphasis—eighteen gestures in all. (The sign for *good morning* is almost a single sign). As one moves from a formal parallel of English to an informally evolved parallel and then to an alternate to English, the number of gestures required for these twenty-eight words falls from thirty-two to twenty-seven to eighteen. Moreover, all of these sign systems include markedly fewer discrete elements than do Cued Speech and the manual alphabet. This advantage would be even greater for messages that contain longer words. This is because signs are relatively independent of word length,

whereas Cued Speech and the manual alphabet necessarily reflect the number of letters, phonemes, and/or syllables in words. I believe, therefore, that the laboriously learned sign systems are simply easier to perceive and execute by most children than fingerspelling and Cued Speech.

A more complex English language sample would probably change the ratio of signs/gestures to words considerably. The ratio of the number of Signed English gestures to the number of English words would be greater than that found in the sample because of the need to represent a larger number of inflections. On the other hand, the almost one-to-one word-sign equivalence found for PSE should become even more favorable to pidgin versions because single signs would be substituted for complete English phrases. Perhaps the greatest change from the tabulated figure might be for ASL. As the complexity and abstractness of the English message increases, the number of signs required to express an equivalent message may approach more closely the number of spoken words because subordination is not handled as efficiently by ASL. This increase in the number of ASL signs that occur as English expression becomes more abstract is evidenced in a set of ASL translations of nine English passages by Hoemann (1976).

Perhaps the most controversial characteristic of contrived systems is the marker system used to represent affixes or word-form changes. Many years of experience with Signed English tend to support earlier concerns that fourteen markers may be too many, rather than too few. For example, the third-person-singular marker provides information that is totally redundant. Hence, many teachers tend not to use it or to use it infrequently. Another group of markers simply does not appear often in the language used with young deaf children (i.e., the participal, adverbial, and adjectival). Finally, many moderately educated parents find it difficult to distinguish between regular and irregular past. Signed English was designed so that the omission of markers does not produce inconsistency or contradiction. But fewer markers create gaps and loss of information. Here, again, the reader's perception of the language acquisition problem is crucial in evaluating this system's limitations. Are parents who cannot distinguish between the regular and irregular past more likely to (a) spell these words accurately, (b) produce the correct phonetic elements of the word, or (c) use the past as in ASL? I doubt it. The children of such parents may have to depend on the school to provide these elements of English.

Another possible problem with Signed English is the time synchrony of the speech and sign signals and the effect this may have on the development of speech and speechreading. The correlation between the time taken to express each of the spoken and signed words in the sample corpus was .58, somewhat below the .70 found between the two spoken renditions. Moreover, the signed words, on the average, took about twice as long to execute. This ratio corresponds closely to that found by Bellugi and Fischer (1972) and Stokoe (1975a). In every sentence, the signer-speaker began to vocalize after he began to sign and finished vocalizing before he finished signing. How characteristic this is of other signer-speakers is unknown.

It may be possible to improve the synchrony of the two signals by training the signer-speaker to handle the length of pauses between words better, as well as to control the time of execution of the signs. There is virtually no information available on training procedures, however, nor is there any on the effects on language development or speechreading. Adults with a good command of English report relying more on lip movements when the hands are badly out of synchrony and/or forming erroneous signs. What a child might do under these circumstances is again unknown. It is possible that the child needs to attend more to the hands in the first

years of life in order to acquire a language foundation as a prerequisite to acquiring some competence in reading lips—the smaller, more ambiguous signal.

Consistent with this possibility, I found in 1976 that, after a one-year interval, twenty deaf children (with an average age of five years, eleven months) showed about the same growth, that of five months, on both a simultaneous and an oral-only presentation of the Peabody Picture Vocabulary Test. Prior to that year, the children had reached a vocabulary level of thirty-four months on the simultaneous version but only thirteen months on the oral-only presentation. It would be surprising, however, if the problem were no more complicated than delayed competence.

A seeming advantage of Cued Speech and the manual alphabet over contrived systems is that they contain elements that might enable the child to use word-attack strategies when learning to read (i.e., representations of sounds and letters). Contrived sign systems may lead naturally to the whole-word processing method. It is not clear, however, that the manual alphabet acquires "meaning" as letters of a word until after reading is begun. Similarly, it is not clear what the correspondence is between the manual cues of Cued Speech and the elements of the printed word if the child has not developed speech. In any event, reading is probably a complex blend of whole-word recognition and phonetic-alphabetic skills. The most effective mix is yet to be determined. Current contrived systems do have some advantages over the signing that was used in 1830, when Thomas Gallaudet first introduced the whole-word reading method. These systems have much larger vocabularies, and affixes are routinely presented on the printed page.

ALTERNATIVE SYSTEMS

In the United States, the most obvious alternative to English is ASL. In the not-too-recent past, this suggestion would have been ridiculed because ASL was viewed as a reduced, ungrammatical, imprecise version of English. The last few decades have clearly put such notions to rest. Increasingly sophisticated linguistic descriptions of ASL have emerged and continue to emerge.

Initially, signs were described by the following three features or parameters (Stokoe, Casterline, and Croneberg 1965): (1) the place on or near the body where the sign was formed, (2) the hand configuration used to form the sign, and (3) the movement of the hand(s). A fourth feature, the orientation of the palm, is now commonly included (Battison 1974). These parameters serve to describe the citation form of the sign. Originally, all that was borrowed from ASL by contrived-system makers was this citation form. With experience, however, they have made accommodations to some of the other features of ASL. Simply stated, ASL is a language of space and time above and beyond the mere sequence of citation forms. Signs are ordered differently than are English words. ASL has a variety of syntactical structures more appropriate for a visual-manual language. It uses space for a variety of language purposes, for example, pronominalization, facial expression, body posture, rate of signing, reduplication, and force of movement all have important functions in ASL. Hoffmeister (see chap. 5) provides an extensive description of these features.

It is a tenable hypothesis that deaf children should learn ASL as their first and primary language. The reasons given for this are that it is a language appropriate for the visual modality and the motor mechanisms employed to transmit in that modality, and its rate of transmission is not tied to that of speech. Therefore, the rate of transmission is more likely to be consistent with the perceptual and motor capabilities of the child without deleterious effects on ASL acquisition. For example, in table 3, only eighteen gestures are required to communicate the twenty-eight-word, eight-sentence message. Furthermore, ASL is the language of most of the adult Deaf community. Indeed, Hoffmeister maintains that fluency in ASL, not hearing status, defines membership in the deaf community, and that that is a second reason for using ASL. It is an integral element of the deaf community or Deaf Culture into which he believes the child will enter as an adult. In an English-speaking society such as the United States, ASL would be used as a first language in a bilingual, bicultural program of instruction. All the research findings for such programs could be used to support ASL in this fashion. There are some formidable difficulties, however.

It should be noted that generalizing from other bilingual, bicultural research findings may not be appropriate for ASL for two fundamental reasons: (1) ASL is not the home language of 97 percent of the children in question; it is not the language of the neighborhood; it does not have an accepted and widely used orthography; and (2) ASL is not a spoken language; hence, transfer from a manual-visual language (ASL) to the written version of English may not be similar to the transfer from another spoken language (e.g., Spanish) to spoken English. Further, practical problems arise.

1. Hearing parents in a notoriously monolingual society such as the United States must accept the idea of learning a new manual-visual language.

2. Parents must learn this new language quickly and well enough to provide an appropriate language environment for the child. Although no data are available, it is generally believed that very few hearing adults who are not born of deaf parents become proficient in ASL. More commonly, some become proficient in PSE. Indeed, it may be that most deaf adults, when speaking to hearing signers, almost unconsciously shift to PSE so that they can be more easily understood.

3. The structure and syntax of ASL does

not parallel that of English. Practically speaking, therefore, training in speech and the use of residual hearing must be either kept distinct from ASL instruction or delayed and treated as part of second-language training. It is not clear what the consequences of a delay in speech and hearing training might be, but it is difficult to conceive of it as favorable.

4. Unless the educational program limits the learning of English entirely to reading and writing, person-to-person interaction, even in a bilingual program, may still benefit from a manual system that parallels speech.

MANUAL COMMUNICATION IN EDUCATION

Over the last decade, a number of research studies have attempted to describe the manual parallel to speech as actually used in instructional settings. The usual procedure has been to videotape an instructor and count the number of sign words and affixes he or she deletes from the manual signal. Sometimes the manual parallel is named, and sometimes it is not. Most of these studies involve two teachers, a few involve considerably more (e.g., Kluwin 1981; Strong and Charlson 1987). The basic research question addressed is how complete the manual parallel is. Findings are clear. All teachers delete something, some more than others. They also delete in predictable patterns (e.g., functional words more than substance words, certain affixes more than others). Gustason (see chap. 6) summarizes most of these studies and notes that some of the more recent studies showed a higher percentage of completion than in the past. Depending on the amount of deletion found, researchers have had varied conclusions. On one extreme, the manual system is deemed a poor parallel to spoken English. On the other, it is thought that the parallel is almost all it should be.

In fact, the research question posed is,

at best, an exploratory or first-stage one. The appropriate research question, however, does not concern completeness, but sufficiency, and sufficiency depends on two other concepts discussed earlier—redundancy, both between the three information channels (sound, lip movement, and sign) and within English itself; and purpose, as an English language model and/or a form of communication. Very simply, if a child can hear and/or speechread a word, an omission or deletion of the redundant manual signal will not affect comprehension. Further, if the child has sufficiently internalized enough English, he or she may be able to "fill in" the missing element without correctly perceiving any of the three sources of information. Moores reviewed sixteen research studies on the comprehension of messages stemming from multiple sources of information. The evidence overwhelmingly showed that large increases in comprehension result from intersignal redundancy. The largest studies showed an increase from about 30 percent for sound alone to about 90 percent for sound, speechreading, and signing (Moores 1987).

Another major source of information about teacher use of manual features should be addressed, that described in chapters 3 and 4 of this volume. Rather than use the direct observation procedure (videotaping) described above, investigators first chose a nationwide sample of students in educational programs for the deaf and asked their teachers to report on what form of manual communication they used with the students. They then provided two sample sentences and asked the teachers to indicate if they would (a) sign each word or affix, and (b) use the same sign for both words in a subset of word pairs (e.g., he-him).

The great advantage of this approach is that the findings were based on a large, nationwide sample. The limitations are that it is not known if the teachers' reports are the same as their actual signing behavior, nor is it known if the two selected sentences are truly representative of larger language samples. In any event, here, too, it is not known if the choice of signs reported was sufficient for communicating to or modeling for the given student. This might even be true for the use of a single sign for *he-him* if enough information were received from sound, speechreading, context, and the meaning of the entire sentence. Perhaps the best available explanation for this variation can be found in chapter 3, wherein are described the correlates of variation in educational setting, children's hearing impairments, teacher sign-learning sources and opportunities, etc. Certainly, manual communication practices vary enormously throughout the United States.

Now we turn to another consideration that makes interpretation of completion-and-use studies difficult. Earlier, it was stated that Manual English serves two purposes: as a model of spoken English and as a form of communication. It was also noted that manual components, on average, took twice as long as oral components to execute. Further, the more complex a manual system is (that is, the greater the number of signs used to parallel a spoken word), the greater the difference in execution rate between the oral and manual systems.

Returning to the modeling issue, it is appropriate to ask who would want to model English manually. In school, it would most likely be those who teach the child, especially those who have the prime responsibility for teaching English. Therefore, it can be expected, as the child gets older and/or deals with other subject matter, that educators will be increasingly less interested in modeling English and more concerned with communicating information. Logically, it would seem that the slower manual system would be modified in these circumstances. And, most probably, it would be the redundant features of English that would be among the first to go. Even the most casual observation of schools for the deaf will support this state-

ment. For example, you will almost never see faculty and staff members communicate with one another in Manual English. They use PSE, simply because they are not in the business of teaching one another English.

What does a teacher try to accomplish when using a manual supplement to speech? Initially, the teacher wants the child to comprehend and use speech and to read and write English. Does the teacher also want the child to learn to express him- or herself in complete Manual English? I think not. Curiously enough, I am not aware of a single statement to this effect in the literature (including my own writings).

I suspect that, at best, a teacher expects only the youngest child to use a complete Manual English system expressively. Indeed most, if not all, teachers would find it perfectly acceptable if even the youngest child is able to express him- or herself perfectly in speech and omits all or most features of Manual English. As children get older, it is doubtful that teachers expect or even desire that their students express interchannel redundancies and intra-English redundancies with their hands. The adult models formal English manually to the child with neither the expectation nor the desire to see the child express him- or herself in complete Manual English. Consequently, it is almost inevitable that the child will use PSE expressively. This is how redundancy and execution rate interact to yield predictable behavior changes. Indeed, as children become more fluent in spoken or voiced English, they should be more likely to eliminate manual redundancies and substitute more efficient, and possibly more graceful, ASL expressions. Further, this probably parallels similar changes in signing behavior by teachers. They, too, are likely to shift to PSE with older children.

In the home, one or both parents might want to model English. Where both parents are hearing, the best available evidence indicates that it is the mother who assumes almost the entire burden of communicating information and modeling

English. Conversely, it is not likely that modeling English would be the child's desire, even if she or he had good command of the language. At best, the child would do it to gain or keep the approval of the teacher or parent. Certainly, a child cannot be expected to model English consciously to his or her peers, who become increasingly important as the child grows older. Common observation appears to support this contention as well. Children do not use Manual English when they communicate with one another.

If this is true, the consequences are important for both evaluation and research. Examine some recent research in this area. Moores et al. (1987) studied factors related to literacy in sixty-five deaf adolescents with parents who were hearing, and the same number of adolescents whose parents were deaf. The students ranged in age from sixteen to seventeen years, eleven months. All had attended residential schools that employed Total Communication (TC) programs during their school years.

The authors measured ASL, English Signing, and spoken English separately by means of separate language proficiency interviews of approximately fifteen minutes in length. The interviewers were highly proficient in each communication mode studied. The ASL interviewer, for example, was a native user. In addition, the authors used a recently devised Manual English morphology test made up of forty-four videotaped sentences. The sentences contained seventy-seven bound morphemes (eight kinds) and ninety-six function words. The student viewed a single sentence and then repeated it. The interviews were measures of language proficiency or fluency. The Manual English morphology test required the student merely to imitate each sentence that had just been seen.

The pattern of levels of proficiency in table 4 is largely the same for both groups of adolescents, whether their parents are deaf or hearing. They were most fluent in ASL, then in English signing, and least in

Table 4. Summary Statistics for Language Proficiency Measures

Proficiency Measures	Children of Deaf Parents		Children of Hearing Parents	
	Mean	SD	Mean	SD
ASL	3.79	0.48	3.31	0.75
Oral Only	1.30	1.48	1.52	1.39
English Signing	2.97	0.80	2.85	0.76
Manual English Morphology Test*	68	20	58	19

* Raw scores expressed as percentage of 173 items performed correctly.

the oral-only mode. The pattern of relationships between language proficiency and the literacy factors of reading and writing was also the same for both groups of adolescents (table 5). The results can be summarized as follows:

1. There were moderate relationships (r's) between English signing and reading (r = .41 and .41) and positive but smaller relationships between English signing and writing (r = .23 and .16).
2. There is no relationship between ASL fluency and reading or writing in either group.
3. There is a curious pattern of relationships between oral English fluency and reading and writing for both groups; moderately positive ones with reading (r = .30 and .42); and smaller negative ones with writing (r = −.22 and −.21). (Could it be that being less fluent orally causes one to write more in the real world and, hence, be a better writer in school?)
4. However, the data that bear most on the point being made here are the substantial correlations between the English Sign Morphology Test and reading (r = .64 and .55) and writing (r = .54 and .35). In other words, being able to merely recognize and imitate Manual English forms is more highly related to English literacy than the fluency displayed in an inter-

Table 5. Correlations Between Language Proficiency Measures and Reading and Writing Factor Scores*

Proficiency Measures	Reading		Writing	
	Children of Deaf Parents	Children of Hearing Parents	Children of Deaf Parents	Children of Hearing Parents
ASL	−.06 (.32)	.04 (.40)	−.02 (.42)	−.10 (.23)
Oral Only	.30 (.01)	.42 (.00)	−.22 (.04)	−.21 (.05)
English Signing	.41 (.00)	.41 (.00)	.23 (.04)	.16 (.12)
Manual English Morphology Test	.64 (.00)	.55 (.00)	.54 (.00)	.35 (.01)

* Chance probabilities in parentheses.

view. This appears to be consistent with the view suggested earlier that receptive skill (i.e., the ability to recognize Manual English) is the primary usage goal of educators.

It should also be noted that the absolute level of performance on the Manual English Morphology Test was rather modest. The adolescents with deaf parents averaged 68 percent and those with hearing parents 58 percent correct. Standard deviations (SDs) were 20 percent and 19 percent, respectively. Average fluency was rather high in both ASL and English signing. As one might expect, there was more variation in fluency in the hearing-parent group (SD = .75) than in the deaf-parent group (SD = .48). Oral fluency was limited in both groups.

I hope this overview will be a useful prelude for what follows.

REFERENCES

Anthony, D. 1971. *Seeing Essential English*, Vol. 1 and 2. Anaheim, CA: Educational Services Division, Anaheim Union School District.

Battison, R. 1974. Phonological deletion in American Sign Language. *Sign Language Studies* 5:1–9.

———. 1976. Fingerspelled loan words in American Sign Language: Evidence for restructuring. Paper presented at the Conference on Sign Language and Linguistics, Rochester, NY.

Bellugi, U., and Fischer, S. 1972. A comparison of sign language and spoken language: Rate and grammatical mechanisms. *Cognition* 1:173–200.

Bornstein, H. 1965. *Reading the manual alphabet*. Washington, DC: Gallaudet College.

———. 1973. A description of some current sign systems designed to represent English. *American Annals of the Deaf* 118:454–470.

———. 1974. Signed English: A manual approach to English language development. *Journal of Speech and Hearing Disorders* 39:330–343.

———. 1976. Modification of sign language for pre-school children. Progress report, OEG-73-6641.

———. 1979. Systems of sign. In *Hearing and hearing impairment*, Ed. L. J. Bradford and W. G. Hardy, 155–172. New York: Grune and Stratton.

———. 1982. Towards a theory of use for Signed English: From birth through adulthood. *American Annals of the Deaf* 127:26–31.

———. 1987. Distinctive features of the manual alphabet. In *Proceedings of the third annual conference on Computer Technology/Special Education/Rehabilitation*, 71–74. California State University, Northridge.

Bornstein, H., and Hamilton, L. 1972. Some recent national dictionaries of sign language. *Sign Language Studies* 1:42–63.

Bornstein, H., and Jordan, I. K. 1984. *Functional signs: A new approach from simple to complex*. Austin, TX: Pro-Ed.

Bornstein, H., and Kannapell, B. 1969. New signs for instructional purposes. Final Report, OEG-2-6-061924-1890.

Bornstein, H., and Pickett J. 1976. Time coordination of spoken and signed English. Unpublished paper, Washington, DC.

Bornstein, H., Saulnier, K., and Hamilton, L. 1973. *Tommy's day*. Washington, DC: Gallaudet University Press.

———. 1983. *The comprehensive Signed English dictionary*. Washington, DC: Gallaudet University Press.

Boyes-Braem, P. 1973. *A study of the acquisition of the dez in American Sign Language*. Working paper, Salk Institute, La Jolla, CA.

Brasel, K., and Quigley, S. 1977. The influence of certain language and communication environments in early childhood on the development of language in deaf individuals. *Journal of Speech and Hearing Research* 20:95–107.

Brown, R. 1973. Development of the first language

in the human species. *American Psychologist* 28: 97–106.

Caccamise, F., and Blaisdell, R. 1977. Reception of sentences under oral, manual, interpreted and simultaneous conditions. *American Annals of the Deaf* 122:414–421.

Charrow, V. 1975. A linguist's view of manual English. Paper given at the World Conference on the Deaf, Washington, DC.

Clark, B., and Long, D. 1976. The effects of using Cued Speech: A follow-up study. *Volta Review* 78: 97–106.

Cokely, D., and Gawlick, R. 1973. Options: A position paper on the relationship between Manual English and sign. *Deaf American* (May):7–11.

Collins-Ahlgren, M. 1974. Teaching English as a second language to young deaf children: A case study. *Journal of Speech and Hearing Disorders* 29:486–499.

Cornett, R. 1967. Cued Speech. *American Annals of the Deaf* 112:3–13.

———. 1969. In answer to Dr. Moores. *American Annals of the Deaf* 114:27–33.

Crandall, K. 1976. English functor morphemes used in Signed English by young children and their parents. Paper presented at the annual convention of ASHA, Houston, TX.

Eagney, P. 1987. ASL? English? Which? Comparing comprehension. *American Annals of the Deaf* 132: 272–275.

Fant, L. 1974. Ameslan. *Gallaudet Today* 5:1–3.

Gilden, D. 1987. Holding hands with Dexter: New technologies for deaf-blind people. In *Proceedings of the third annual conference on Computer Technology/Special Education/Rehabilitation*, 241–246. California State University, Northridge.

Goldman-Eisler, F. 1968. *Spontaneous speech.* London, England: Academic Press.

Goodman, L., Wilson, P. S., and Bornstein, H. 1978. National survey of sign language programs in special education. *Mental Retardation* 16:104–106.

Gregory, J. F. 1987. An investigation of speechreading with and without Cued Speech. *American Annals of the Deaf* 132:393–398.

Gustason, G., Pfetzing, D., and Zawolkow, E. 1978. *Signing Exact English:* Suppl. 1 and 2. Los Angeles, CA: Modern Signs Press.

Hafer, J. C., and Wilson, R. M. 1986. *Signing for reading success.* Washington, DC: Gallaudet University Press.

Hall, A. 1977. Personal communication.

Hoemann, H. 1976. *The American Sign Language.* Silver Spring, MD: National Association of the Deaf.

Jensema, C., and Trybus, R. 1978. *Communication patterns and educational achievement of deaf students* (Series T, No. 2). Washington, DC: Office of Demographic Studies, Gallaudet University.

Johnson, C. 1976. Communication characteristics of a young deaf adult population. *American Annals of the Deaf* 121:409–424.

Jordan, I. K., Gustason, G., and Rosen, R. 1976.

Current communication trends at programs for the deaf. *American Annals of the Deaf* 121:527–532.

———. 1979. An update on communication trends in programs for the deaf. *American Annals of the Deaf* 124:350–357.

Kautsky-Bowden, S. M., and Gonzales, B. R. 1987. Attitudes of deaf adults regarding preferred sign language systems used in the classroom with deaf students. *American Annals of the Deaf* 132:251–255.

Kluwin, T. 1981. The grammaticality of manual representation in classroom settings. *American Annals of the Deaf* 126:417–421.

Kramer, J., and Leifer, L. 1987. The talking glove: An expressive and receptive "verbal" communication aid for the deaf, deaf-blind, and non-vocal. In *Proceedings of the third annual conference on Computer Technology/Special Education/Rehabilitation*, 335–340. California State University, Northridge.

Leutke-Stahlman, B. 1988. Documenting syntactically and semantically incomplete bimodal input to hearing-impaired students. *American Annals of the Deaf* 133:230–234.

McIntire, M. L. 1974. A modified model for the description of language acquisition in a deaf child. Master's thesis, California State University, Northridge.

McNeil, D. 1966. The capacity for language acquisition. *Volta Review* Reprint No. 852:5–22.

Moores, D. 1969. Cued Speech: Some practical and theoretical considerations. *American Annals of the Deaf* 114:23–27.

———. 1972. Communication: Some unanswered questions and some unquestioned answers. In *Psycholinguistics and total communication: The state of the art*, Ed. T. J. O'Rourke. Silver Spring, MD: National Association of the Deaf.

———. 1987. *Educating the deaf: Psychology, principles and practices.* 3rd ed. Boston: Houghton Mifflin.

Moores, D., Kluwin, T., Johnson, R., Coc, P., Blennerhassett, L., Kelly, L., Sweet, C., and Fields, L. 1987. *Factors predictive of literacy in deaf adolescents with deaf parents; factors predictive of literacy in deaf adolescents in total communication programs.* Project No. NIH-NINCDS-83-19; Contract No. NO1-NS-4-2365.

Musselwhite, C. R. 1985. *Songbook: Signs and symbols for children.* Asheville, NC: Author.

O'Rourke, T. J. 1970. *A basic course in manual communication.* Silver Spring, MD: National Association of the Deaf.

Pudlas, K. A. 1987. Sentence reception abilities of hearing impaired students across five communication modes. *American Annals of the Deaf* 132: 232–236.

Quigley, S. 1969. *The influence of fingerspelling on the development of language communication and educational achievement in deaf children.* Urbana, IL: Institute for Research on Exceptional Children, University of Illinois.

Quigley, S., Wilbur, R., Power, D., Montanelli, D.,

and Steinkamp, M. 1976. *Syntactic structures in the language of deaf children*. Final Report, OEG-0-9-232175-4370.

Raffin, J., Davis, J., and Gilman, L. 1969. Inflectional-morpheme acquisition by deaf children using Seeing Essential English. Paper presented at the Annual Convention of ASHA, Houston, TX.

Reich, P., and Bick, M. 1976. An empirical investigation of some claims made in support of visible English. *American Annals of the Deaf* 121:573–577.

Ries, P. 1986. Characteristics of hearing impaired youth in the general population and of students in special educational programs for the hearing impaired. In *Deaf children in America*, Ed. A. N. Schildroth, & M. A. Kauchmer. San Diego: College Hill Press.

Schlesinger, H., and Meadow, K. 1972. *Sound and sign: Childhood deafness and mental health*. Berkeley: University of California Press.

Solovjev, I., Shif, Z., Rozanove, T., and Yaskova, N. 1971. *The psychology of deaf children*. Moscow: Pedagogica.

Stokoe, W. C. 1970. Sign language diglossia. *Studies in Linguistics* 21:27–411.

———. 1974. The view from the lab: Two ways to English competence for the deaf. *Gallaudet Today* 5:31–32.

———. 1975a. Face-to-face interaction: Sign to language. In *Organization of behavior: Face to face interaction*, Ed. A. Kendon, R. Harris, and M. Key, 315–337. The Hague: Mouton.

———. 1975b. The use of sign language in teaching English. *American Annals of the Deaf* 120:417–421.

Stokoe, W. C., Casterline, D. C., and Croneberg, C. G. 1965 & 1976. *A dictionary of American Sign Language on linguistic principles*. Silver Spring, MD: Linstock Press.

Strong, M., and Charlson, E. S. 1987. Simultaneous communication: Are teachers attempting an impossible task? *American Annals of the Deaf* 132:376–382.

Wampler, D. 1971. *Linguistics of visual English*. Santa Rosa, CA: Early Childhood Education Department, Aurally Handicapped Program, Santa Rosa City Schools.

Washington State School for the Deaf. 1972. *An introduction to Manual English*. Vancouver, WA: Author.

Woodward, J. 1973. Some characteristics of Pidgin Sign English. *Sign Language Studies* 3:39–46.

CHAPTER 3

Communication in Classrooms for Deaf Students: Student, Teacher, and Program Characteristics

Thomas E. Allen, Michael A. Karchmer

This chapter explores the variety of communication modes employed during the academic instruction of deaf students in schools throughout the United States. An alternate, separate analysis was made of the *different* manual techniques used in the classroom. That analysis is described in chapter 4 of this volume.

Several analyses were made of survey data collected in the spring of 1985 by the Center for Assessment and Demographic Studies (CADS) at Gallaudet University. The purpose of this survey was to study, in detail, variations in communication modes as they occur in the instruction of academic material to deaf students. Communication mode is highly related to characteristics of the students, their teachers, and their educational programs. In fact, communication, student, and classroom variables are so highly intertwined that

statements about causal effects—for example, about the advantages of integrating deaf with hearing students or the effectiveness of a particular communication strategy—are extremely difficult to demonstrate empirically.

Simply put, the data show that nonmanual modes are most commonly used in integrated ("mainstream") settings with and by students who have less-than-severe hearing losses and intelligible speech. Manual communication is overwhelmingly prominent among nonintegrated programs that serve students with profound hearing losses.

Three analyses will be presented in this chapter. The first is a description of the characteristics of deaf students in different educational settings. Four types of settings will be considered: residential schools for the deaf, day schools for the deaf, local schools in which deaf students *are not* academically integrated with hearing students, and local schools in which deaf students *are* integrated, at least to some extent, during academic instruction. The second analysis explores variations in communication modes employed in these settings and examines within each setting the relationships among communication and student variables. The third explores reported qualitative differences in the signing of teachers within the different settings. This analysis considers self-reported features of teachers' signs, teachers' assessments of their own receptive and expressive sign competence, and sources of teachers' sign acquisition.

METHOD

Sample

Data for this study are from the 1985 CADS survey. The sample for the study was drawn from those programs that supply data to the Annual Survey of Hearing-Impaired Children and Youth. The Annual Survey, conducted yearly since 1968, collects demographic, audiological, and educational information on the vast majority of deaf and hard-of-hearing students receiving special educational services in schools throughout the United States. In 1985, the year of the study, the database for the Annual Survey contained information on 50,731 students.

Sampling for this study was based on students from the previous year's (*1983–1984*) Annual Survey database. From this population of students, 4,500 were randomly selected and assigned to one of three subject-area stratification groups: reading (or English), mathematics, and social studies. This stratification was adopted to ensure that teachers from a variety of academic contexts were represented in the sample. The educational programs enrolling these students were sent questionnaires labeled with the sampled students' names and the name of the targeted sub-

ject area. School administrators were requested to distribute the surveys to the appropriate teachers. The surveys asked questions about specific communication practices used during the academic instruction of the targeted subject area to the sampled student.

The file created for the analysis contained information from this communication survey and from the 1984–1985 Annual Survey on 2,363 students. In terms of the stratification, 791 (33.7 percent) forms were returned from students selected for the English subsample, 772 (32.9 percent) from students selected for the mathematics subsample, and 781 (33.3 percent) from students selected for the social studies subsample. The remaining eighteen were returned by teachers who failed to indicate the area taught (Woodward, Allen, and Schildroth 1985).

Operational Definitions of Education Setting Groups

The central purpose of all the analyses presented will be to examine differences among types of educational programs serving deaf students. Questions pertaining to program type appeared on both the Annual Survey and the communication questionnaire. Studies of the responses to both questionnaires led to the following operational definitions of program type in the current analysis.

Residential Schools.   A student was classified as a residential school student if *either* the teacher answering the communication questionnaire or the school personnel answering the Annual Survey reported that the school was a residential school. (Ninety-five percent were classified as residential students by both the communication and the Annual Surveys.)

Day Schools.   Students were classified as being day school students only when *both* the communication and the Annual Surveys indicated day school as the program type for individual students, because only

114 (44 percent) were similarly classified by the Annual Survey. (These 114 students compose the Day School sample for the current study. The others were, by and large, judged to be in attendance at local schools that also serve hearing students.)

Local Schools. Students enrolled in local schools serving both hearing and deaf students (both public and private) were initially classified as "local" students. They were further classified as to whether they were integrated with hearing students during instruction. A question on the Annual Survey asked respondents to report whether individual students were integrated with hearing students during any part of their academic instruction, either full- or part-time. Teachers were asked on the communication survey whether the specific classroom situation toward which the communication questions were directed was integrated. Given these two integration questions, three subgroups of local school students were defined:

1. *Local, not integrated*. These students were reported as not being integrated by *both* the Annual and communication surveys.
2. *Local, integrated, but not in target*. These students were reported to the Annual Survey as receiving some academic integration, but teachers responding to the communication survey indicated that the specific class about which questions were asked was nonintegrated.
3. *Local, integrated, in target*. These students were reported by teachers to the communication survey as being integrated with hearing students during the specific classroom situation toward which questions on the survey were directed.

Relationship of Setting Groups to Analyses

Group definitions within the local school settings will vary slightly within this chapter, depending on the research issues being addressed by each analysis. Figure 1 summarizes the relationship among the groups for the three analyses.

In Analysis 1, that of student characteristics, the important distinction within the local school setting is whether the student was integrated at all with hearing students during academic instruction. Since this analysis is not concerned with specific classroom behavior of individual teachers, the two groups defined as "local, integrated" are combined.

In Analysis 2, it is important to keep those students who were integrated in the specific English, mathematics, or social studies classes toward which the communication questions were directed separate from those who were integrated during other classes but not during the target class. For this analysis, the data for these two groups will be analyzed separately. Students who were reported by the Annual Survey as being integrated for part of the day, but were not reported by teachers as being integrated in the target class, are considered as a separate group.

In the analysis of teacher variables, the most important distinction within the local schools is whether the teacher was working in an integrated setting. For this analysis, it is less relevant whether students who were not integrated might be integrated in other academic contexts. Thus, for Analysis 3, the students who were reported as being integrated by the Annual Survey, but who were not integrated in the target class, are combined with the "local, not integrated" group.

Student Characteristics

1. *Placement level*: Students were categorized into one of five educational placement levels—preprimary, elementary, junior high, high school, or ungraded.
2. *Sex*: Students were categorized as male or female.
3. *Ethnic background*: The students' ethnic backgrounds were categorized us-

	Residential School	Day School	Local School		
			Local, Not Integrated	Integrated, Not in Target	Integrated, in Target
ANALYSIS #1 Student Characteristics	✔	✔	✔	Combined	
ANALYSIS #2 Communication Strategies	✔	✔	✔	✔	✔
ANALYSIS #3 Teachers' Signing Experiences	✔	✔	Combined		✔

Figure 1. Summary of analysis groups.

ing a coding scheme that allowed for multiple responses.

4. *Hearing loss*: Students were categorized as having one of six degrees of unaided hearing loss (see table 4 for categories). For most of the students for whom audiological data had been reported to the Annual Survey, the categorization was computed as the student's average hearing threshold in the better ear across the speech frequency range (known as the better ear average, or BEA). For students with no reported audiogram data, estimates of hearing loss were made by personnel filling out the Annual Survey on each child. For some of the analyses, the students with hearing thresholds below 71 dB have been combined to form a category called "less than severe."

5. *Additional handicaps*: The Annual Survey contains a checklist of educationally significant additional handicaps. Students were first dichotomized into those with additional handicaps and those with no additional handicaps; then those with additional handicaps

were studied with respect to the specific handicaps reported.

Communication Characteristics

1. *Student mode of classroom communication*: Teachers were asked to report the student's mode of communication in the classroom during the instruction of the targeted class.
2. *Teacher mode of classroom communication*: Teachers were asked to report their own mode of communication with the sampled student during classroom instruction of the targeted subject area.
3. *Teacher ratings of student speech intelligibility*: Teachers were asked to judge how intelligible the student's speech would be to an average "person on the street."

Teacher Characteristics

1. *Certification*: Teachers were asked if they had special education certification or, if not, whether they had

taken any special courses related to deafness.

2. *Years of experience teaching deaf students*: Teachers were asked to indicate the number of years experience they had with deaf students.

3. *Hearing status*: Teachers were asked to report whether they were hearing, hard of hearing, or deaf.

4. *Amount of social interaction with deaf adults*: Teachers were asked to report how much social interaction they had with deaf adults. (Responses to this question were assessed only for those teachers who reported that they signed to their students during instruction).

5. *Self-ratings of expressive and receptive signing ability*: Teachers were asked to judge their receptive and expressive signing skills in comparison with their ability to use spoken English.

6. *Source of sign skill acquisition*: A checklist of possible sources was provided. Teachers were asked to indicate all the sources that contributed to their learning to sign and which was most important.

7. *Degree of English*: To determine the degree to which teachers might be incorporating features of English into their signs, they were presented with two short English sentences: "I am looking at him," and "He is looking for me." For each of the twelve syntactic elements in these sentences— *I, am, look, –ing, at, him, He, is, look, –ing, for*, and *me*—teachers indicated

how they would communicate it to the named student in the classroom. Additionally, teachers were asked whether they would use the .same or different signs for the pairs *I* and *me*, *is* and *am*, *he* and *him*, and *look* in both sentences. Each of the teacher's responses to these sixteen questions was coded "1" if it represented an English grammatical or vocabulary choice or "0" if it did not. The sixteen dichotomously scored English elements were subjected to a Rasch psychometric analysis. The results of the psychometric analysis are presented by Woodward and Allen (1987). The product of this procedure was a scaled score assigned to each teacher's responses indicating the degree of English. This score is evaluated in the current analysis.

RESULTS

Student Characteristics Within Program Type

Placement Level.   Table 1 shows comparison of placement levels by program type. Large differences in the placement levels of students attending the different types of programs are evident; *students attending residential schools were an older group than those attending other types of programs.* Sixty percent of the residential school students were in either junior high or high school, compared to only 13 percent of the local, non-

Table 1.   Placement Level of Student Within Program Type

Placement Level	Residential School		Day School		Local, Not Integrated		Integrated Full- or Part-time		Total	
Preprimary	41	6%	23	20%	100	35%	61	6%	225	10%
Elementary	193	27%	54	47%	129	45%	441	42%	817	38%
Junior High	103	15%	17	15%	22	8%	200	19%	342	16%
High School	316	45%	13	11%	14	5%	324	31%	667	31%
Ungraded	56	8%	7	6%	21	7%	34	3%	118	5%
Total	709	100%	114	100%	286	100%	1060	100%	2169	100%

Table 2. Sex of Student Within Program Type

	Residential School		Day School		Local, Not Integrated		Integrated Full- or Part-Time		Total	
Male	405	57%	63	55%	147	52%	544	51%	1159	53%
Female	305	43%	51	45%	138	48%	516	49%	1010	47%
Total	710	100%	114	100%	285	100%	1060	100%	2169	100%

integrated group, and 50 percent of the local, integrated group. While these data cannot be interpreted longitudinally, they suggest that elementary school students, in greatest need of special education support in the local, nonintegrated programs, are perhaps not well-served by the local programs once they reach junior high school. Either they move to local, integrated programs or they change to residential schools, as evidenced by the higher proportion of junior- and senior-high-school students in these programs. Research is needed to evaluate the likely school migration patterns of elementary, deaf, nonintegrated students.

Sex. As can be noted in table 2, males comprised a slightly higher percentage of residential school students (57 percent) than of other program groups. The lowest percentage for males (51 percent) could be found in the local, integrated setting. Day schools and local, nonintegrated settings

enrolled 55 percent and 52 percent males, respectively.

Ethnic Background. The distributions of ethnic background within program type appear in table 3. While residential schools and local, integrated settings contained similar percentages of white, non-Hispanic students (71 percent and 73 percent, respectively), the minority composition of these two program types differed markedly. While residential schools comprised 22 percent black and 6 percent Hispanic students, local, integrated programs comprised 12 percent black and 11 percent Hispanic students. Day schools and local, nonintegrated programs had higher concentrations of minority students than residential and local, integrated programs. Only 53 percent of the day school and 54 percent of the local, nonintegrated groups were white, non-Hispanic students. The minority compositions of these program types differed also. While the day schools

Table 3. Ethnic Background of Student Within Program Type

Student's Ethnic Background	Residential School		Day School		Local, Not Integrated		Integrated Full- or Part-Time		Total	
White, non-Hispanic	501	71%	60	53%	154	54%	778	73%	1493	69%
Black	153	22%	16	14%	74	26%	126	12%	369	17%
Hispanic	39	6%	32	28%	45	16%	113	11%	229	11%
Native American	2	0%	0	0%	0	0%	2	0%	4	0%
Asian Pacific	7	1%	2	2%	9	3%	32	3%	50	2%
Other or not reported	7	1%	5	4%	5	1%	17	2%	34	1%
Total	709	100%	113	100%	286	100%	1060	100%	2168	100%

Note. The percentages within program type may add up to more than 100 due to the presence of multi-ethnic responses to the survey.

were 14 percent black and 28 percent Hispanic, the local, nonintegrated group was 26 percent black and 16 percent Hispanic.

The larger concentrations of minority students in day schools and local, nonintegrated programs, compared to the residential schools, may represent geographical differences along an urban–rural dimension. Day schools and the larger special education programs exist in urban schools where there are likely to be larger percentages of minority students. Residential-school education may represent the only option for students living in rural areas. The overrepresentation of white, non-Hispanic students in local, integrated programs (especially compared to local, nonintegrated programs) may represent differences in achievement test scores and other measures used to select students for integration.

Hearing Loss. Table 4 shows the strong association between hearing loss and program type. While 93 percent of the residential school students had severe or profound hearing losses, only 49 percent of the local, integrated students had this severity of loss. In fact, 35 percent of the local, integrated students had normal hearing or mild or moderate losses, while only 1 percent of the residential school students were in that range. While the day schools and local, nonintegrated groups had distributions that fell between these two extremes, their students were much more similar to those of the residential

schools than to those in local, integrated settings.

These findings demonstrate the importance of considering audiological differences among students in different program types in any discussion of communication differences that are noted.

Additional Handicaps. A similar percentage of residential school and local, integrated students report the presence of additional handicaps (29 percent and 26 percent, respectively); however, as table 5 demonstrates, the distributions for specific handicaps differ. Of those students with handicaps in the residential schools, 21 percent report uncorrected visual problems, compared to only 7 percent of those with additional handicaps reported in integrated programs. In the local, integrated group, 42 percent of those with additional handicaps report specific learning difficulties, compared to 36 percent among those with additional handicaps in the residential schools. Finally, there is greater prevalence of reported emotional/behavioral problems among the additionally handicapped students in the residential schools compared with the local, integrated group.

Overall, the day school and local, nonintegrated groups show higher percentages of students with additional handicaps (with 33 percent and 37 percent, respectively). *Compared with the residential and local, integrated programs, higher proportions of physical handicaps can be noted in these self-contained day programs.* Of those with ad-

Table 4. Level of Hearing Loss Within Program Type

Level of Hearing Loss	Residential School		Day School		Local, Not Integrated		Integrated Full- or Part-Time		Total	
Normal: <27 dB	0	0%	2	2%	3	1%	112	11%	117	5%
Mild: 27–40 dB	3	0%	1	1%	8	3%	122	12%	134	6%
Moderate: 41–55 dB	9	1%	2	2%	10	4%	128	12%	149	7%
Moderate–Severe: 56–70 dB	37	5%	10	9%	42	15%	173	17%	262	12%
Severe: 71–90 dB	148	21%	24	21%	77	27%	205	20%	454	21%
Profound: ≥91 dB	512	72%	75	66%	141	50%	302	29%	1030	48%
Total	709	100%	114	100%	281	100%	1042	100%	2146	100%

Table 5. Additional Handicapping Conditions Within Program Type

Handicapping Condition	Residential School		Day School		Local, Not Integrated		Integrated Full- or Part-Time		Total	
Presence of Additional Handicaps										
No	504	71%	76	67%	179	63%	773	74%	1532	71%
Yes	204	29%	38	33%	107	37%	276	26%	625	29%
Total	708	100%	114	100%	286	100%	1049	100%	2157	100%
Specific Handicaps										
Legal blindness	5	2%	2	5%	13	12%	11	4%	31	5%
Visual problem	43	21%	3	8%	15	14%	18	7%	79	13%
Brain damage	9	4%	1	3%	11	10%	11	4%	32	5%
Epilepsy	8	4%	1	3%	5	5%	6	2%	20	3%
Orthopedic problem	12	6%	4	11%	15	14%	20	7%	51	8%
Cerebral palsy	13	6%	2	5%	13	12%	25	9%	53	9%
Heart disorder	15	7%	6	16%	10	9%	12	4%	43	7%
Other health impairment	20	10%	5	13%	14	13%	24	9%	63	10%
Mental retardation	29	14%	6	16%	32	30%	53	19%	120	19%
Emotional/behavioral problem	53	26%	10	26%	15	14%	42	19%	120	19%
Learning disability	74	36%	17	45%	17	16%	115	42%	223	36%
Other	16	8%	2	5%	4	4%	13	5%	35	6%
Total	203	100%	38	100%	106	100%	276	100%	623	100%

Note. The percentages listed for specific handicaps are based on the number of students within each program type reporting *any* additional handicaps. Since multiple responses were allowed for students with more than one additional handicap, the percentages in any column may add up to more than 100.

ditional handicaps in local, nonintegrated programs, 30 percent are reported with mental retardation. In contrast, 45 percent of those with additional handicaps in the day schools are categorized with learning disabilities.

It should be stressed that the differences noted in these additional handicap distributions should not be overinterpreted. In the case of the prevalence of visual problems among residential school students, the finding is an artifact of the cohort of rubella students still enrolled in the spring of 1985. For some of the other categories, especially those in the cognitive and behavioral domains, distinctions are based on unknown assessment strategies with unknown psychometric properties. It is possible that assessment bias might correlate with program type, such that a given individual described as learning disabled in one type of setting might be classified as mentally retarded in another. Additional handicap assessment and its implications for educational programming are important issues requiring further study.

Communication Characteristics

Before studying the relationships of each of the communication measures to program type, it is useful to explore their interrelatedness without consideration of program variation. Table 6 presents a cross-tabulation of hearing loss with teacher ratings of speech intelligibility; table 7 presents a cross-tabulation of teacher-rated speech intelligibility with the student's mode of communication in the classroom; and table 8 examines the association of student communication mode to hearing loss.

Clearly, as can be seen from table 6, hearing loss is strongly related to teacher

Table 6. Association of Speech Intelligibility with Hearing Loss

Type of Hearing Loss	Intelligible		Nonintelligible		Total	
Less-than-severe	637	90%	73	10%	710	100%
Severe	273	56%	216	44%	489	100%
Profound	258	24%	841	76%	1099	100%
Total	1168	51%	1130	49%	2298	100%

ratings of speech intelligibility. For students with less-than-severe hearing loss (BEA < 71 dB), 89.7 percent are judged by teachers to have intelligible speech. For students with severe impairments (BEA between 71 and 90 dB), 55.8 percent are judged by their teachers as having intelligible speech. Among those with profound loss (BEA > 90 dB), only 23.5 percent are rated by teachers as having intelligible speech.

While hearing loss is related to speech intelligibility, the latter is, in turn, highly related to the communication mode the student uses in the classroom (as evidenced by table 7); of those with intelligible speech, only 33.7 percent used sign language in the instructional context; among those judged by teachers to have nonin-

telligible speech, 87.5 percent used sign language in the classroom.

Finally, student communication mode (table 8) is highly related to hearing loss. (Obviously, none of these three two-way associations is statistically independent of the other two; that fact is the central point of this chapter.) While, overall, 34.9 percent of the deaf students in the sample used speech in the classroom, this finding is misleading. A full 77.5 percent of those students with a less-than-severe hearing loss used only speech as their mode of communication in the classroom, while only 10.5 percent of those with profound loss used speech all the time. As tempting as it is to use the 35 percent figure in describing the percentage of deaf students enrolled in "oral" programs, it must be

Table 7. Association of Speech Intelligibility with Communication Method

Intelligibility	Student Signs		Student Speaks		Other[a]		Total	
Intelligible	397	34%	761	64%	23	2%	1183	100%
Nonintelligible	997	88%	57	5%	86	7%	1140	100%
Total	1396	60%	818	35%	109	5%	2323	100%

[a] Cued speech, gestures, writing, etc.

Table 8. Association of Student Communication Mode with Hearing Loss

Hearing Loss	Student Signs		Student Speaks		Other		Total	
Less-than-severe	140	20%	553	77%	21	3%	714	100%
Severe	330	67%	139	28%	25	5%	494	100%
Profound	927	84%	116	10%	62	6%	1105	100%
Total	1397	60%	808	35%	108	5%	2313	100%

presented in such a way as to indicate the very strong relationship between speech use and degree of hearing loss.

We now examine the relationship of these variables to program type. Given the sizeable relationship between hearing loss and program type (table 4) and the noted interrelationships among the hearing loss, communication mode, and speech intelligibility variables, we can predict that each of these communication variables will covary strongly with program. The results are presented in tables 9, 10, and 11.

Student Communication Mode. Table 9 reveals a strong relationship between program type and student communication mode. Ninety-one percent of the residential school students in the survey used signs (either with or without speech), while only 18 percent of the students integrated in the target class signed to their teachers. In the integrated, in-target group, 76 percent used speech only. The relationship of communication mode to program type is phenomenally systematic: The prevalence of student signing in the classroom decreases as a function of degree of integration experienced by the student—91 percent of the residential school students sign; 76 percent of the day school students; 70 percent of the local, nonintegrated students; 62 percent of the students who are not integrated in the target class but who are integrated in other academic contexts; and 18 percent of the students integrated in the target area.

Teacher Communication Mode. As can be seen from table 10, the relationship between teacher communication mode and program type is equally strong. Interestingly, fewer students sign themselves than have teachers who sign to them. Overall, 68 percent of the students in the survey had teachers who reported signing in instruction, while 61 percent of the students were reported as signing. Combining the three signing categories in table 10, we find the following: In residential schools, 96 percent of the students had teachers who signed during instruction of the target course area; in day schools, 81 percent of the students had signing teachers; in local, nonintegrated programs, 82 percent of the students had signing teachers; in nonintegrated classes for students who were integrated for other academic courses, 69 percent had signing teachers; and in integrated classes, only 23 percent of the students had signing teachers.

Among the signing teachers, differentiation was made as to whether they spoke while they signed and, if not, whether they used simultaneous lip movements. Virtually none of the students, except those in residential schools, had signing teachers who did not use simultaneous communication. In the residential schools, 11 percent had teachers who reported not using lip movements. Linguistically, these findings imply a low rate of possible ASL use in the classroom.

Other communication methods were reported very infrequently. Cued Speech was

Table 9. Communication Mode Student Normally Uses in Class Within Program Type

Communication Mode	Residential School		Day School		Local, Not Integrated		Integrated Not in Target		Integrated in Target		Total	
Speaks and signs	381	54%	64	57%	122	43%	208	49%	81	13%	856	40%
Signs only	265	37%	21	19%	78	27%	55	13%	30	5%	449	21%
Communicates through interpreter	0	0%	0	0%	0	0%	1	0%	24	4%	25	1%
Speaks only	39	6%	26	23%	61	21%	155	36%	478	76%	759	35%
Other	22	3%	2	2%	25	9%	9	2%	17	3%	75	3%
Total	707	100%	113	100%	286	100%	428	100%	630	100%	2164	100%

Table 10. Communication Mode Teacher Normally Uses in Class by Program Type

Communication Mode	Residential School		Day School		Local, Not Integrated		Integrated Not in Target		Integrated in Target		Total	
Sign and speak	570	82%	86	80%	219	81%	282	69%	120	22%	1277	63%
Sign/no speech, with lip movement	78	11%	0	0%	1	0%	2	0%	4	1%	85	4%
Sign/no speech, no lip movement	20	3%	1	1%	2	1%	0	0%	0	0%	23	1%
No sign, with interpreter	1	0%	0	0%	0	0%	1	0%	31	6%	33	2%
No sign—Speech	24	3%	21	19%	44	16%	121	30%	386	71%	596	29%
No sign—Cued Speech	0	0%	0	0%	3	1%	3	1%	1	0%	7	0%
Total	693	100%	108	100%	269	100%	409	100%	542	100%	2021	100%

used with less than 1 percent of the students in the entire data-base (seven students were reported as having teachers who used Cued Speech), and only 6 percent of the students who were integrated with hearing students in the target class were reported to have teachers who used a sign interpreter.

Teacher Ratings of Speech Intelligibility. Table 11 shows the distribution within program type of the responses to the question about students' speech intelligibility. As with the other communication variables, strong relationships can be noted. While 30 percent of the residential school students were rated by their teachers as having intelligible speech, 81 percent of the students integrated in the target class were judged as having intelligible speech. Two of the other three settings had intelligibility rates between these extremes, but speech intelligibility at the local, noninte-

grated setting is almost identical to that found in the residential schools.

Summary of Communication Variables. Bar charts showing group differences of selected characteristics appear in figure 2. The unique characteristics of the students who were "integrated in target" are vividly indicated.

Further Analysis of Variable Relationships

Figure 3 shows the relationship of program assignment to the combined variables of hearing loss and rated speech intelligibility. The first division of the population, represented by the three graphs, is into three hearing-loss groups: less than severe, severe, and profound. A second division is made, represented by the separate groups of bars within the graph, so that different levels of speech intelligibility could be studied within hear-

Table 11. Teacher Rating of Students' Speech Intelligibility Within Program Type

Intelligibility Rating	Residential School		Day School		Local, Not Integrated		Integrated Not in Target		Integrated in Target		Total	
Very intelligible	44	6%	18	16%	23	8%	113	27%	297	47%	495	23%
Intelligible	168	24%	23	20%	69	24%	125	29%	212	34%	597	28%
Barely intelligible	172	25%	28	25%	55	19%	91	21%	52	8%	398	19%
Not intelligible	194	28%	31	27%	74	26%	72	17%	39	6%	410	19%
No attempt to speak	119	17%	13	12%	66	23%	25	6%	27	4%	250	12%
Total	697	100%	113	100%	287	100%	426	100%	627	100%	2150	100%

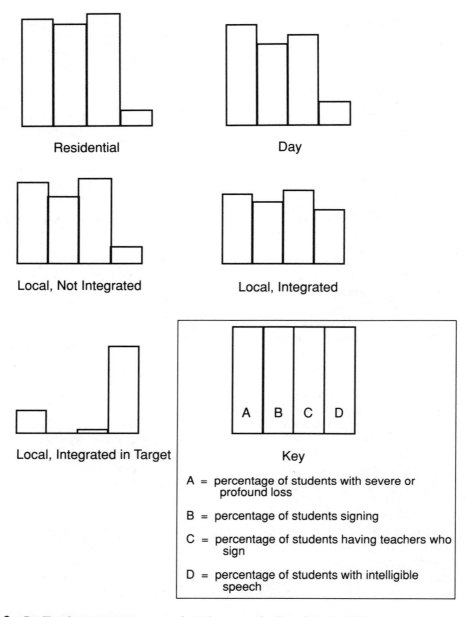

Figure 2. Profile of program types on selected communication characteristics.

ing-loss groups. The final division, represented by the grouped bars themselves, is by program type. In this figure, the actual numbers are represented for each subgroup defined by these divisions.

The first important conclusion to be drawn from figure 3 is that the population is decidedly bimodal. A large percentage of the entire population (well over a third)

falls into one of two groups: less than severely deaf with intelligible speech in integrated programs (where we know that nonmanual education predominates), or profoundly deaf with nonintelligible speech in the residential schools (where we know that manual communication predominates).

Other facts that are apparent from figure

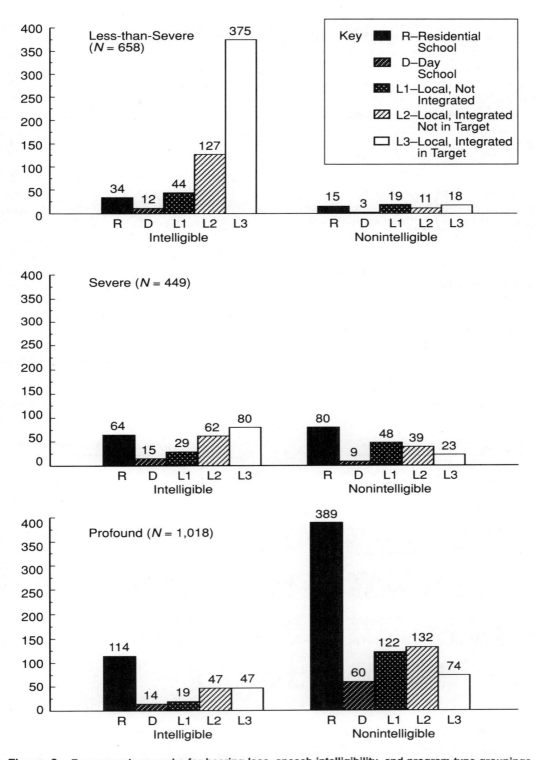

Figure 3. Frequency bar graphs for hearing loss, speech intelligibility, and program type groupings.

3 are as follows: among those students with less-than-severe loss, 90 percent are judged as having intelligible speech. Furthermore, the overwhelming majority either are in integrated classes or are integrated in classes other than the target. Among the severely impaired, there is little systematic pattern. The students are roughly evenly divided into the intelligible and nonintelligible groups, and they appear in all program types. This lack of a discernible pattern makes these students extremely interesting from a planning, placement, and policy point of view. For the less-than-severe and profound groups, speech and hearing determines program placement. For those students who have severe but not profound losses, other factors are obviously important.

The profound group is overwhelmingly judged as having nonintelligible speech (76 percent); however, there was a cluster of 114 profoundly deaf students in residential schools who were rated as having intelligible speech. Further research is needed to ascertain the reasons deaf students with intelligible speech elect to attend residential schools. Another interesting subgroup is the seventy-four profoundly deaf students with nonintelligible speech in integrated classes. It is difficult to say much about this subgroup, since it comprises only 3.5 percent of all the students in the survey.

Figure 4 shows the relationship of speech intelligibility to sign use for students in different program settings. The figure reveals an interaction between program type and sign use with respect to intelligibility. In integrated programs, the rated speech intelligibility determined communication mode: 63.5 percent of the students who have nonintelligible speech sign in instructional settings, while only 7.3 percent of the integrated students who have intelligible speech, as rated by their teachers, use sign in the instructional context. In the residential schools, virtually everyone

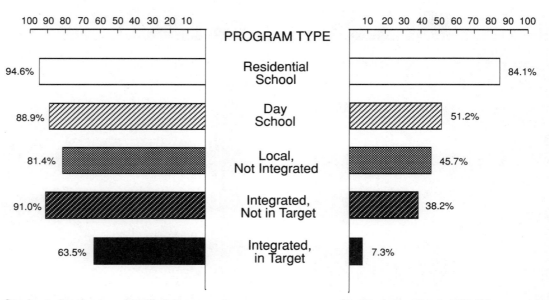

Figure 4. Percentage of students who communicate using sign in different intelligibility groups within program type.

signed, including 94.6 percent of those with nonintelligible speech and 84.1 percent of those with intelligible speech. Therefore, while speech intelligibility is highly related to communication overall, the strength of the relationship is dependent on the nature of the educational program with respect to the level of academic integration.

Table 12 examines the relationship of student and teacher modes of communication in the different program settings. In all settings, when students sign in the classroom their teachers do also. In all but the integrated-in-target settings, more than 95 percent of the students who signed in the instructional context also had teachers who signed. In the integrated-in-target setting, 7 percent of the signing students had teachers who spoke only, and 6 percent had teachers who used some other method (most notably an interpreter). This finding should be viewed in light of the fact that only 20 percent of the integrated-in-target students were signers.

For speaking students, teachers exhibited variation by program in their mode of communication. In residential schools, 30 percent of the speaking students had signing teachers. Again, it should be noted that speaking students comprised only 5 percent of the residential school population. In the integrated-in-target group, 95 percent of the speaking students had speaking teachers. In the other three program types the percentage of speaking students who had speaking teachers ranged from 76 to 86 percent. These results indicate that, throughout the different settings, quite a large number of speaking students have signing teachers. This situation has received very little attention from the research community.

Teacher Characteristics

Up to this point, we have considered, in general terms, whether or not teachers in the different programs signed to their students, and we have referred to signing teachers from the five settings as if they were a homogeneous group of skilled signers. Clearly, the teachers of the students in these five types of programs vary with respect to their own experiences with

Table 12. Distribution of Teacher Communication Methods Within Each Program Type for Students Who Employ Different Methods[a]

Student: Teacher:	Residential School			Day School			Local, Not Integrated			Local, Integrated Not in Target			Local, Integrated in Target		
	Signs	Speaks	Other	Signs	Speaks	Other	Signs	Speaks	Other	Signs	Speaks	Other	Signs	Speaks	Other
Signs	100%	0%	0%	99%	1%	0%	99%	1%	0%	97%	3%	0%	87%	7%	6%
			92%			78%			74%			64%			20%
Speaks	30%	70%	0%	14%	86%	0%	18%	76%	6%	15%	82%	2%	4%	95%	1%
			5%			21%			19%			33%			73%
Other[b]	Too few students report "other" communication modes to warrant presenting figures broken down within program type														
			3%			2%			8%			2%			7%
	N = 691			N = 107			N = 268			N = 409			N = 540		

[a] The overall distribution of student communication mode within each program type is presented below the diagonal in each cell.

[b] "Other" includes use of interpreter, Cued Speech, and miscellaneous other means indicated by respondents on survey forms.

Table 13.   Teacher's Hearing Status[a]

	Residential School		Day School		Not Integrated in Target		Integrated in Target		Total	
Hearing	519	73%	98	86%	683	96%	610	97%	1910	88%
Hard-of-Hearing	44	6%	10	9%	23	3%	15	2%	92	4%
Deaf	144	20%	6	5%	6	1%	4	1%	160	7%
Total	707	100%	114	100%	712	100%	629	100%	2162	100%

[a] Percentages indicate the number of students having teachers who show a given characteristic. For example, 73% of the residential school students in the survey had hearing teachers. This does not imply that 73% of the residential school teachers are hearing.

deafness. This varied experience might influence qualitative aspects of the teachers' signing. The intent of this final section of the analysis will be to describe some of these differences.

Hearing Status of Teachers.   Twenty percent of the residential students reported in the study had deaf teachers, compared to only 1 percent of the integrated students (table 13). Also, only 1 percent of the local, *not* integrated-in-target group had deaf teachers. These findings should be viewed in conjunction with the age differences noted above. If it is true that more and more younger students at all levels of hearing loss are attending local schools for their elementary school experience, and that residential schools are becoming high schools for profoundly deaf, less academically able students who cannot obtain appropriate services in the local schools, it is also true that young deaf students are not seeing deaf teacher role models in the elementary grades. This also implies that the

signing experienced by these younger students is limited to that of hearing teachers in primarily self-contained classrooms.

Years of Experience Teaching Deaf Students.   Overall, teachers with considerable experience are teaching deaf students. Combining program types (table 14), 67 percent of the deaf students in the survey had teachers with more than five years' experience. However, experience was related to program type. Fifty-three percent of the residential school students had teachers with more than ten years' experience, while only 34 percent of the students in integrated classrooms had teachers with this much experience. Similarly, only 4 percent of the residential school students had teachers with less than two years' experience, compared to 20 percent of the local, integrated students. Of all the program types, day schools had the least experienced staffs. Only 30 percent of the day school students had teachers with more than ten years' experience, and 45 percent

Table 14.   Years Experience Teaching Deaf Students[a]

Teaching Experience	Residential School		Day School		Not Integrated in Target		Integrated in Target		Total	
Less than 2 years	28	4%	22	19%	69	10%	122	20%	241	11%
2–5 years	117	17%	30	26%	181	25%	131	21%	459	21%
6–10 years	186	26%	28	25%	218	31%	153	25%	585	27%
More than 10 years	376	53%	34	30%	243	34%	212	34%	865	40%
Total	707	100%	114	100%	711	100%	618	100%	2150	100%

[a] See note to table 13.

Table 15. Teachers' Self-Rating of Expressive Signing Ability by Program Type[a,b]

Teachers' Self-rating	Residential School		Day School		Not Integrated in Target		Integrated in Target		Total	
Cannot sign	2	0%	0	0%	0	0%	1	1%	3	0%
Use English much better	108	16%	27	31%	148	29%	40	32%	323	23%
Use English a little better	203	31%	32	37%	186	37%	41	33%	462	34%
Use signs as well	299	45%	27	31%	165	33%	39	32%	530	38%
Sign a little better	21	3%	0	0%	1	0%	0	0%	22	2%
Sign much better	33	5%	1	1%	3	0%	2	1%	39	3%
Total	666	100%	87	100%	503	100%	123	100%	1379	100%

[a] See note to table 13.
[b] This table is limited to analysis of students whose teachers report signing to them during classroom instruction.

had teachers with five or fewer years' experience teaching deaf students.

Self-ratings of Expressive Signing Ability. Table 15 shows the distribution of responses to the question asking teachers to rate their own signing ability. The sample for this table has been restricted to those teachers who reported that they signed to their students during instruction. Over half of the residential school students (who had signing teachers) had teachers who reported using signs as well as or better than they used spoken English. This compares to only 33 percent of the integrated students (in signing classrooms). The day school and the local, nonintegrated teachers were similar in their response in this rating to the local, integrated teachers.

The presence of deaf teachers in residential schools explains only some of these differences. When the sample is limited to *hearing* teachers who sign to their students in the classroom, the percentages of students having teachers who rate their expressive signing ability as high or higher than their English ability are 32 percent for residential and 30 percent for local, integrated settings. Thus, in addition to the presence of deaf teachers in the residential schools, there is a tendency for hearing teachers to rate their signing more highly than do signing teachers in integrated settings.

Self-ratings of Receptive Signing Ability. Table 16 shows the distribution of teacher responses to the question about their receptive sign language abilities. Although in every group teachers rate their receptive skills lower than their expressive skills, the same pattern can be noted: a higher per-

Table 16. Teachers' Self-Rating of Receptive Signing Ability by Program Type[a]

Teachers' self-rating	Residential School		Day School		Not Integrated in Target		Integrated in Target		Total	
Can't understand signs	0	0%	0	0%	0	0%	1	1%	1	0%
Understand English much better	148	22%	36	41%	198	40%	47	39%	429	31%
Understand English a little better	243	37%	29	33%	220	44%	52	43%	544	40%
Understand signs as well	235	35%	21	24%	77	15%	20	16%	353	26%
Understand signs a little better	16	2%	0	0%	1	0%	0	0%	17	1%
Understand signs much better	22	3%	1	1%	5	1%	2	2%	30	2%
Total	664	100%	87	100%	501	100%	122	100%	1374	100%

[a] See notes to tables 13 and 15.

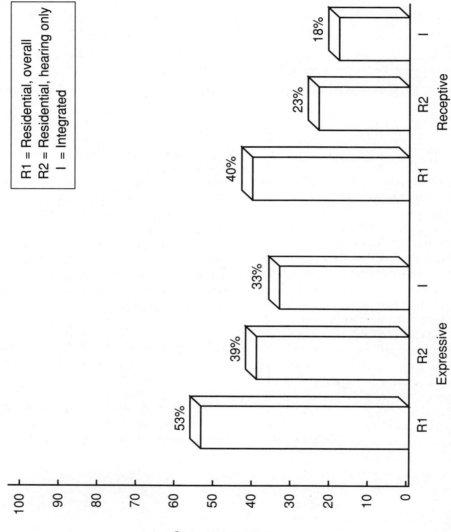

Figure 5. Comparison of self-ratings of communication skills for signing teachers in residential and integrated settings.

centage of teachers in the residential schools rate their receptive sign skills as being equal to or better than their English skills. While 40 percent of the residential students had teachers who rated their receptive skills equal to or better than their English skills, only 18 percent of the integrated students had signing teachers who rated their receptive skills that high. When the residential school group was limited to those with hearing teachers, the percentage of students with highly self-rated teachers dropped to 23 percent. This percentage, while much lower than the 40 percent reported for the entire group, is still five percentage points higher than that reported for the integrated students.

The percentages of students in signing classrooms from residential and integrated programs who have teachers rating their expressive and receptive sign skills equal to or better than their English skills are plotted in figure 5. The differences that have been discussed can be readily noted.

Source of Sign Language Acquisition. On the communication survey, teachers were asked to indicate on a checklist which of several sources were important to their acquiring signing skills. Then they were

asked to indicate which of these was the single most important source of their skill. The results of the analysis of these variables are presented in tables 17 and 18 (again, it should be remembered that the analysis is limited to those students who had teachers who reported that they signed in the instructional context).

Overwhelmingly, sign classes were reported as the modal source of sign acquisition. However, in the residential schools, this source was selected less often than in the other three settings. In the residential schools, 70 percent of the students had teachers who indicated that sign classes contributed to their acquisition, compared to the other three settings, whose comparable percentages ranged from 91 percent to 97 percent. In the residential schools, deaf students, co-workers, and deaf friends contributed more significantly than in the other program types.

Deaf students were indicated more often as the most important source in the residential schools (29 percent), followed by sign classes (21 percent) and deaf friends (19 percent). This pattern differed markedly from that of the other settings. In the integrated group, for example, sign classes were the most important source (47 per-

Table 17. Sources of Teachers' Sign Learning Within Program Type[a,b]

	Residential School		Day School		Not Integrated in Target		Integrated in Target		Total	
Deaf parents	53	8%	1	1%	28	6%	4	3%	86	6%
Hearing parents	21	3%	0	0%	8	2%	2	2%	31	2%
Deaf students	449	67%	52	60%	318	63%	72	59%	891	65%
Self-instruction	321	48%	42	48%	289	58%	67	55%	719	52%
Deaf child	15	2%	0	0%	12	2%	1	1%	28	2%
Deaf spouse	45	7%	4	5%	13	3%	0	0%	62	4%
Colleagues	425	64%	46	53%	305	61%	52	43%	828	60%
Sign language classes	467	70%	84	97%	468	93%	111	91%	1130	82%
Deaf relatives	80	12%	6	7%	23	5%	12	10%	121	9%
Deaf friends	425	64%	34	39%	229	46%	67	55%	755	55%
Hearing friends	117	18%	17	20%	116	23%	32	26%	282	21%
Other	93	14%	4	5%	39	8%	9	7%	145	11%
Total	666	100%	87	100%	503	100%	122	100%	1378	100%

[a] See notes to tables 13 and 15.

[b] Since respondents could check more than one source, the percentages for any one column may be greater than 100.

Table 18. Teachers' Single Most Important Source of Sign Learning[a]

	Residential School		Day School		Not Integrated in Target		Integrated in Target		Total	
Deaf parents	39	6%	0	0%	9	2%	2	2%	50	4%
Hearing parents	0	0%	0	0%	1	0%	0	0%	1	0%
Deaf students	181	29%	13	16%	86	18%	13	11%	293	22%
Self-instruction	22	4%	1	1%	34	7%	14	12%	71	5%
Deaf child	3	0%	0	0%	0	0%	0	0%	3	0%
Deaf spouse	6	1%	1	1%	4	1%	0	0%	11	1%
Colleagues	75	12%	9	11%	31	6%	5	4%	120	9%
Sign language classes	133	21%	38	46%	246	50%	56	47%	473	36%
Deaf relatives	11	2%	0	0%	3	1%	3	3%	23	1%
Deaf friends	117	19%	16	20%	55	11%	22	19%	257	14%
Hearing friends	0	0%	0	0%	1	0%	0	0%	3	0%
Other	43	7%	4	5%	20	4%	4	3%	85	5%
Total	630	100%	82	100%	490	100%	119	100%	1321	100%

[a] See notes to tables 13 and 15.

cent), followed by deaf friends (19 percent) and self-instruction (12 percent). In both nonintegrated day settings, also, sign classes were the most important source.

Amount of Social Interaction with Deaf Adults. As might be predicted from the above findings, the teachers of residential school students report more social interaction with deaf adults (Table 19). Teachers of 39 percent of the residential school students in signing classrooms report having "All or Nearly All" or "A Lot" of their social interaction with deaf adults. This compares to 20 percent of the teachers of integrated students and only 11 percent of the nonintegrated. This last difference is interesting, as it indicates greater social

immersion with deaf adults among teachers in integrated classrooms where sign is used than among teachers in local, nonintegrated classrooms. It should be kept in mind, however, that the twelve integrated students with signing teachers represent only 23 percent of the total number of integrated students in the study. The remaining 77 percent were reported by teachers who used speech only as their instructional mode of communication.

In nonintegrated classrooms, 89 percent of the students were reported as having teachers who had "None or Nearly None" or "A Little or Some" of their social interaction with deaf adults. As we have seen, this group comprised teachers of most of the younger students from the data set

Table 19. Amount of Teachers' Social Interaction with Deaf Adults by Program Type[a]

Social Interaction	Residential School		Day School		Not Integrated in Target		Integrated in Target		Total	
None or nearly none	59	9%	24	28%	190	38%	43	36%	316	23%
A little or some	346	52%	54	62%	258	51%	54	45%	712	52%
A lot	187	28%	7	8%	45	9%	22	18%	261	19%
All or nearly all	70	11%	2	2%	9	2%	2	2%	83	6%
Total	662	100%	87	100%	502	100%	121	100%	1372	100%

[a] See notes to tables 13 and 15.

with severe or profound impairments. Future research should be directed to assessing the effects on younger students of teachers with little or no experience with deafness beyond their formal schooling.

Degree of English in Teachers' Signs. Up to this point, this chapter has been concerned only with the modal (i.e., manual communication versus speech) characteristics of communication in the classroom. The linguistic properties of the signs that are used have not been discussed. While extremely important, such properties are difficult to determine through survey research such as this. Nonetheless, a group of questionnaire items was designed to assess the degree to which teachers incorporated features of English into their signing with deaf students. The method section of this chapter describes these questions briefly; the resulting "English features" scale has been described elsewhere (Allen and Woodward 1987; Woodward and Allen 1987).

A one-way analysis of variance (ANOVA) was performed using the "English features" scale as the dependent measure and "Program Type" as the independent measure. It should be obvious from all the preceding analyses that this ANOVA can in no way imply a causal relationship. Programs differ on virtually every variable that has been discussed so far. The purpose of this analysis was to determine, within the limitations of the questionaire and scaling procedure used, whether students from the different settings had teachers who reported different levels of incorporation of English features into their signing of simple sentences.

The means and standard deviations of the "English features" scale score for the different program types are presented in table 20. The ANOVA revealed significant differences among groups (F [4,103] = 4.59, p = .001). Three multiple comparisons were run to determine which of the pairs of group means differed significantly. Using the tests for Least Significance Differences

Table 20. Means and Standard Deviations of English Features Scale for Different Program Types

Type of Program	Mean	Standard Deviation
Residential School	1.99	1.83
Day School	2.34	1.91
Local, not integrated	2.54	1.66
Local, integrated, not in target	2.30	1.90
Local, integrated, in target	2.59	1.79

and Duncan's Multiple Range Test, it was found that students in residential schools had teachers who reported incorporating significantly fewer English features in their signing of the elements of the scale items than teachers of students in each of the three local school setting types. No other pairs of programs had means that differed significantly. Based on the more conservative Scheffe's procedure, the only significantly different comparison was between residential and local, nonintegrated programs, indicating that students in residential schools had teachers who reported incorporating fewer English features in the scale items than did the students in nonintegrated local school programs.

Again, it should be reiterated that residential school students differed from local school students as to their age, ethnicity, hearing status, and additional handicap status. Furthermore, their teachers differed as to hearing status, amount of experience with deaf students, and the sources of their sign language skills. Thus, it is not at all surprising that their "sign languages" might differ linguistically. The questionnaire items were not behavioral measures, and reliance on the scale values will depend on validation against observational measures, which has not been done. Nonetheless, the findings are provocative. Assessment of the educational implications of differences in the linguistic properties of sign language is a rich area for future research. However, such research will be very difficult to design. As we have shown, all variables are correlated with all others. Isolating the effects of a variable as subtle as linguistic variation (controlling for all other variables) and determining its impact on educational variables (which are themselves difficult to measure) will be a challenge for researchers for many years to come.

REFERENCES

Allen, T., and Woodward, J. 1987. Teacher characteristics and the degree to which teachers incorporate features of English in their sign communication with hearing impaired students. *American Annals of the Deaf* 132:61–67.

Woodward, J., and Allen, T. 1987. Two analyses of the ASL to English continuum. In *Proceedings of the second annual Pacific Linguistics Conference*, eds. S. De Lancey and R. Tomlin. Eugene: University of Oregon.

Woodward, J., Allen, T., and Schildroth, A. 1985. Teachers of deaf students: An ethnography of classroom communication. In *Proceedings of the first annual meeting of the Pacific Linguistics Conference*, eds. S. Delancey and R. Tomlin. Eugene: University of Oregon.

CHAPTER 4

Sign English in the Education of Deaf Students

James Woodward

This chapter focuses on the type of signing that has been called Sign English or Pidgin Sign English (PSE). This is the type of signing that skilled deaf and hearing signers often use with each other in discussing formal topics. It is often described by nonlinguists as signing English conceptually. The signer uses signs from American Sign Language (ASL) in English word order (with some manual representation of English function words and without any manual representation of English inflections), while using as many ASL grammatical characteristics as possible. Sign English may be used with voice and/or extensive mouthing of English words.

Sign English has developed out of the language contact between ASL and English and cannot be understood without reference to the bilingual, diglossic continuum between these languages in the U.S. Deaf community. This chapter includes a discussion of that continuum, a summary of some linguistic characteristics of Sign English, a discussion of the current use of Sign English in the education of deaf stu-

dents, and a presentation of some hypotheses about the future role of Sign English in the education of deaf students.

THE ASL-TO-ENGLISH DIGLOSSIC CONTINUUM

Diglossia

Stokoe (1970) first pointed out the existence of diglossia in the U.S. Deaf community, using Ferguson's (1959) classic paper as a model. Stokoe defined the formal variety as English (represented manually) and the conversational variety as ASL and demonstrated that varieties of signing English and ASL have the sociolinguistic characteristics typical of languages in diglossic situations. For many deaf signers, Sign English is the formal variety in the diglossic situation. Other deaf signers use much more English-like signing as the formal language variety.

Signing that approaches English along the continuum serves as the formal variety in the diglossic situation and tends to be used in formal conversations, such as in church, the classroom, lectures, and with hearing people. Signing that approaches ASL tends to be used in smaller, less formal, more intimate conversations. Publicly, English is often considered superior to ASL. Much formal grammatical description has been given of English (in its spoken or written form), but only relatively recently has any research on ASL been done. Some signers feel that standardization is necessary, but sign language diglossia appears as stable as other diglossic forms.

There appears to be only one possible point of conflict between diglossia in the U.S. Deaf community and in hearing communities—how the languages are acquired. In hearing diglossic situations, the conversational variety is learned first at home and the formal variety at school. Recent evidence from the Center for Assessment and Demographic Studies (CADS) at Gallaudet University suggests that only about 4 percent of the deaf population has two deaf parents and an additional 3 percent has one deaf parent. Thus, ASL is not generally learned in the home by most deaf children. However, while the home is the initial locus of enculturation for hearing children, many deaf children of hearing parents are enculturated primarily in residential schools. Given this, we can now say that the conversational variety is generally learned early in the initial locus of enculturation. Until now, many deaf children of hearing parents learned ASL, in informal settings, from their peer-group deaf children of deaf parents or from older deaf children who had already been enculturated into the Deaf community. English (signed, spoken, or written) was learned in more formal classroom situations.

The Sign-to-English Continuum

The notion of a language continuum in the Deaf community was pointed out by Stokoe (1972), Moores (1972), and Woodward (1972). Varieties of ASL were seen at one end of this continuum, which, as Stokoe (1973) pointed out, is probably multidimensional, and varieties of Manual English at the other.

Let's examine one example of variation between ASL and English signing.

FINISH ME	ASL
EAT	
EAT FINISH ME	ASL
ME FINISH EAT ME	ASL
ME FINISH EAT	ASL
I FINISH EAT	ASL
I END EAT	ASL
I HAVE EAT	ASL
I HAVE(V) EAT	ASL
I HAVE(V) EAT FINISH	Manual English

In this example, meaning *I have eaten*, purer ASL can sign EAT and FINISH simultaneously by using both hands, while no English variety does. Also notice that ASL does not have the same word order as English. English uses a different perfective marker than ASL. ASL has one form for the first person singular pronoun; English has two. Certain types of English signing use an initialized handshape (*V*) on HAVE. All of this variation is systematic. If people use the initialized sign for the English pronoun *I*, they will use English word order. If people use an initialized perfective marker, they will also use the sign for *I* and English word order. Depending on the social background of the signer and the appropriate language variety to choose, a person will use more ASL-like signing or more English-like signing. Of course, the use of any particular type of signing is dependent on the signer's knowledge. People can't use a language variety they do not know.

It has been shown (Battison, Markowicz, and Woodward 1975; Woodward 1973a, b, c, d, 1974) that variation along the Sign-to-English continuum is nondiscrete, but regular, rule-governed, and describable in terms of modified scalogram analysis (Bailey 1973; Bickerton 1973) and variable rules (Fasold 1970; Labov 1969). This variation correlates with gross social variables, such as whether a person is deaf or hearing, has deaf or hearing parents, learned signs before or after the age of six, and attended some or no college (Woodward 1973a).

SOME LINGUISTIC CHARACTERISTICS OF SIGN ENGLISH

The intermediate varieties along the continuum between ASL and English are particularly interesting theoretically. For example, the sentence "ME FINISH EAT" has English word order but an ASL pronoun and an ASL perfective marker. Some native signers will consider this sentence ASL, while others will consider it English-like signing.

To resolve this problem, H. Markowicz and I (Woodward 1973c; Woodward and Markowicz 1980) posited that these intermediate varieties along the ASL-to-English diglossic continuum have certain linguistic and sociological characteristics of pidginized language varieties and thus have referred to intermediate varieties between ASL and English as Pidgin Sign English. It is important to note that these studies did not consider Sign English a separate language from ASL and English, but rather a mechanism to describe the regularity of intermediate language varieties that were not easily classifiable as ASL or English. A continuum, by its very nature, does not have discrete internal boundaries. Sign English merely describes the fact that there is often no clearcut division between ASL and English and allows one to talk about English-like ASL and ASL-like English for deaf people and ASL-like English for a few hearing people and English-like English for most hearing people.

These studies indicate that Sign English demonstrates the reductions (Samarin 1971) and admixtures (Hymes 1971) in morphology and phonology that are typical of pidginized language varieties. Sign English retains certain grammatical characteristics of both ASL and English and some of the phonological characteristics of ASL, although the number of redundancies is reduced.

Deaf signers retain more ASL characteristics in their Sign English than do hearing signers, who retain more English characteristics. However, due to the incapability of the visual channel to directly transmit oral phonological information, there is almost no retention of English phonology in Sign English. In Sign English phonology there are more distinctive handshapes at the phonological level than in ASL; however, the signing space is somewhat restricted for deaf signers and greatly restricted for hearing signers. No English suprasegmentals can be retained in Sign English because of the incompatibility of the visual and oral channels. Suprasegmentals that are distinctive at the phonological level in ASL are redundant in Sign English. Deaf signers, because of their ASL base, tend to use more of these redundancies than hearing signers, who almost always come from an English base. Thus, the Sign English production of hearing people is much more reduced than that of deaf people. Hearing signers are often said to sign without expression or to mumble.

There is considerable debate as to whether Sign English should be described as a pidgin language (Woodward 1973c), a pidginized language variety (Woodward and Markowicz 1980; Woodward 1980), "foreigner talk" (Cokely 1983), a language variety resulting from possible hybridization or pidginization that may be developing along a "pre-pidgin continuum" (Bochner and Albertini 1988), etc. It is likely that "foreigner talk," hybridization, pidginization, nativization, and creolization may all be involved to some extent, depending on the topics, participants, setting, etc., influencing the use of Sign English in a specific conversation. Despite this controversy, most linguists would agree that Sign English occurs frequently in deaf/ hearing interaction and that it is a mixture of certain ASL and English characteristics.

It is important to note that there has been very little descriptive research done on the grammatical characteristics of Sign English. The little that has been done has been based primarily on ethnographic observations of the interactions of skilled deaf and hearing signers. There are no large-scale studies of Sign English as there have been of ASL. Ceil Lucas and Clayton Valli, both of the Linguistics Department at Gallaudet University, are currently working on a large corpus of data on Sign English variation. This study should provide a good basis for validating or rejecting the information that has previously been published regarding grammatical characteristics of Sign English. More than likely, Lucas and Valli's data will indicate that there is a very complex set of patterns for Sign English that will vary considerably according to topic, participants, and setting. For now, we have to rely on previous studies.

To date three studies of grammatical characteristics of Sign English have been published (Woodward 1973c; Woodward and Markowicz 1980; Reilly and McIntire 1980). The authors focus on the type of signing that skilled deaf and hearing signers often use with each other for discussing formal topics. This type of signing can be used with voice and/or extensive mouthing of English words and is often described by nonlinguists as signing English conceptually, or signing in English word order while using as much ASL as possible. The following specific characteristics of Sign English have been noted in the literature.

Use of Copulas. ASL does not have a copula (the verb "to be"); English has a highly inflected copula. Sign English has variable use of a copula, with varying form. For example, Sign English used by older persons borrows the ASL sign TRUE and uses this as an uninflected copula. Signers may also fingerspell English copula forms. Some new copula forms that were developed for artificial systems designed for representing English are sometimes used in Sign English by younger signers.

Progressive Aspect. To express progressive aspect (continuous action), Sign English makes use of a mixture of ASL and English characteristics. ASL tends to use verb reduplication (repetition) to mark progressive aspect. English tends to use the form *be* + verb + *-ing*. In Sign English, no sign occurs for *-ing*. The *be* form is variable. ASL verb reduplication is also variably included.

Perfective Aspect. ASL uses the sign FINISH to indicate perfective aspect (completed action). In many varieties of ASL, FINISH normally follows the verb. English tends to use the form *have* + tense + verb + *-en*. In Sign English, FINISH is used before the verb and both FINISH and the verb remain uninflected; *-en* is not represented in Sign English.

Negative Incorporation. Several verbs in ASL may be negated by an outward twisting movement of the hand(s) from the place where the sign is normally made. English does not have this characteristic. In Sign English, verbs are normally negated by NOT + verb. The verbs KNOW and WANT may incorporate the negative into the verb sign instead of using NOT + verb. This varies from signer to signer and may vary within one signer depending on the social context of the conversation.

Agent–Beneficiary Directionality. ASL has a large number of verbs that express the relationship between agent and beneficiary by direction in three-dimensional space. Movement of the hand(s) is from the agent toward the beneficiary. English relies on word order and/or prepositions to express such relationships as "the woman gave the book to the man" or "the woman gave the man the book." In Sign English, the last version of the sentence would be preferred to the first because it allows for more ASL (agent–beneficiary directionality) and less dependence on English function words.

Articles. While ASL has demonstratives such as THAT, it does not have articles, such as English *a* and *the*. Sign English has variable use of articles, probably conditioned by surrounding environments. Older and less educated signers use articles less frequently. Articles in Sign English are generally fingerspelled, not signed.

Number Incorporation. In ASL, numbers are often incorporated into pronoun signs. While there is also number incorporation in Sign English pronouns, it does not appear to be as extensive as in ASL.

CURRENT CLASSROOM USE OF SIGN ENGLISH

In assessing the current use of Sign English in the education of deaf students, it is useful to examine certain data from the 1985 CADS Communication Study. The population for the study was drawn from those programs supplying data to the CADS Annual Survey of Hearing-Impaired Children and Youth, which collects demographic and educationally relevant data on more than 50,000 deaf students.

From the 1983–1984 Annual Survey database, 4,500 students were randomly selected and assigned to one of three subject area stratification groups: reading, mathematics, and social studies. Questionnaires were sent to the programs enrolling these students, with instructions to distribute them to the reading, mathematics, or social studies teachers of the students. Students were stratified in this way to ensure that teachers in a variety of academic contexts were represented in the database. Since sampling was carried out on an individual-student basis, some teachers received two or more questionnaires. Because the primary aim of this analysis was to describe the signing patterns of teachers, duplicate responses for these teachers were eliminated from the database. Also, the data set was limited to teachers who signed or signed and spoke directly with their students rather than using other methods of communication. Finally, teachers with missing or incomplete data were

eliminated from the database. The resulting file contained information on 1,187 teachers.

The questionnaire was constructed to describe the communication patterns used in classroom situations between teachers and deaf students and to distinguish the language codes and channels of communication used (Woodward, Allen, and Schildroth 1985). Teachers were asked whether or not they used signing during their instruction of individual students randomly selected for the survey. For teachers who signed, several additional questions were asked to determine where they fit along the ASL-to-English continuum. (The responses by percentage are on the right side of the page after each choice).

Questions	*Responses*
1. When teaching this student in the classroom, do you normally:	
a. Speak and sign at the same time	92.6%
b. Sign only	6.8%
c. Other	0.6%
2. If you sign only, do you use lip movements for most or all English words?	
a. Yes	81.6%
b. No	18.4%
3. The following list consists of phrases which have been used to characterize types of signing. Which of these best describes the signing you use when teaching this student? (Choose only one.)	
a. American Sign Language (ASL or Ameslan)	11.1%
b. Pidgin Sign English (PSE)	24.3%
c. Seeing Essential English (SEE I)	2.7%
d. Signing Exact English (SEE II)	25.9%
e. Signed English	31.8%
f. Linguistics of Visual English (LOVE)	0.2%
g. Other	4.1%

4. Read the following two English sentences:
He is looking at me.
I am looking for him.

a. When communicating the meaning of the two English sentences above to the *named student* in the classroom, indicate how you would communicate each of the following:
(a. Would fingerspell; b. Would use separate sign or gesture; c. Would include as part of another sign; d. Would omit).

1. He	(a,b,c, or d?)	I	(a,b,c, or d?)
2. is	(a,b,c, or d?)	am	(a,b,c, or d?)
3. look	(a,b,c, or d?)	look	(a,b,c, or d?)
4. −*ing*	(a,b,c, or d?)	−*ing*	(a,b,c, or d?)
5. at	(a,b,c, or d?)	for	(a,b,c, or d?)
6. me	(a,b,c, or d?)	him	(a,b,c, or d?)

b. When communicating the meaning of the two English sentences above to *this* student in the classroom, indicate how you would normally sign the following words:
(a. Would use the same sign for each; b. Would use a different sign for each; c. Would not sign one or both of these words).

1. He and Him	(a,b, or c?)
2. I and Me	(a,b, or c?)
3. Am and Is	(a,b, or c?)
4. Look in both sentences	(a,b, or c?)

These questions allowed the researchers to divide teachers into five basic groups: (1) those whose responses indicated that they do not follow the grammatical patterns of any researched sign variety on the continuum between ASL and English, (2) those whose responses indicated that they are probably ASL users, (3) those whose responses indicated that they use grammatical structures characteristic of Sign English, (4) those whose responses indicated that they manually represent English inflections in addition to English function words but do not use an artificial sign system designed to represent English, and (5) those whose responses indicated that they use an artificial sign system designed to represent English (SEE I, SEE II, LOVE, Signed English, etc.).

Teachers were classified as signing inconsistently (not on the continuum) for one of two reasons: (1) they reported that they manually represented English inflections but did not manually represent English function words and/or English content words, or (2) they reported that they manually represented English function words but did not represent English content words.

Teachers were classified as probable ASL users if they reported three characteristics in their signing: (1) that they signed only (without voice), (2) that they used ASL, (3) that they used no separate manual representation of −*ing*, *is*, *am*, or *at*. The majority of teachers who claimed they used ASL did not follow the rules of ASL when reporting how they would sign specific sentences (Woodward and Allen 1987).

Teachers were classified as probable Sign English users if they had the following characteristics: (1) they could not be classified as ASL users by the above characteristics, (2) they reported no manual representation for English inflections, (3) they reported manual representation of all English content words and some or all English function words or they reported no manual representation of English function words but reported manual representation of some or all English content words.

Teachers in the fourth group reported that they manually represented all English morphemes for the given sentences. However, they used ASL vocabulary wherever possible.

Teachers were classified as using one of the artificial sign systems designed to represent English if they met the following conditions: (1) they reported using a *separate sign* for each of the English morphemes; (2) they reported using a *different sign* each for *he* and *him*, *I* and *me*, and *am* and *is*; (3) they reported using the *same sign* for *look* in both sentences. The majority of teachers in this group who claimed they used one of the artificial sign systems designed to represent English did not follow the principles of these systems when reporting how they would sign specific English sentences (Woodward and Allen 1988). It is interesting to note that proponents of Signed English explicitly advocate omitting English inflections and function words and using ASL sign vocabulary if the teacher is sure that the student has demonstrated mastery of the English constructions in question (cf. Bornstein 1982). It is impossible to know from these data if some teachers who say they are using Signed English but do not report actually following its principles are intentionally not using the artificially designed principles of Signed English because the student they are signing with has achieved mastery of English or because the teachers themselves are not competent in these principles. Whichever is the case, it is clear that the majority of teachers who claim they are using Signed English are not using the artificially designed characteristics of Signed English but are approximating grammatical and lexical structures common to Sign English.

As shown in figure 1, the responses of the 1,187 signing teachers indicate that the majority of teachers would use a variety of Sign English to communicate the meaning of "He is looking at me," to their students. (Due to rounding, the percentages indicated do not total 100 percent).

Use ASL (Woodward and Allen 1987)	25	(2.1%)
Use Sign English grammatical characteristics	586	(49.4%)
Manually represent English function words and affixes (no invented signs)	358	(30.2%)
Use artificial sign system (SEE I, SEE II, Signed English, LOVE) (Woodward and Allen 1988)	167	(14.1%)
Inconsistent Signing (not on continuum)	51	(4.3%)

Figure 1.   How teachers fit on the ASL-to-English continuum for "He is looking at me." (N = 1,187)

Table 1.   Sign English Versions of "He is looking at me."

	Group	What Is Manually Represented	Percentage of Teachers (N = 586)
English-like Sign English	1	He is look at me	53.8% (315)
	2a	He is look me	11.1% (65)
	2b	He look at me	5.5% (32)
	3	He look me	20.1% (118)
	4a	He look	7.0% (41)
ASL-like Sign English	4b	look me	0.7% (4)
	5	look	1.9% (11)

Note. Due to rounding, percentages do not total 100 percent.

Teachers who used Sign English grammatical characteristics in signing "He is looking at me," varied in the frequency of their use of these characteristics. Table 1 shows the variation found.

The majority of teachers using Sign English (53.8 percent) manually represented all English words in the sentence. Variations in the teacher's signing was patterned. As expected, English function words were less likely than content words to have a separate manual expression. *At* was most often deleted, followed by *is*, then *me*, and then *he*. It is likely that there is no directionality in groups 1 and 2, while directionality is highly likely in groups 3 to 5. Teachers in groups 3 to 5 are using forms of Sign English that are very close to ASL, but they are not using ASL. The great majority (86.2 percent) of these 174 teachers are speaking and signing at the

Table 2.   Relationship of Hearing Status to How Teachers Manually Represent "He is looking at me."

Hearing Status	Sign English Grammar (No inflections)	Non-Sign English Grammar (Inflections)
Deaf	73.9% (68/92)	26.1% (24/92)
Hard of Hearing	62.5% (30/48)	37.5% (18/48)
Hearing	50.3% (488/971)	49.7% (483/971)

Note. Chi-square = 20.78, *df* = 1, *p* < .0000.

same time. The rest claim they are using English, not ASL.

As table 2 indicates, hearing status is an important variable in how much English the teachers reported representing in their signing. Deaf teachers were more likely to report such use, followed by hard-of-hearing teachers, then by hearing teachers.

For hearing teachers, a number of other variables are related to how much English they reported representing in their sign-

ing, for example, type of program, grade level taught, number of years teaching deaf students, and age of sign language acquisition. Table 3 illustrates these relationships.

Hearing teachers having the following characteristics tended to report signing with grammatical characteristics typical of Sign English—teaching in a residential school, teaching in a high school or at an ungraded level, teaching in the Northeast region of the United States, having fewer

Table 3.   Relationship of Background Variables to How Hearing Teachers Manually Represent "He is looking at me."

Background Variable	Sign English Grammar (No inflections)	Non-Sign English Grammar (Inflections)
Type of Program (Chi-square = 17.87, $p < .0000$)		
Residential	59.0% (217/368)	41.0% (151/368)
Nonresidential	44.8% (269/601)	55.2% (332/601)
Grade Level Taught (Chi-square = 38.66, $p < .0000$)		
Preschool	45.6% (62/136)	54.4% (74/136)
Elementary	42.1% (155/368)	57.9% (213/368)
Junior High	46.8% (66/141)	53.2% (75/141)
High School	59.9% (161/269)	40.1% (108/269)
Ungraded	78.2% (43/55)	21.8% (12/55)
Region (Chi-square = 20.29, $p < .0002$)		
Northeast	64.2% (131/204)	35.8% (73/204)
Midwest	45.7% (96/210)	54.3% (114/210)
South	47.2% (188/398)	52.8% (210/398)
West	45.9% (73/159)	54.1% (86/159)
Years Teaching Deaf Students (Chi-square = 16.47, $p < .0009$)		
Fewer than 2 Years	56.6% (47/83)	43.4% (36/83)
2 to 5 Years	59.2% (141/238)	40.8% (97/238)
6 to 10 Years	50.0% (143/286)	50.0% (143/286)
More than 10 Years	43.1% (156/362)	56.9% (206/362)
Age Learned to Sign (Chi-square = 15.65, $p < .0013$)		
Before age 6	76.5% (13/17)	23.5% (4/17)
6 to 17 Years Old	64.2% (43/67)	35.8% (24/57)
18 to 21 Years Old	52.6% (212/403)	47.4% (191/403)
Older than 21	45.2% (217/480)	54.8% (263/480)
Social Interaction with Deaf Adults (Chi-square = 6.24, $p < .0125$)		
None or a Little	48.6% (412/847)	51.4% (435/847)
A Lot or All	61.3% (73/119)	38.7% (46/119)

Use ASL (Woodward and Allen 1987)   25 (2.1%)

Use Sign English grammatical characteristics   617 (52.0%)

Manually represent English function words and affixes (no invented signs)   319 (26.9%)

Use artificial sign system (SEE I, SEE II, Signed English, LOVE) (Woodward and Allen 1988)   167 (14.1%)

Inconsistent Signing (not on continuum)   59 (5.0%)

Figure 2. How teachers fit on the ASL-to-English continuum for "I am looking for him." (*N* = 1,187)

than ten years of experience teaching deaf students, and reporting a lot of social interaction with Deaf adults. Hearing teachers not having these characteristics reported using manual representations of English inflections.

As shown in figure 2, the responses of the 1,187 signing teachers indicate that the majority of them would use a variety of Sign English to communicate the meaning of "I am looking for him" to their students. (Due to rounding, percentages do not total 100 percent).

Teachers who used Sign English grammatical characteristics in signing "I am looking for him," varied in the frequency of their use of these characteristics. Table 4 shows the variation found.

The majority of teachers using Sign English (56.7 percent) manually represented all English words in the sentence. Variations in the teacher's signing was patterned. English function words were less likely than content words to have a separate manual expression. *Am* was most often deleted, followed by *for*, then by *I*, and then by *him*. It is likely that there is no shift in eye gaze in groups 1 and 2, while such a shift is likely in groups 3 to 5. Teachers in group 2b are using a form of Sign English that is similar to some forms of ASL; however, these teachers are not using ASL. The great majority (91.6 percent) of these 118 teachers are speaking and signing at the same time. The rest claim they are using English, not ASL. While teachers in groups 3 to 5 are using forms of Sign English that are very close to ASL, they are not using ASL. The great majority (94.4 percent) of these ninety teachers are speaking and signing at the same time. The rest claim they are using English, not ASL. Table 5 indicates the relationship of hearing status to signing among these teachers. The relationship is similar to that found in table 2. Table 6 illustrates the relationship of other variables to the proportion of English in the signing of hearing teachers. The relationships of teacher characteristics to grammatical tendencies were similar to those for table 3.

THE FUTURE OF SIGN ENGLISH IN THE EDUCATION OF DEAF STUDENTS

It is clear from the data presented in this chapter that signing that uses grammatical characteristics of Sign English is

Table 4. Sign English Versions of "I am looking for him."

	Group	What Is Manually Represented	Percentage of Teachers (*N* = 617)
English-like Sign English	1	I am look for him	56.7% (350)
	2a	I am look him	9.6% (59)
	2b	I look for him	19.1% (118)
	3	I look him	12.6% (78)
	4a	I look	0.2% (1)
ASL-like Sign English	4b	look him	1.0% (6)
	5	look	0.8% (5)

Table 5. Relationship of Hearing Status to How Teachers Manually Represent "I am looking for him."

Hearing Status	Sign English Grammar (No inflections)	Non-Sign English Grammar (Inflections)
Deaf	71.1% (64/90)	28.9% (26/90)
Hard of Hearing	64.6% (31/48)	35.4% (17/48)
Hearing	54.1% (522/965)	45.9% (443/965)

Note. Chi-square = 11.19, *df* = 2, *p* < .0037.

currently used widely in the education of deaf students. Can we expect this same situation to continue in the future, or can we expect a shift in classroom communication preferences? For there to be a shift in communication trends, one of the current methods of classroom communication (i.e., oralism, Cued Speech, ASL, and artificial signs systems designed to represent English) would have to greatly increase or decrease in usage.

Table 6. Relationship of Background Variables to How Hearing Teachers Manually Represent "I am looking for him."

Background Variable	Sign English Grammar (No inflections)	Non-Sign English Grammar (Inflections)
Type of Program (Chi-square = 16.42, *p* < .0001)		
Residential	62.5% (228/365)	37.5% (137/365)
Nonresidential	48.8% (292/598)	51.2% (306/598)
Grade Level Taught (Chi-square = 29.51, *p* < .0000)		
Preschool	50.8% (67/132)	49.2% (65/132)
Elementary	47.8% (175/366)	52.2% (191/366)
Junior High	50.7% (73/144)	49.3% (71/144)
High School	60.6% (163/269)	39.4% (106/269)
Ungraded	83.0% (44/53)	17.0% (9/53)
Region (Chi-square = 20.29, *p* < .0002)		
Northeast	68.0% (138/203)	32.0% (65/203)
Midwest	49.3% (100/203)	50.7% (103/203)
South	51.4% (206/401)	48.6% (195/401)
West	49.4% (78/158)	50.6% (80/158)
Years Teaching Deaf Students (Chi-square = 24.31, *p* < .0000)		
Fewer than 2 Years	65.9% (54.82)	34.2% (28/82)
2 to 5 Years	64.0% (149/233)	36.0% (84/233)
6 to 10 Years	53.4% (156/292)	46.6% (136/292)
More than 10 Years	45.5% (162/356)	54.5% (194/356)
Age Learned to Sign (Chi-square = 18.57, *p* < .0003)		
Before 6	76.5% (13/17)	23.5% (4/17)
6 to 17 Years Old	70.2% (47/67)	29.9% (20/67)
18 to 21 Years Old	57.2% (230/402)	42.8% (172/402)
Older than 21	48.2% (229/475)	51.8% (246/475)
Social Interaction with Deaf Adults (Chi-square = 7.80, *p* < .0052)		
None or a Little	52.3% (437/836)	47.7% (399/836)
A Lot or All	66.1% (82/124)	33.9% (42/124)

The proportion of students who normally receive only aural/oral instruction has remained stable since 1972. Reliable statistics are not available from before that time. Jensema and Trybus (1978) reported on a study of communication patterns of 657 teachers of deaf students for the 1972–1973 school year. They found that 31.2 percent of the teachers reported speech without signing as their normal method of classroom communication. In the 1985 CADS Communication Study, 32.7 percent of the 1,934 teachers surveyed indicated that they used aural/oral instruction with no sign language interpreter as their normal method of classroom communication. Similar proportions of students receiving only aural/oral instruction can be seen in the CADS Annual Surveys that have included questions on the use of sign language in instructional programs. In 1982–1983, 34.0 percent of 46,393 students were enrolled in programs that did not incorporate the use of sign language in instruction; in 1984–1985, the proportion was 37.1 percent of 48,043 students; and in 1986–1987, the proportion was 37.2 percent of 44,099 students (Arthur Schildroth, personal communication 1988). There seem to be no compelling reasons to expect a significant increase in oralism (with a possible decrease in Sign English use). One might argue that the "Deaf President Now" movement at Gallaudet University could eventually cause a decrease in oralism (with a possible increase in Sign English use). However, the programs that have not shifted to signing for the last fifteen years or more would be unlikely, in my opinion, to do so now, unless there was a change in their own administration.

Figures for Cued Speech usage are not as available as those for usage of the aural/oral method. The available figures suggest that Cued Speech has not been and still is not widely used on a national level. Corbett and Jensema (1981) found that 2.4 percent of 4,887 surveyed teachers reported using Cued Speech as a usual method of classroom instruction. In the 1985 CADS Communication Study, 0.2 percent of the 1,934 teachers surveyed indicated that they used Cued Speech as their normal method of classroom instruction. A similar proportion of students receiving Cued Speech instruction can be seen in the one CADS Annual Survey that has included questions on the use of Cued Speech in instructional programs. In 1986–1987, 0.2 percent of 44,099 students were enrolled in programs that incorporated the use of Cued Speech in the students' instruction (Arthur Schildroth, personal communication, 1988). A decrease in Cued Speech usage would not affect Sign English use. A dramatic increase in Cued Speech usage might cause a decrease in Sign English usage, although I suspect it would more likely affect oral teachers than signing teachers. However, I do not believe there is any reason to suspect that such a dramatic increase would occur in the foreseeable future.

Figures on ASL usage are even harder to come by. Some linguists (e.g., Lee 1982 and Cokely 1983) have claimed anecdotally that as a result of linguistic research on ASL, classroom use of ASL is increasing, especially among deaf teachers. Empirical research has not supported these claims. The most reliable data come from a 1987 report on ASL users in the 1985 CADS Communication Study (Woodward and Allen 1987). The report concluded that actual ASL usage is much lower than claimed because many teachers do not know what ASL is. While 140 teachers in the study claimed to be using ASL, only twenty-five might have been using ASL, and only six of these clearly did use ASL. Linguistic studies of ASL apparently have had little affect on its usage in classroom situations. A decrease in classroom use of ASL would not affect the use of Sign English. While there is currently much discussion about the possible use of ASL for classroom instruction, many technical problems must be overcome before actual classroom use can dramatically increase.

Little is known, also, about the use of artificial sign systems designed to represent English. While two earlier studies (Jordan, Gustason, and Rosen 1976, 1978) reported that the majority of programs surveyed claimed to use Total Communication (read "simultaneous communication"), the authors could only suggest the type of English signing used. Based on sign language books used as references by the programs, the authors suggested that many of these programs were using one of the four major artificial sign systems designed to represent English. While this may have been the case, the hypothesis as presented was flawed, since there can be no guarantee that teachers follow the principles in the reference books located at the school.

A more recent empirical study, by Woodward and Allen (1988), indicates that actual use of artificial sign systems is much lower than claimed use. While 722 teachers claimed to be using one of the artificial sign systems designed to represent English, only 167 teachers actually followed the principles of these systems in reporting how they would sign two sample sentences. Clearly, use of these systems has not increased since Jordan, Gustason, and Rosen's studies. If one accepts their figures, the use of these systems has greatly decreased. A more likely explanation, in my opinion, is that their figures were too high and the percentages of use have remained roughly the same through the 1970s and 1980s. I see no reason to expect a future increase in the use of these artificial sign systems.

From the data discussed in this chapter, I expect that signing that uses grammatical characteristics of Sign English will probably continue to be widely used in the education of deaf students. In some cases, this will be a conscious choice; in others, it may simply be the natural outcome of the linguistic and cultural contact of ASL and English.

What I would like to see happen is a clear separation and use of both ASL and English in the education of deaf students. Sign English serves as a natural bridge be-

tween two communities that use different languages. It should be remembered that most adults who use Sign English already know ASL, English, or both. Most deaf children do not come to school with full competence in either ASL or English. While Sign English has characteristics of both ASL and English, it is neither one, but a mixture of the two languages. Sign English may be useful for communication with deaf children, but it is not going to teach them ASL or English.

Elsewhere, I have pointed out that bilingual education is a very desirable alternative in the education of deaf students (Woodward 1980). I believe that the systematic use of ASL and English (in its written form) for instructional purposes is important for the majority of deaf students, whether or not they have deaf parents. Many deaf children will grow up and interact with both the hearing and the Deaf worlds. I believe their education should prepare them to do both. I also believe that hearing children be given every opportunity to become bilingual in English and ASL, if they so desire.

While my beliefs about the desirability of bilingual education are rooted in my training in sociolinguistics and in my research in Deaf communities in the United States and abroad, my experience also leads me to believe that this is not likely to happen in the United States in the near future. In addition to the information already discussed here, there are two other important reasons for this belief. First there is a strong emphasis on the use of speech in the education of deaf students. Overall, 35.5 percent of the teachers in the 1985 CADS Communication Study reported speaking without signing; 59.4 percent of the teachers reported speaking and signing at the same time. Thus, almost 95 percent of the teachers normally used their voice during classroom instruction. ASL cannot be used with speech. As long as speech is emphasized in normal classroom communication, ASL will not be used and bilingual education cannot occur. *Status quo* use of Sign

English will continue as the easiest and most natural accompaniment to spoken English.

Second, the 1985 CADS Study found that the large majority of teachers of deaf students are hearing (89.1 percent), learned signs at college age (84.6 percent), and rate their receptive and expressive signing skills lower than their spoken or written English skills (79.9 percent and 70.8 percent, respectively). Only 6.7 percent of the teachers in this study classified themselves as deaf. Given this situation, there is little likelihood of ASL being used or bilingual education occurring. Sign English is likely to continue as the easiest and most natural communication tool for hearing teachers to use with their deaf students.

NOTE

1. Research on this chapter was supported in part by Sign Language Research, Inc.

REFERENCES

Annual Survey of Hearing-Impaired Children and Youth. 1983–1984. Washington, DC: Center for Assessment and Demographic Studies, Gallaudet University. Database.

Bailey, C. 1973. *Variation and linguistic theory.* Washington, DC: Center for Applied Linguistics.

Battison, R., Markowicz, H., and Woodward, J. 1975. A good rule of thumb: Variable phonology in American Sign Language. In *Analyzing variation in language,* eds. R. Shuy and R. Fasold, 303–311. Washington, DC: Georgetown University Press.

Bickerton, D. 1973. The structure of polylectal grammars. *Georgetown University Monographs in Language and Linguistics* 25:17–42.

Bochner, J., and Albertini, J. 1988. Language varieties in the deaf population and their acquisition by children and adults. In *Language learning and deafness,* ed. M. Strong, 3–48. New York: Cambridge University Press.

Bornstein, H. 1982. Towards a theory of use for Signed English: From birth through adulthood. *American Annals of the Deaf* 127:26–31.

CADS communication study. 1985. Washington, DC: Gallaudet University. Database.

Cokely, D. 1983. When is a pidgin not a pidgin? An alternative analysis of the ASL-English contact situation. *Sign Language Studies* 38:1–24.

Corbett, E., and Jensema, C. 1981. *Teachers of the deaf:*

Descriptive profiles. Washington, DC: Gallaudet University Press.

Fasold, R. 1970. Two models of socially significant linguistic variation. *Language* 46:551–563.

———. 1984. *The sociolinguistics of society.* Oxford, England: Basil Blackwell Publisher, Ltd.

Ferguson, C. 1959. Diglossia. *Word* 15:325–340.

Hawking, J. 1983. A re-examination of sign language diglossia. *American Annals of the Deaf* 128:48–52.

Hymes, D. 1971. *Pidginization and creolization of languages.* Cambridge, England: Cambridge University Press.

Jensema, C., and Trybus, R. 1978. *Communication patterns and educational achievement of hearing impaired students.* Office of Demographic Studies Publication, Series T, Number 2. Gallaudet University, Washington, DC.

Jordan, I. K., Gustason, G., and Rosen, R. 1976. Current communication trends at programs for the deaf. *American Annals of the Deaf* 121:527–532.

———. 1978. An update on communication trends at programs for the deaf. *American Annals of the Deaf* 124:350–357.

Labov, W. 1969. Contraction, deletion, and inherent variability of the English copula. *Language* 45:715–762.

Lee, D. 1982. Are there really signs of diglossia? Re-examining the situation. *Sign Language Studies* 35:127–151.

Markowicz, H., and Woodward, J. 1978. Language and the maintenance of ethnic boundaries in the Deaf community. *Communication and Cognition* 11:29–38.

Moores, D. 1972. Communication: Some unanswered questions and some unquestioned answers. In *Psycholinguistics and total communication: The state of art,* ed. T. J. O'Rourke, 1–10. Silver Spring, MD: American Annals of the Deaf.

Reilly, J., and McIntire, M. 1980. ASL and PSE: What's the difference? *Sign Language Studies* 27:151–192.

Samarin, W. 1971. Salient and substantive pidginization. In *Pidginization and creolization of languages,* ed. D. Hymes, 117–140. Cambridge, England: Cambridge University Press.

Stokoe, W. 1970. Sign language diglossia. *Studies in Linguistics* 21:27–41.

———. 1972. *Semiotics and human sign languages.* The Hague: Mouton.

———. 1973. Sign language syntax and human language capacity. Paper presented at the Summer Institute in Linguistics, Ann Arbor, MI.

Woodward, J. 1972. Implications for sociolinguistic research among the deaf. *Sign Language Studies* 1:1–7.

———. 1973a. *Implicational lects on the deaf diglossic continuum.* Doctoral dissertation, Georgetown University, Washington, DC.

———. 1973b. Interrule implication in American Sign Language. *Sign Language Studies* 3:47–56.

———. 1973c. Some characteristics of Pidgin Sign English. *Sign Language Studies* 3:39–46.

———. 1973d. Some observations on sociolinguistic variation and American Sign Language. *Kansas Journal of Sociology* 9:191–200.

———. 1974. A report on Montana-Washington implicational research. *Sign Language Studies* 4:77–101.

———. 1980. Some sociolinguistic problems in the implementation of bilingual education for deaf students. In *Second National Symposium on Sign Language Research and Teaching*, eds. F. Caccamise and D. Hicks, 183–209. Silver Spring, MD: National Association of the Deaf.

Woodward, J., and Allen, T. 1987. Classroom use of ASL by teachers. *Sign Language Studies* 54:1–10.

———. 1988. Classroom use of artificial Manual English sign systems by teachers. *Sign Language Studies* 55:60.

Woodward, J., Allen, T., and Schildroth, A. 1985. Teachers and deaf students: An ethnography of communication. In *Proceedings of the first annual meeting of the Pacific Linguistics Conference*, eds. S. Delancey and R. Tomlin, 479–493. Eugene. University of Oregon.

Woodward, J., and Markowicz, H. 1980. Some handy new ideas on pidgins and creoles: Pidgin sign languages. In *Sign and Culture*, ed. W. Stokoe, 55–79. Silver Spring, MD: Linstok Press.

CHAPTER 5

ASL and Its Implications for Education

Robert J. Hoffmeister

The use of American Sign Language (ASL) in the education of deaf children has had a varied history of support and denial. This chapter will explain the users of the language, the problems that ASL has encountered, the support for its use, and why it is necessary as the language of instruction for all deaf children in school. A significant portion is dedicated to explaining some of the structural properties of ASL, the knowledge of which is essential to an understanding of its function and use.[2]

ASL is a language that has been misunderstood, misused, and misrepresented over the past 100 years. It is structured very differently from English. The structure of ASL is based on visual/manual properties, in contrast to the auditory/spoken properties of English. ASL is able to convey the same meanings, information, and complexities as English. The mode of expression is different, but only at the delivery level. The underlying principles of ASL (i.e., the fact that the language is able to describe "who is doing what to whom," "who is doing what where," question

forms, negation, etc.) are based on the same basic principles found in all languages. ASL is able to identify and codify agents, actions, objects, locations, subjects, verbs, aspects, tense, and modality, just as English does. ASL is therefore capable of stating all the information expressed in English and of doing this within the same conceptual frame. ASL is able to communicate the meaning of a concept, through a single sign or through a combination of signs, that may be conveyed by a word or phrase (combination of words) in English. The description of ASL herein includes a definition of the composition of a sign.

ASL is acquired differently than most of the languages of the world. It is usually learned through a peer transmission process rather than from an intergenerational passage within families. Since less than 5 percent of deaf persons have deaf parents, and since most schools do not formally teach or recognize ASL, the only source available is deaf children. The most fluent users of ASL are children who have deaf parents and children who have attended residential schools since age five or six. These children are the native or near-native users of the language who guarantee its survival.

ASL has been in existence for almost 200 years. Although it became the language of instruction for five decades, it has not been used in the educational system for the past 150 years (Lane 1984, 228). Yet it is still used by the majority of deaf adults in their everyday lives as the preferred mode of communication.

As noted by Moores and Stedt (see chap. 1), ASL has been embroiled in controversy over both its social and its pedagogical use since it was officially introduced in the United States in the early 1800s. It is documented as being a mixture of the French Sign Language brought to America by Laurent Clerc, a Deaf teacher from France, and the local sign system used by deaf children in the newly established schools (Lane 1984). It has evolved over the years and has been heavily influenced by both French Sign Language and Signed French. Groce (1987) suggested that a base ASL developed on Martha's Vineyard among the Deaf community and slowly, through contact with Deaf people in other areas, became integrated with the language of the schools. Lane (1984) suggested that in families with deaf children, the "home sign" language was brought to the schools by the students. In the mid- to late nineteenth century, ASL was suppressed because the educational system selected speech as the means for instructing deaf children. This resulted from the mistaken assumption that the use of ASL would interfere with the acquisition of English. During that time the issue became so controversial that a major purge of ASL resulted. This movement to suppress ASL was led by Alexander Graham Bell, who feared the development of a Deaf race. Bell's fear stemmed from his belief that

> The immediate cause is undoubtedly the preference that adult deaf-mutes exhibit for the companionship of deaf-mutes rather than

that of hearing persons. Among the causes that contribute to bring about this preference we may note: (1) segregation for the purposes of education, and (2) the use, as a means of communication, of a language which is different from that of the people. . . . Nearly all the other causes I have investigated are ultimately referable to these (Bell 1883, 46).

Ultimately, he feared the expansion and continuation of the adult Deaf community. The continuation and preservation of the Deaf community depended on the use of a signed language. Bell proposed that by "changing his [the deaf child's] social environment," (i.e., segregating deaf children from one another), one could achieve the removal of this language from schools. He hypothesized that successfully removing the language and establishing policies prohibiting public display of ASL in the community, along with banning marriage between two consenting deaf adults, "would go a long way towards checking the evil" (p. 45), which he defined as the formation of "a Deaf variety of the human race." Bell admitted that the social restrictions, banning of marriages, and proposed sterilization of young deaf women were repressive and probably could not be legislated. However, his work was at the forefront of the movement to repress the use of signed language in schools. This fear of the Deaf community's existing on its own and having its own culture was primarily responsible for driving ASL and the Deaf community underground.

During this period of oppression (1885–1935), Deaf teachers were fired and not hired (Corbett 1981). ASL became the "inferior," unaccepted language. The continuation of ASL was provided by nonacademic people: Deaf adults who were hired as dormitory supervisors and maintenance personnel. Ironically, these oppressive views are still held today, as evidenced by the need to propose legislation to recognize ASL as a language (Wilcox and Corwin 1988).

The initial linguistic descriptions of ASL included assumptions that the language related directly to English. These discussions presented ASL at one end of the diglossic continuum and English at the other, implying that ASL was a dialectal variant of English (Stokoe 1970; Woodward 1973). Further discussion presented issues of how the language is used in its different register forms. The dialects could then be compared to some standard of the community. ASL was proposed as equivalent to the low dialect, and English was the high dialect, using Ferguson's criteria (Stokoe 1970). Although this comparison may have been unintentional, researchers providing this discussion gave educators support for the use of a "high" form of the dialect in schools. Therefore, the dialect that most closely resembled English was chosen as the method of instruction in schools. Thus Total Communication (TC) (which in practice has become the simultaneous use of signed English and spoken English) was born.

Artificially created sign systems (such as Signed English) were created because of the unsupported notion that deaf children had to "see" a signed form of English in order to acquire English-language skills. The developers of these systems also believed that ASL could not be used as the language of instruction. Although these views may not be explicitly stated, they are the underlying premises at the root of the move to prevent the pedagogical use of ASL (Johnson, Liddell, and Erting 1989).

Currently, the TC programs in the United States that use signed forms of English have brought a visual communication system to many deaf children at an early age. The premise that the use of these created signed systems will enable deaf children to learn English is based on several assumptions.

1. It is possible to represent a spoken language using a visual mode, including the essential prosodic features of a language (Gustason, Pfetzing, and Zawolkow 1972, 1978);
2. Teachers and parents will follow a "more complete" representation of English, including its morphological endings, at all times (Bornstein and Saulnier 1984a, 1987; Gustason, Pfetzing, and Zawolkow 1972, 1978); and
3. Deaf children will use this invented system, as it is presented, to learn English (Bornstein and Saulnier 1984a, 1987; Gustason, Pfetzing, and Zawolkow 1972, 1978).

It has been noted that the majority of teachers do not adhere to a Signed English (SE) system when communicating with their deaf students (Woodward and Allen 1988). Several research studies have investigated the young deaf child's exposure to a SE system. Results indicate that deaf children modify the system to include more ASL-like features (Hoffmeister 1978, 1982; Hoffmeister and Goodhart 1978; Goodhart 1984, Mounty 1986; Raffin 1976; S. Supalla 1988; T. Supalla 1982; Schick 1987). This shift toward more ASL-like signing is called "nativization" (Anderson 1983). This supports the theoretical notion that children have an innate capacity to learn a language through the bioprogram (Bickerton 1982). The bioprogram operates on language input (which may be impoverished or vastly reduced from the original or superstrate language) and assists the child in making the input language more efficient. Deaf children operating on the SE input appear to take advantage of ASL principles in several ways. For example, they use space as a grammatical device, decompose "frozen" forms into their classifier components, and use a freer word order because their use of agreement markers in space permits them more "freedom" than is found in SE. It appears that even in the presence of input that has been artificially created to represent English visually, the language mechanism tends to operate on the visual components of the input rather than the auditory code it is supposed to mirror.

ASL has not received adequate study and examination due to prejudice and ignorance. Because ASL does not have a written form, linguists and educators did not consider it a real language. In spite of this, the Deaf community has maintained, supported, and been proud of ASL. It is used as a symbol of membership and prestige in the Deaf community.

Languages can be categorized into different types, such as world class, local, creoles, and pidgins, depending on social, political, and educational variables. In many countries, more than one language is used. Generally, there is a dominant language (e.g., English in the United States), and one (or more) minority language (e.g., Spanish and its variants in the United States). Users of the minority language often want to maintain their language to identify with their cultural heritage. Language provides the minority group with a means of passing on the culture to their children and of identifying membership in their group. If language transmits culture, it also transmits attitudes about the culture. Membership in a group can be determined by the user's skill in the language.

The TC movement has provided an interesting dilemma for Deaf persons. Prior to this movement, Deaf adults could easily identify members of the Deaf community by the way they used a signed language; that is, a person's knowledge and use of ASL places him or her either inside or outside the boundaries of the community. Deaf persons who are fluent users of ASL are viewed as core members of the Deaf community. Those who use forms of English-based sign, whether it is SE or some pidginized version of ASL, are considered to be more on the periphery of community membership. People's ability to use ASL also identifies where they have grown up and what type of school program they have attended. For example, fluent users of ASL tend to come from residential schools, while more English-based signers tend to come from public schools.

Language use is also a form of power. One's control over language can also work to the benefit of one's group. In the Deaf community, English is not viewed negatively and, while it is not the language of power, its use in the community can assist members in gaining leadership roles. There are various levels of prestige and participatory roles in the Deaf community. Because the Deaf and hearing communities coexist, interaction between them is essential. When contact is required between Deaf and hearing persons—for example, in educational, professional, or sociopolitical systems—the form of signed language is more English-like. When contact with the hearing community is not required, such as in the clubs or sports organizations of the Deaf community, ASL is the predominant language. Leadership in these different aspects of the community is usually not held by the same Deaf people. At the club level, leadership is usually restricted to individuals who are fluent in ASL. In the contact situation, members of the community who have fluency in both English and ASL are more eligible to become leaders. These contact leaders tend to be more educated and knowledgeable about "hearing ways," while the club leaders tend to be more "grass-roots" and have less contact with hearing people.

Membership in the Deaf community is based on hearing loss and use of a signed language. However, a member does not have to be fluent in ASL and have a significant hearing loss. The sign language used by the person usually displays the attitude she or he has toward the Deaf community and whether she or he wishes to be part of this community. Users of SE who do not modify their language form toward ASL are not considered full members of the community. They are tolerated until they make the appropriate language modifications, implying that they have made the appropriate attitudinal changes. For example, young Deaf adults who have graduated from public school (including many of the TC programs) may still hold many "hearing" values when they attempt to join the Deaf community. This is displayed in their use of SE. Initially, they will be considered deaf but "THINK-HEARING." THINK-HEARING is a sign formed by using the same handshape and movement as in the sign HEARING, but is placed at the forehead rather than at the mouth. This THINK-HEARING deaf person has not internalized the values of Deaf culture and the Deaf community.

ASL STRUCTURE

Since Stokoe (1960) first delineated the parameters of a signed language almost three decades ago, extensive research has resulted in sophisticated descriptions of ASL. ASL is similar in structure to many other languages. Languages vary by type and name due to a number of influences. The evolution of a language can be extremely complex and many of the original components may still exist in the evolved language. For example, in Dutch or Flemish, the base language is German but, due to changes in dialect involving all levels of the language, the evolved language has become different from its base language. Yet, one is still able to recognize the Germanic influence in the languages.

Languages tend to focus on different elements that are important to the cultures in which they are encapsulated. Lexical choices reflect those items that have prominence in both the culture and the language, thus, lexical items in one language may not have equivalents in another. However, all languages are able to express the same semantic content.

Modality of expression will influence how users of a language construct its lexical items and choose to increase its efficiency. Efficiency is necessary for the production of the same semantic content within approximately the same amount of time by different languages. Clearly, it may take more time to fill in the cultural background if the languages do not share this information.

ASL is a spatial-visual language that requires visual perception for its decoding and encoding. It is produced by the hands, arms, body, and face. Its production involves movement in space. Any movements in the space within two to three feet of the body are possible. However, the hands and arms usually perform in the space within twelve inches of either side of the body and about eighteen inches in front. Vertical signing space extends from the waist to about six inches above the head. These dimensions have been referred to as the "sign bubble" (Lacy 1975). The sign bubble influences the production of signs. For example, signs performed at the outer edges of the bubble tend to be two-handed, use large movements (whole forearm involvement), and have identical handshapes. This perceptual predictability reduces the visual scanning that can slow down reception during input. As signs move toward the center of the signing space, more detailed movements are possible (e.g., wiggling of the fingers), handshapes may differ, and single-handed signs may involve multiple movements (such as KING, QUEEN, and PROUD). To reduce visual-perceptual load when both hands have different handshapes, the constant or base hand (usually the one that doesn't move) uses one of the basic handshapes: A, B, O, G, S, and C.

As the signs are formed on or near the head, more complicated handshapes and movements may be involved. The eyes of the listener are usually focused at the signer's chin; therefore, more detail may be produced without overloading the perceptual system. Signs on or near the face have shorter movements along a path, the fingers can change (e.g., from G to X, as in SUMMER), or the fingers can wiggle while the hand moves to the rear (as in A-LONG-TIME-AGO).

The Phonological Component: Basic Units in the System

Modality influences the units of language. In spoken languages the units of sound are called phonemes and depend on the articulators—the lips, tongue, oral cavity, and teeth—for their production. The movement of air is also required for the production of sounds. Different placement of the articulators creates different paths, changing the velocity and direction of the air and creating different phonemes. The oral cavity acts as a basic locator of resonation for dividing up the phoneme categories (e.g., nasals and sonorants), while the lips, teeth, and tongue combine to create divisions in categories such as sibilants and fricatives. The tongue and the oral cavity operate to divide up the consonants and vowels. Different placement of the articulators, combined with the velocity and path of the air stream, results in predictable phoneme categories. That is, of all the possible sets of sounds, only a small number are used in a particular language.

Individual languages have rules that restrict the combinations or sequences of meaningful sounds. For example, English restricts the sequencing to up to three consonant sounds, while Russian permits sequences of up to four consonants. This type of restriction is not modality-defined but language-defined. There are, however, some modality constraints on the production of sequences of sounds. For example, one cannot produce two sounds simultaneously. Because of this linear restriction certain sounds may influence those that follow or precede them. Sounds are used in combination to produce meaning units called morphemes. Although these examples describe spoken language units, the same divisions apply to ASL.

In ASL, the basic units of the language are the handshape, location, movement, and orientation of the hands. These function as the articulators of the language. As with spoken languages, the possibilities for combining these articulators are infinite. There are many handshapes that can be used; however, only a few are relevant to a particular signed language. For example, some handshapes in Japanese Sign Language are not used in ASL (Klima and Bellugi 1979). Of all the possible handshapes, nineteen are used in ASL. These are subject to the orientation of the palm. Only a small subset of possible locations is actually used. Finally, there is movement. Because of the modality, movement

is critical to sign formation. However, as with all the other articulators, only a small subset of movement is relevant to ASL. Some movements are restricted to a twisting of the wrist, resulting in a rotation of the hand. At another level, it may involve the whole hand moving from one location to another. Movements may be embedded inside one another. For example, the whole hand may be moving while the fingers wiggle simultaneously, as in ONCE-IN-A-GREAT-WHILE.

Morphemes are the smallest units of meaning in a language. When at least two parameters of handshape, location, movement, and orientation are produced, we have a morpheme in ASL. A sign may contain one morpheme or many. There are two kinds of morphemes, bound and free. Free morphemes are able to stand alone. Bound morphemes are those that must be attached to other morphemes for their production. For example, the morpheme *work* is a free morpheme but the bound morpheme *-ing* must be attached to *work* to carry the meaning of *working*. In spoken languages some individual sounds are morphemes (for example, the sounds *s* and *z* are plural morphemes). In ASL, a parameter is always a phoneme (the basic unit), but not always a morpheme. For example, the handshape *B* as a unit must be placed in a particular spatial location to have meaning. Handshape and location may combine with movement to produce meaning, but the individual parameters may not carry meaning. BLUE and FISH have identical handshapes and movements, but different locations of the hand, hence different meanings.

The common frozen forms that hearing people learn are signs. However, many signs are multimorphemic in construction. As in spoken languages, morphemes may stand alone or be affixed to each other to create new signs or words. Bound morphemes may precede, follow, or be inserted between free morphemes. In TWO-WEEKS-AGO, the free morpheme TWO precedes the free morpheme WEEK and the bound morpheme AGO. TWO is a prefix, AGO is a suffix. AGO is the movement morpheme that begins at the tip of the fingers (the end of the movement in WEEK) and proceeds in an arc toward the signer's body, forming a complex sign unit. This example depicts the sequential nature of ASL production.

ASL is generally composed of sequences of morphemes, but in some instances they occur simultaneously. The occurrence of simultaneous production is not foreign to spoken languages. When *man* is pluralized to *men*, the plural is embedded within the production of the word form. In ASL this phenomenon may occur in many forms that are produced by a single hand. Since both hands may be used at the same time, two morphemes may be produced simultaneously. For example, if each hand represents an individual and the sign LOOK is produced by the right and left hand, the following meanings are possible:

1. $LOOK_{lh} + LOOK_{rh}$: orientation-palms out: "They [dual] look out there."
2. $LOOK_{lh} + LOOK_{rh}$: orientation-palms facing each other: "They [X and Y] look at each other."

Bound morphemes in ASL are more difficult to see because we do not have a written representation of the language that provides a way to segment different parts of signs.

Morphological Components in ASL:Verbs

In the traditional explanations of ASL linguistics, verbs were thought of as belonging to three category types (depicted in figure 1): body-anchored verbs (those having contact with the body, such as eat), directional verbs (when body contact does not occur and the hand moves from one location to another, such as, GIVE), and locational verbs (when the verb or hand-shape occurs in one location in space such as, BREAK). In earlier research, a verb that moved from one location to another was

Body-Anchored
KNOW

Locational
BREAK

Directional
GIVE

Figure 1. Examples of three types of verbs in ASL.

Note. Reprinted by permission of the publisher, from L. Lane, *The Gallaudet Survival Guide to Signing* (1987):26, 75, 96. Washington, DC: Gallaudet University Press.

considered one morpheme and was not assigned separate meaning components for the movement and the location. That is, in a verb such as GIVE the movement and its beginning and end points were all considered one unit. Recent research views the multiple locations and variations in movement as separate morphemes (Gee and Kegl 1984; Supalla and Newport 1978).

Initial research in ASL focused attention primarily on the handshape of the sign. Because the handshape was easily perceptible and descriptions of spoken languages influenced analysis, movement was not seen as a primary component of meaning. Klima and Bellugi (1979) provided an extensive analysis of movement morphemes that are part of the ASL verb-modulation system. They described a number of morphemes that attach to the basic verb to give a variety of meanings.

Each verb in ASL has a basic movement. Some researchers make the claim that movement *is* the verb in ASL (see Gee and Kegl 1983, 1984), to which additional movements may be added. These are bound morphemes and they act like affixes in spoken languages. For example, in WORK, two S handshapes are placed in neutral space with the base hand (BH) located under the dominant hand (DH), so that the heel of the DH is directly over the back of the BH. The basic movement of the verb is a downward motion of the DH, ending in contact with the BH. A straight upward motion, returning the DH to its starting position, completes the movement in the verb WORK. Repetition of movement, when added to the base movement, produces meaning variation in the verb equal to the present progressive or "working over time."

Verb modulation in ASL can be divided into two categories, punctual and nonpunctual. Punctual modulations have the effect of suggesting a beginning and end to the activity, or an over-and-over-again intent. Nonpunctual modulations suggest unclear beginning and ending points, or for-a-long-time intent. Both of these movements can apply to active and stative verbs. Klima and Bellugi (1979) describe the application to stative verbs as modulation of adjectival predicates.

Six modulation morphemes have been identified. They all relate to duration of the verbs over time and are classified as durative modulations. Each of the movement morphemes is depicted in figure 2. The *protractive, durational,* and *continuative* morphemes are examples of nonpunctual modifications. They have fluid repetitions and suggest an event that occurs over time. The punctual category includes the *incessant, habitual,* and *iterative* morphemes, all of which have restrained repetitions, some with short holds. These movements suggest an activity or state that begins and ends regularly. These morphemes are added to the base movement in the production of the verb.

Directional and locational verbs have other movement morphemes that may be added and affect the distribution of the verb's activity. They are affixed to the verb's end points and distinguish between notions of distributing to or acting on discrete elements and a group of elements. For example, *discrete* has the meaning of verb + "to each one," where the movement of the verb's path returns to individual locations in space already established in the conversation. The *collective* morpheme refers to verb + "to all of you" and consists of a horizontal, slightly arcing motion added to the end point of the base motion of the verb. Not all verbs are capable of accepting these two morphemes. Thus, the semantic domain of each verb will determine which verbs are able to accept specific morphemes. The semantics of the verb must include the capability of distributing the activity individually and collectively. The following is an example of these morphemes with the verb *give*.

GIVE + DISCRETE
motion is repeated from signer to each of four previously established locations—"I give X to each one of you"

GIVE + COLLECTIVE
motion is a smooth, continuous arc from left to right about two feet long—"I give X to all of you"

In examples just given, the morphological processes within the verb are all in-

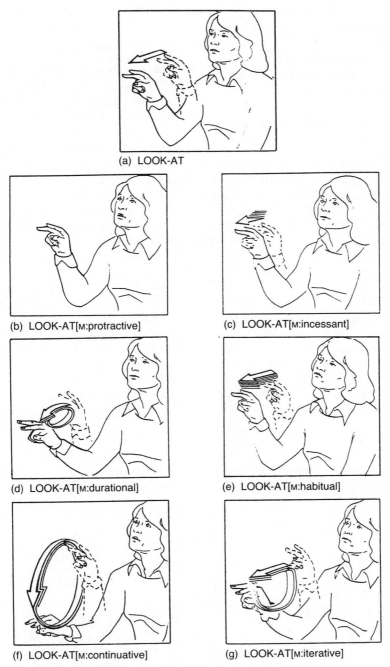

(a) LOOK-AT

(b) LOOK-AT[M:protractive]

(c) LOOK-AT[M:incessant]

(d) LOOK-AT[M:durational]

(e) LOOK-AT[M:habitual]

(f) LOOK-AT[M:continuative]

(g) LOOK-AT[M:iterative]

Figure 2.   Examples of inflections for temporal aspect on LOOK-AT.

Note. Reprinted by permission of the publishers, from *The Signs of Language* by E. Klima and U. Bellugi, p. 293, Cambridge, MA: Harvard University Press. Copyright © 1979 by the President and Fellows of Harvard College.

flectional. Derivational processes, which change one class of morphemes to another, are also readily available in ASL.

These are also depicted by changes in movement. T. Supalla (1978) explains that verbs have continuous paths in their base movement, and by shortening and re-peating the movement one can change verbs to nouns. An example is illustrated in figure 3, which depicts the verb COM-PARE and its corresponding change to COMPARISON.

Semantic Families: Related Morphemes in ASL

Movement Families. As in most lan-guages of the world, there are families of words that have an underlying meaning or are related by phonological similarities. For example, in English, one can add "magna" to different words to establish the family of "very large." This process also exists in ASL, and families may be related by movement, handshape, and lo-cation. Movement can be related positively and negatively to the root meaning. Move-ment here refers to the whole hand mov-ing from one location to another, opening and closing of the fingers, and movement of the individual fingers.

Depicted in figure 4 are examples of up-ward movement, suggesting an underly-ing positive meaning, and downward movement, suggesting a negative mean-ing. The production of APPEAR-DISAP-PEAR provides one example. Changes in what Wilbur (1987) refers to as local move-ments, such as the change from a single movement to a repeated one, result in an underlying change from an action that has an ending to one that may occur over time.

Movement variation within the hand it-self presents other possible groupings of semantic families. The wiggling or re-peated movement of the fingers suggests an extension of the basic meaning, as in FINE/FANCY/FORMAL, suggesting that FINE is the base and the wiggling of the fingers extends the meaning to *extra-fine*. Another example is BLOW-UP, in which the wiggling fingers extend, meaning "*to explode*" or "a very large *blow-up*." Another variation in local movement is the opening and closing of the fingers (either into a first or contacting the thumb), which implies "letting go" when opened and "getting" when closed. For example, when this is combined with an outward movement of the hand, the underlying meaning could be "to release in the direction of this move-ment or to an object in this direction," as in BAWL-OUT, in which the hands open and are directed toward the person being admonished. When the hands close, as in "to take regularly," the underlying mean-ing is that of the sign WELFARE. When the movement is one of a grasping form or with fingers contacting the thumb, it has the underlying meaning of *taking* as in

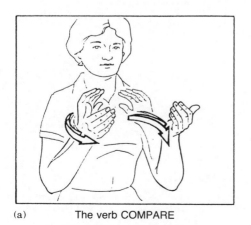
(a)   The verb COMPARE

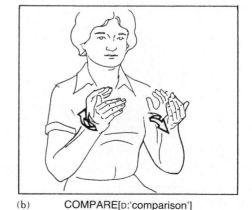
(b)   COMPARE[ᴅ:'comparison']

Figure 3. An example of a verb becoming a noun.

Note. Reprinted by permission of the publishers, from *The Signs of Language* by E. Klima and U. Bellugi, p. 296, Cambridge, MA: Harvard University Press. Copyright © 1979 by the President and Fellows of Harvard College.

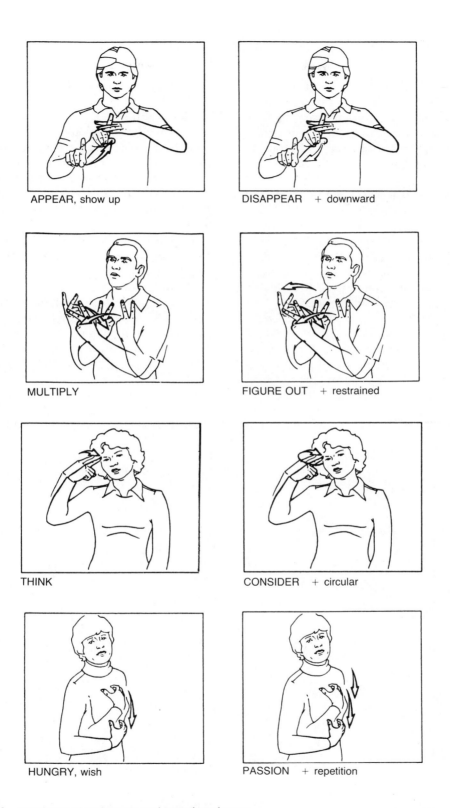

APPEAR, show up

DISAPPEAR + downward

MULTIPLY

FIGURE OUT + restrained

THINK

CONSIDER + circular

HUNGRY, wish

PASSION + repetition

Figure 4. Examples of movement and meaning change.

Note. Adapted by permission of the publisher, from *A Basic Course in American Sign Language*, T. Humphries, C. Padden, and T. O'Rourke, (1980):41, 103, 107, 210. Silver Spring, MD: T.J. Publishers.

LEARN or PICK UP/ONE. In LEARN, the "taking" implies the grasping of information and bringing it to the brain. In PICK UP/ONE, the implication is one of choosing an object in space as in "picking out this particular object."

Handshape Families. Some semantic families involve handshapes. The handshape 8 is related to the underlying theme of emotions. FEEL, SYMPATHIZE, SENSITIVE, and EXCITE are all related to "coming into contact with one's feelings." When we add the opening or the "loss of contact," the negative feelings are presented, as in HATE and AWFUL. The G handshape has many underlying semantic meanings, but one in particular is its relationship to WH questions. This may have to do with the transfer of movement from the body to the sign itself, a process described by Frishberg (1975) as part of the historical changes that have occurred in ASL. The movement of the G handshape for WHERE (index finger moves from side to side, with a pivoting movement at the wrist) may have resulted from an old sign form that involved a point in neutral space and a shaking of the head from left to right. The left-to-right movement has transferred from the head to the hand and has become the current sign form for WHERE.

Two handshapes that have a semantic theme attached to their use are the V and the bent V. The V handshape has an underlying semantic intent of "to see." When variations in local movement and across different locations are produced, various meanings (all using the idea of "to see") are represented. The bent V handshape adds a negative interpretation to the semantics of "to see." For example, in figure 5, the bent V is used to indicate BLIND, as in "can't see," and DOUBTFUL, as in "one's difficulty in seeing." Other mean-

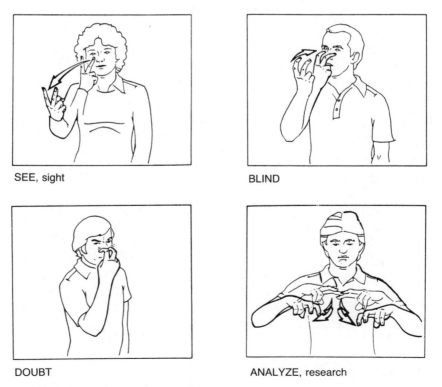

SEE, sight

BLIND

DOUBT

ANALYZE, research

Figure 5. Examples of variation of the V handshape.

Note. Adapted by permission of the publisher, from *A Basic Course in American Sign Language*, T. Humphries, C. Padden, and T. O'Rourke, (1980):42, 182, 189, 229. Silver Spring, MD: T.J. Publishers.

ings using the metaphorical extension of "to see" can be derived by adding other movements and locations, such as in AN-ALYZE, which consists of both palms down in neutral space, changing from V to bent V, suggesting that one is looking again and again at many details in this location. ASL offers a large number of meanings and variations within its movement and handshape parameters.

Location Families.   In addition to semantic families related to handshape and movement, there are some semantics related to location. Specifically, locations related to gender in ASL form the basis for many signs that describe family or kinship. The half of the face from the nose up is reserved for male and the lower half for female. Many kinship terms begin with the first part of the sign indicating male or female, as in the signs for BROTHER and SISTER.

The back of the hand serves as another location that implies "foundation." The signs for INSTITUTION, CHURCH, NATION, and MOUNTAINS all have the underlying semantics of "solid base as in rocks."

In addition, Wilbur (1987) pointed out that sign forms produced on or near the nose have a negative intent, as in UGLY, STINK, and IGNORE.

Influence of Spoken Language

The influence of English is probably most easily seen when the processes of semantic families are extended to include meanings borrowed from English. The initialization process is related to the productive components found in ASL and, in particular, the semantic families. As in all languages, there is a process that involves the borrowing of lexical items from one language by another. For example, a significant number of French and Greek words are used in English, such as "restaurant," "gourmet," and "delta." In ASL, a similar borrowing mechanism occurs through the initialization process, which can be seen most easily in the semantic families. For

example, holding location and movement constant, the underlying semantic representation for *group* can be found in these signs: FAMILY, ASSOCIATION, GROUP, CLASS, CATEGORY, and WORKSHOP. For these forms the location is in neutral space, at chest level, and the movement is a circle made with both hands in initial contact, when each hand making a 180° arc, ending in contact. Other families using initialization are in the sign forms for KING, QUEEN, LORD, and PRINCE; and for MONDAY, TUESDAY, WEDNESDAY, FRIDAY, and SATURDAY. This process of borrowing the first letter of words found in spoken languages is not new to ASL or other signed languages. Many ASL sign forms are originally based in French Sign Language, and their etymology includes handshapes based on French words. For example, the A in OTHER is borrowed from the French *autre* (Hoffmeister, Moores, and Ellenberger 1975). Other signed languages also have been found to borrow forms (Kourbetis and Hoffmeister 1986, 1987).

Particular handshapes that form semantic categories have been extended from the original meaning and may change over time. Some meanings may actually be expanded to include a wider application than originally intended; some sign forms become more restricted as to what meanings may be included. This is due to the evolution of the language and must be attended to when ASL is discussed as a pedagogical tool. Knowledge of the historical development of ASL will permit an understanding of what areas are open to change and how the language allows these changes to occur. (For an extensive discussion on the historical development and linguistic changes in ASL, the reader is referred to Frishberg 1975, Fischer 1975, and Wilbur 1987.)

Pronominal System

Personal Pronouns.   A pronoun is a form that may be used in place of a noun form for an object or to refer to the location of the noun. Pronouns refer to the categories to which noun referents belong. In some languages, lexical forms may be used to represent objects based on their membership in the above categories (Allan 1977). Because of its shifting reference capabilities, the pronoun system is context-dependent. Pronouns are cognitively anchored, that is, they are directly tied to both the environmental context and its mapping within the conversation. To understand the pronoun referent, one must be aware of how one makes reference to the speaker/signer, listener, and objects outside the present environment, and the speaker/signer must be aware of the listener's perspective. In addition, pronoun forms are able to refer to many objects, which means they have shifting reference.

Pronoun forms may occur as free or bound morphemes, depending on the language. They may be used as alternatives to nouns (reference) or to call attention to any object (deictic). Pronouns serve to omit the redundancy of naming the object every time it is mentioned. The pronoun may carry information related to the noun referent it is replacing. In English, it carries information about the noun's gender and number. In some languages, pronouns may carry information that cannot be attached to the noun. For example, in English, the reflexive is a pronoun form; *self* may only be attached to a pronoun root, as in John ate the fish himself, or John himself ate the fish.

In English, the pronoun may also contain syntactic information relevant to the particular sentence, conveyed by the morphological principles of English. In other languages, pronouns may also carry other information, such as size and shape, matter and material. When pronouns convey this information they form the category called classifiers.

In ASL, pronominal forms may also occur deictically or indexically to call the listener's attention to a referent. They may occur anaphorically to refer to something previously mentioned. They are of two types, independent (free) or attached (bound). Independent proforms are the set of personal pronouns, such as I/ME, YOU, HE/SHE/IT. The actual form consists of the G or one handshape pointing in the direction of the object being referred to. These independent proforms require that the object be present when reference is being made. If the object is not present, another process must be used, which requires that an arbitrary location in space be named. This location functions as a marker, so that if the speaker/signer wishes to refer to that object again, the G hand may be directed toward the previously established location.

Table 1 presents a listing of various handshapes and their meanings in the ASL pronominal system.

Pluralization. The bound morphemes for pluralization involve the addition of two types of movement to the pronominal forms in figure 6. A discrete plural involves two specific movements to two different locations. For example, a movement back and forth between the speaker and listener expresses the meaning of YOU AND ME. In

Table 1.   Selected Pronominal Forms in ASL

| Handshape | Direction of Hand | | |
	+ Speaker/Signer	− Speaker/Signer + Listener	− Speaker/Signer − Listener
G	I/ME	YOU	HE/SHE/IT
B	MY/MINE	YOUR/S	HIS/HERS/ITS
A	MYSELF	YOURSELF	HIMSELF/HERSELF
K (palm in)	TWO-OF-US	TWO-OF-YOU	TWO-OF-THEM
3 (palm in)	THREE-OF-US	THREE-OF-YOU	THREE-OF-THEM

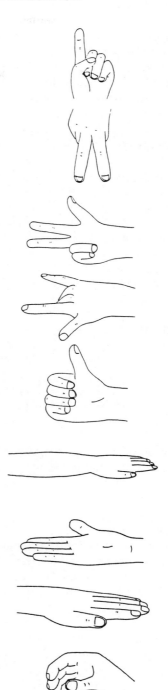

1. General person (animate): G-hand, usual orientation is fingertip up

2. Person by legs: v-hand, usual orientation is fingertips down for "stand," "walk," "kneel," but may have other orientations

3. Vehicle: 3-hand, orientation is fingertips sideways (as opposed to the numeral "3," which has its citation orientation fingertips up), may be used for cars, motorcycles, boats, trains, etc.

4. Plane ⊔ handshape, may be used for airplanes

5. Stationary object taller than it is wide (also may be used as dummy general object): A-hand, used in place of objects such as bottle, house, lamp.

6. Stationary object taller than it is wide that cannot be moved by an independent source or that is intended to be stationary: arm extended upward from elbow to fingertips, B-hand, used for buildings, trees, walls, etc.

7. Flat objects that can be moved: B-hand, palm up, can be used for book, paper, mirror, etc.

8. Flat object that is not supposed to be moved: B-hand, palm down, can be used for bridge, floor rooftop, ground, etc.

9. Hollow, curved object with rim: c-hand, palm facing sideways, can be used for glasses, cups, jars, etc.

Figure 6. Examples of some major ASL classifiers.

Note. Reprinted by permission of the publisher, from R. Wilbur, *American Sign Language: Linguistic and Applied Dimensions*, (1987):90. San Diego: CA: College-Hill Press.

the sign form for BOTH-OF-US, the hand-shape is a fist with the index and second finger extended and the palm facing the signer. The two movements involve the two extended fingers on the same hand. A point with the index finger to the listener or to a third party is then followed with a point to the signer with the second finger. The handshape remains constant throughout the motions. This incorporates the two discrete pointing motions that are also available to indicate "you and me." However, the sign YOU-AND-ME is produced using only the index finger. Through direction of movement one can include the speaker/signer, listener, and other objects, or they can be excluded. This individual or discrete reference indicates an "each-of" meaning. A continuous movement across all the objects being depicted indicates a group of objects. This is called the horizontal sweep, indicating "all of."

ASL inflectional morphology is working at its fullest within the pronominal system. It has developed through the production of forms that result in very efficient use of visually perceived time and space. When the pronominal system is expanded, additional information can be incorporated, not only into the signs, but into the entire sentence.

Classifiers. Classifiers are pronoun forms that symbolize referents by the category to which the referents belong. They contain more information than the pronoun forms available in English (Wilbur 1987). Classifiers include information about composition, animacy, and arrangement and functions of objects. Many other languages include classifiers within their pronominal systems. They represent nouns based on the salient visual-tactile characteristics of the referents that are found universally across classifier-type languages (T. Supalla 1985). Allan (1977) described seven categories for classifiers in spoken languages. To date, the following four are known to exist in ASL: (1) material (animate vs. inanimate); (2) shape (salient one-dimensional, two-dimensional, three-dimensional, vertical/horizontal extent, salient top/underside surfaces, round, flat); (3) size (small/large); and (4) arrangement (heaps, pleats) (Wilbur 1987, 89). ASL classifiers are handshapes and graphic representations that must combine with a predicate[3] root (specific movement) to be produced within the system.

Wilbur outlined three basic classifier types, and T. Supalla (1985) discussed five. Both researchers agree on the following classifier types: (1) semantic classifiers, which represent a class of objects; (2) size and shape specifiers (SASS), which represent the size, shape, and extent of objects; and (3) "handle," or instrument, classifiers, which represent how the object functions and include visual and geometric characteristics. T. Supalla (1982, 1985) suggested two more: (4) body classifiers, which represent the whole body as a classifier form; and (5) body-part classifiers, which represent limbs.

Semantic classifiers are more abstract in their reference to objects. They are handshapes that represent characteristics of object groupings, such as "bipedal" motion movement involving two feet or legs, an upright person, a vehicle, or an airplane (see figure 6). These semantic classifiers directly represent objects and are produced using single-handed forms.

SASSes are morphemes that carry information about the size and shape of the noun and, in many instances, its extent. For example, the G handshape may be used to represent a long, thin object, such as a railing on a fence. If the fence were composed of flat boards adjacent to one another, it might be represented by using the first two fingers (the H handshape). This increase in the use of fingers represents thickness. Size and shape may also be demonstrated by tracing shapes in space. Shapes may be modified in a variety of ways by varying the size of the tracing, modifying extent by using two or four fingers, or varying length and distance by opening the G handshape to an L.

The handle classifiers (Kegl and Wilbur 1976), or instrument classifiers (T. Supalla 1985), are forms that represent the action when handling the actual objects. For example, BROOM is produced by two S handshapes, as if holding a broom, and the movements are comparable to a sweeping action.

Three predicate roots to which classifier handshapes attach have been proposed by T. Supalla (Ibid.): existence (produced as holds in sign space), location (produced as if stamping a spot by the hand), and motion (producing linear paths, arcs, and circles). These have been further modified by Schick (1985, 1987), to suggest that the movement root be retained and location and existence be combined into one root, since both include a hold in space. To choose a handle classifier, a signer must decide to identify the common characteristic that will be used to represent the object, and then how to demonstrate this by handshape and movement across similar objects. Wilbur has suggested that this is a "distillation" of real-world representation (1987, 93). In the description of a movement root, it is important to understand that it consists of two movements— path of referent and extent of referent. The path refers to movement from one location to another, and extent refers to the descriptive details of the object being represented. For example, the G handshape (palm down) could be used to represent the path of an animal running away from the signer, where the movement is in a straight line away from the chest with the hand pointing out about eighteen inches. The representation is "animal is moving along this path." A change in the direction of the movement to the right in a straight line, as if the signer is tracing an imaginary line at chest level, transforms the representation into "a long, thin, polelike object." With the addition of a path movement to this representation, the meaning becomes "long, polelike object moves to another location." (For a more detailed discussion of classifiers and their importance in ASL, the reader is referred to Macdonald 1982, S. Supalla 1989, T. Supalla 1978, 1985, 1986, and Wilbur 1987.)

Sentence Level Structures

Syntax, or the ordering of morphemes in ASL, is quite complex, because it involves the interaction of morphological and ordering rules. There is evidence that ASL is a language whose underlying grammatical frame is Subject-Verb-Object (SVO) (Fischer 1975, Padden 1983). When one chooses to transform sentences into different surface orders, the changes must be marked. Marking these changes is a way to understand the meaning and signal that it is a structurally changed sentence. English is very different on the surface from ASL, in that it primarily uses free morphological markers and a rigid word-ordering system to indicate sentential relationships. Internal morphology, or bound morphemes that mark case, are found only in the pronoun system.

In ASL, when basic word order is varied, there must be a way of recovering the information that a noun phrase (NP) or sentential case role has been moved. This is done through the use of the indexing system (Hoffmeister 1978, 1979, 1980, 1987a; Padden 1983). When characters or locations are introduced in ASL, they usually are produced in some location relative to the signer and within the sign bubble (Lacy 1975). Lexical nouns designate arbitrary locations in space on the horizontal line, at chest level, called the Sign Shelf. Complex stories with many characters and different events may need more than one shelf to locate all the NPs. These NPs serve as loci (Liddell 1980) to represent the arbitrarily attached noun and may be used for a variety of morphosyntactic mechanisms in ASL.

The following is an example of how the syntactic system in ASL is able to represent semantic and grammatical functions within sentences.

MAN$_1$ BOSTON$_2$ BRUSSELS$_3$ #$_{1+2}$ FLY-BY-AIRPLANE $_3$#

The movement for the verb "to fly" begins in location [#1 + 2], which not only marks the grammatical functions within the sentence (MAN and BOSTON are in the same location), but also includes the classifier as instrument (the man flies by airplane from location 2 to location 3). The path extends between locations 2 + 3, signifying Boston to Brussels. The end of the movement is displayed with the handshape for AIRPLANE in location 3. The handshape and the locations in relative position with one another are in agreement. This agreement or sentence-level process marks the roles of subject, object, source, and goal. The handshapes are classifier forms that are inserted in the verb complex.

As the examples suggest, the system can become quite complex from what might appear to be simple gestural movements and handshapes. Complex sentences, such as those with topicalized, relative, and embedded clauses, also require the use of nonmanual forms (Liddell 1978). For example, embedded relative clauses may be marked by a slight head tilt backwards while the clause is produced on the hands and, when the main clause is begun, the head returns to the upright or conversationally normal position. (For a more detailed discussion of this principle, the reader is referred to Liddell 1980.)

IMPLICATIONS FOR EDUCATION

The field of deaf education has established, through its implementation of a TC philosophy, an educational framework that requires a closer look at the use of language. The change from oral to TC programs has created a situation that is difficult to define or evaluate.

TC programs generally combine spoken English with some form of English-based sign (or sign-supported speech [SSS]), as explained by Johnson, Liddell, and Erting (1989). Support for the use of these sign systems appears in parallel hypotheses presented in bilingual education programming:

1. Because ASL is different from English, the "linguistic mismatch" will hinder the learning of English;
2. If an English-based sign system is not used, there will be an "insufficient exposure" to the majority language (English) (adapted from Cummins 1986, 20).

Cummins disputed both hypotheses by citing research that shows that when the minority language has high status in the education program and is strongly reinforced in the wider society, students who are instructed using the minority language for all or part of the day will perform as well in English academic skills as students instructed exclusively in English (Ibid.). Cummins continued to explain that what is needed is a "personal redefinition" by teachers of the importance of the minority language and culture. For educators of the deaf, this means that it is critical to fully understand ASL in its linguistic and cultural domains. Teachers should be able to distinguish ASL and English linguistic properties, visual and spoken modalities, and cultural issues in the Deaf and hearing communities.

Moving from One Language to Another

An effective bilingual/bicultural program will employ teachers familiar with the properties of both languages. There is no one-to-one correspondence in form between spoken English and ASL; however, there is correspondence in relation to meaning. In all languages, translation from one language to another is dependent on the meaning being expressed rather than the individual matching of words. The view that SE is an acceptable translation of English is held by those who are not aware of the translation, interpretative, and cultural factors that exist when two languages convey the same information. These factors, by acting as filters and adjusters, allow a bilingual person to adjust to each of the two languages. The interpretation may not be identical because of the cultural factors. Often, one culture views the meaning of a form as positive or neutral, and another culture perceives it negatively. When this occurs the interpretation from one language to another may vary the meaning slightly so that it is acceptable to both cultures. In addition, for an accurate interpretation, the translator should also be bicultural or, at the very least, have an extensive understanding of the culture of the second language (Cummins 1986).

Bilingual/Bicultural Programming

Bilingual/bicultural programming as defined here is the use of ASL as the first language and written English as the second. Equal status is afforded both languages; however, equal use is not.

It is well documented that the young deaf child has great difficulty learning and using English (Rodda and Grove 1987; Moores 1987). Studies comparing deaf children of deaf parents with deaf children of hearing parents provide evidence that, if a child is presented with a fluent ASL model, she or he will learn it naturally. The child will then use form and function learned in the first language (ASL) to acquire the form and function of the second one (English).

Cummins (1984, 1986) presented a model that suggests the need to develop strengths in both languages in bilingual children. Pattison (1982) suggested that, in the development of literacy skills, it is necessary to view the use of English in the social and academic settings as two distinct dialects and, possibly, two languages. He argued that the child must learn how to interact fluently in both dialects to be academically successful. Both researchers present convincing arguments that recognize the difficulty in becoming literate in monolingual academic situations, and suggest that it is far more difficult in the bilingual settings

that exist in the United States today. For the deaf child, as for any bilingual child, four languages—or two distinct dialects of both languages—must be learned to achieve success. According to this model the deaf child must learn at least three languages, although school systems theoretically expose him or her to only one (Hoffmeister 1989a, b).

The use of artificially created sign systems or sign-supported speech systems are attempts to restrict the deaf child to a monolingual input in the classroom. These artificial systems hinder the deaf child's success in school. SE systems have been reported to reduce the complexity of the spoken language from which the model is derived (S. Supalla 1986, 1989; Leutke-Stahlman 1988). Information that serves to provide a cohesive, complex system is omitted, and a basic, low-level structural input becomes the model (Marmor and Petitto 1979). The result is a low-level monolingual (English) presentation in a bimodal (spoken English and SE) framework for deaf children (Greenwald 1984). The complexity of the English input is reduced, diminishing the opportunities for a deaf child to learn metalinguistic strategies for understanding the signed forms based on the spoken model (including English-based sign systems). The presentation of complex utterances is necessary so that the child will have enough data from which to derive information and will include structures that challenge him or her (DeVilliers 1987).

The evidence shows that deaf children who are fluent in ASL and English experience superior achievement in school. Studies of deaf children of deaf parents and their use of both English and ASL provide solid evidence for the positive effects of bilingualism on formalized testing and school success (Moores 1987; Quigley and Paul 1984). The fact that deaf children of deaf parents score significantly higher than deaf children of hearing parents on measures related to school achievement, including reading, mathematics, and world knowledge, relates to their metaknowledge of both languages.[4]

This advanced development is also strongly related to the environment that supports bilingual/bicultural input. The fact that a deaf child of deaf parents has access to a set of cultural norms, values, and beliefs enables that child to gain a sense of place in the world. This allows him or her to participate in social interaction where content and function are focal, in addition to structure and form. The child is able to obtain a great deal of information that is not necessarily explicit in language form but occurs through language use. For example, lexical forms that are considered negative within the family and the culture are learned through appropriate interaction and discussion; they may not be explicitly discussed within the conversation. Nuances signalled by nonmanual forms (such as the negative head shake) are included when various lexical forms are presented. Teachers not fluent in ASL may not realize that these signals must accompany certain forms and therefore may not transfer this information to the deaf child. In spoken languages nuances are also delivered through the use of intonation, stress, and facial expression. However, facial expression in a spoken language does not present the same semantic frame of meaning as in a signed language. This results not only in a language conflict, but also in a cultural one (Mather 1987).

Theoretical Framework-Bilingual Program

A bilingual/bicultural program for deaf students must have strategies to empower the students and deemphasize the influence of the dominant culture. Cummins (1986, 21) suggests the following theoretical criteria for establishing a bilingual/bicultural program.

1. Minority students' language and culture should be incorporated into the school program;

2. Minority community participation should be encouraged as an integral component of children's education;
3. The pedagogy should promote intrinsic motivation for students to use language actively in order to generate their own knowledge; and
4. Professionals involved in assessment should become advocates for minority students, rather than legitimizing the location of the "problem" in the students.

Strategies for Incorporating Minority Language and Culture. The recognition of deaf people as members of a linguistic and cultural minority group is not widely acknowledged within the educational system. The circumstances surrounding the deaf child's abilities and the variation in environmental factors, such as level of hearing loss, etiology, home language, and age of identification of the hearing loss, all contribute to complicating eligibility decisions. All deaf children, regardless of the level of hearing loss, should be enrolled in a bilingual/bicultural program. The primary goal is to allow the deaf child maximum input to acquire fluency and communicative competency in a first language (ASL), which will enable him or her to successfully acquire English as a second language.

The programmatic structure should distinguish between learning the curriculum and acquiring a first and second language. The goal of formal language instruction is for the child to learn the differences between ASL and English, not only in modality but in structure. ASL structure should be taught so that the young deaf child can identify nouns, verbs, classifiers, pronouns, and adjectives. Deaf children who are exposed to ASL in the classroom and at home will be able to discuss the properties of ASL and then learn how they relate to properties of a spoken language (English).

The ability to talk about one's language, both its form and function (metalanguage), has been found to be important to learning and acquiring literacy skills (Menyk 1988; Flood and Salus 1984). Cummins (1979) supported the notion that sociocultural factors influence the development of language learning and academic skills. Clearly, this is supported by the numerous studies that rank deaf children of deaf parents at a significantly more advanced level than deaf children of hearing parents. However, deaf children of deaf parents are still not on a level equal to that of hearing children. This inequality has more to do with sociocultural elements missing in programs than the limitations of the abilities of deaf children. Low expectations, directly connected to attitude toward deaf adults and their use of ASL, result in an environment that does not challenge the deaf child.

Studies examining attitudes toward Deaf people, and curricula that depict expectation levels in schools, easily explain why deaf children of deaf parents are not at the same scholastic level as hearing children (Erting 1985, 1982; Hoffmeister 1978; Hoffmeister and Shettle 1983; Johnson, Liddell, and Erting 1989). The literature regarding the educational needs of deaf children contains frequent references to adaptation of materials and curricula to suit the needs of the young deaf child. It is here that a bilingual/bicultural program will be of most benefit. Attitudes and expectations will be raised significantly with a concurrent increase in academic achievement within the program.

Including Minority Community Members in Programming. A bilingual/bicultural program for deaf children will require a professional staff well-trained in the use of ASL and English and able to demonstrate the linguistic and cultural similarities and differences in both languages. This background will allow language variation among deaf children to be accepted and will establish a precedent for ASL to be used consistently and approached positively.

Providing equal status to both languages and communities inside the school system will avoid bicultural ambivalence and reduce the internalization of inferior status held by many Deaf adults who are products of the current system. Administrators must be careful to avoid promoting a philosophy of equality and presenting to the students an organizational structure of conflicting expectations. Staffing should consist of equal numbers of Deaf and hearing teachers. One member of the team should be a speech pathologist specifically trained in bilingual approaches, to assist in the development of speech and articulation skills.

Providing Intrinsic Motivation for Deaf Students. The deaf child uses vision in much the same way as the hearing child uses hearing. A deaf child learns to categorize, store, and recall information through the visual channel. The most efficient language learning will be that which is most conducive to processing by the eyes (Bahan 1989; S. Supalla 1989). The young deaf child (regardless of whether he or she has hearing or deaf parents) who has been exposed to ASL-like signing is able to use ASL principles to convey information (Goodhart 1984; Gee and Goodhart 1986). These principles should be capitalized on in the instructional setting. Instructors who are knowledgeable about the system will be able to detect the use of ASL by their students and begin discussions about the language. The curriculum should be developed around ASL principles and ways in which to assist the child in recognizing their use and importance. These program elements create a positive self-image in deaf children, enabling them to feel accomplished and ready to tackle the difficult job of learning English. Moreover, the young deaf child will now have a language that can be used and talked about in school. This language can form the basis for delivering information and acquiring literacy skills.

The acquisition of literacy skills by deaf

children is an area that requires further research. Literacy includes, but should not be limited to, English reading and writing skills. The definition of literacy needs to be expanded to include storytelling in the Deaf community. The issue of how to introduce English and how much emphasis should be placed on its use within bilingual programs has been addressed by several investigators (Leutke-Stahlman 1986; Bahan 1989; Johnson, Liddell, and Erting 1989).

For the deaf child, reading in a bilingual/ bicultural program is a two-part process; it requires both understanding what a story or a narrative is and understanding the reference of the written word. Most teachers and parents are uncertain of how ASL can be used to introduce reading.

Parents are encouraged to read to their hearing children whether the children understand the story or not (Lapp and Flood 1978; Wells 1985, 1989). The basic premise is to create knowledge of both the content of a story and its structure. For deaf children, this may be done by presenting a pictorial sequence and a story in ASL. The child will understand the narrative process, which is inherent in learning to read. Once the deaf child is presented with a story model and is able to tell stories in ASL, the next step is to associate this with English by adding print. Pictures may be matched to print in the same way signed information corresponds to the pictures. The child now has a language foundation, a story base, a meaning-transfer strategy, and a model. Given these basic components in ASL, application to printed English is now based on previous knowledge. The deaf child is no longer confronted with the task of simultaneously learning the structure, meaning, and strategies of storytelling through the nonnative language. This approach may include some access strategies that relate to cultural information. Teachers need to be taught how to construct, expand, and modify stories in ASL, motivating stu-

dents to create their own stories. Their pride in their stories, language, and culture will be reflected not only in the classroom but within the community and home.

Assessment. Critical to the establishment of a good bilingual/bicultural program is a qualified assessment team. Measuring skills in deaf students is a complicated process, which cannot be fully described in a few short paragraphs. The following issues must be considered when evaluating deaf students:

1. skills of the examiner
2. type of test
3. language of the test
4. language used to administer directions (Hoffmeister 1988b).

A team approach is necessary to effectively evaluate the deaf child (Greenwald, Hoffmeister, and Kourbetis 1985). At least one of the examiners must be a Deaf professional trained to test deaf children, to allow for wide variation in the child's skills. The ASL and English communication skills of the examiner must be more advanced than those of the child being tested. The test instrument must be reviewed for both obvious and subtle bias against the child. Bias may appear in the form of questions relating to sound (i.e., music, telephone) or to culture (i.e., etiquette judgments based on gestures, such as pointing). All testing must be videotaped for review by the team after completion. Drawing conclusions during the testing process can result in misdiagnosis, since information is often hidden in other communicative signals (e.g., nonmanual expressions such as eye gaze). Having a Deaf examiner available to administer the test instructions will ensure that the deaf child understands the task he or she is expected to perform (Greenwald, Hoffmeister, and Kourbetis 1985).

The team approach will enable the testing situation to be reviewed from a variety of perspectives. This input will help avoid the inevitable discriminatory assessment conducted by "well-intentioned individuals" (Cummins 1986, 30; Greenwald, Hoffmeister, and Kourbetis 1985).

Parental Programming. The unique nature of the deaf child's family circumstances requires that parental participation be an essential component to the educational process. Over 90 percent of the parents of deaf children are hearing and will not necessarily support the principles and theories behind a bilingual/bicultural program for their children. Parents often fear that their deaf child will not absorb parental values and beliefs. Their fear that their child will not be part of their future inhibits their acceptance of this educational approach (Hoffmeister 1979; 1988a, 1989b; Hoffmeister and Shettle 1983). Therefore, the bilingual/bicultural approach requires that hearing parents be assisted in learning about ASL and the Deaf community. One way to do this is for them to learn stories in ASL, which requires contact with Deaf adults and the Deaf community, enhancing the parents' awareness of cultural and individual differences. This allows parents to feel more comfortable with their child and not view their differences negatively. To ease the parents' adjustment, a Deaf professional should be assigned to visit with the parents of preschoolers in their homes on a regular basis. At the elementary level, group meetings should be established at school. Parents who meet frequently with Deaf adults will be able to exchange cultural information and learn directly about the effects of deafness on children. As contact with Deaf adults increases, hearing parents will become more comfortable with ASL and with the impact caused by their child's deafness. Parents who have a positive outlook toward ASL, Deaf adults, and the Deaf community will transfer these feelings to their child. These attitudes will assist deaf children in their attempt to learn language. The deaf child will view both English and ASL as viable ways of communicating. This approach requires careful planning to establish a curriculum that presents English and ASL on an equal basis.

NOTES

1. I am indebted to Ms. Janey Greenwald and Mrs. Aurora Wilbur-Leach for their support, assistance, perseverance and most of all for their friendship. A word of gratitude is owed Dr. Donald F. Moores, for without his encouragement, guidance and direction, I would not have had the courage to attempt this document. To Dr. Ronnie Wilbur for her support, willingness to share ideas and listen to my radical meshuggaas. Finally, to Ben Bahan, Steve Nover, and the Deaf community who continue to teach and inspire me.

2. Because *language* and *English* are often used interchangeably in the literature, I would like to clarify the use of the following terms: *language* is used to describe conventional or shared communication that has been developed naturally and over time by groups of people, while *English* refers specifically to spoken and written English. *Signed languages* (such as ASL) refer to the natural or conventional signed languages of the world and would be included under the term *language*, while *Signed English* (SE) or *sign systems* designate artificially created forms of a visual language, and cannot be considered languages in the true sense of the word.

3. The term *predicate* refers to a verb form that may include information about subject, direct object, and/or indirect object, as well as information usually represented in English by prepositional phrases and adverbs (Wilbur 1987; 86).

4. Cummins (1984, 1986) explains that measuring conversational fluency in ASL (L_1) is not a good predictor of academic success. Moores (1988) suggests that there is no correlation between ASL and English academic skills. However, only conversational fluency (LPI) was used to measure ASL skills. There were numerous tests/measures in this study, examining a wide range of metalinguistic and metacognitive skills for English in the deaf subjects, yet none of the tests measured these same skills in L_1. If Cummins' data are correct, I would hypothesize that those deaf children who were "high" in "English-academic" skills (reading, writing) would also score "high" on tests of metalinguistic and metacognitive processing (knowledge about the language) in ASL if they were fluent signers. This is supported by the fact that many of the "high" scorers were deaf children of deaf parents.

REFERENCES

Allan, K. 1977. Classifiers. *Language* 53:285–311.

Andersen, R. 1988. A language acquisition interpretation of pidginization and creolization. In *Pidginization and creolization as language acquisition*, ed. R. Andersen. Rowley, MA: Newbury House. Armstrong.

Bahan, B. 1989. Literacy, ASL and the deaf child. Paper presented at the Conference on Literacy, Language, and Deafness, March 19, Newport, RI.

Bell, A .G. 1883. *Memoirs of a deaf variety of the human race*. Washington, DC: National Academy of Sciences.

Bellugi, U., and Klima, E. 1985. The acquisition of three morphological systems in American Sign Language. In *Educating the hearing-impaired child*, eds. F. Powell, T. Finitzo-Heber, S. Friel-Patti, and D. Henderson. San Diego: College Hill Press.

Bickerton, D. 1982. *Roots of language*. Ann Arbor: Karoma Press.

Bernstein, H. and Saulnier, K. 1981. Signed English: A brief follow up to the first evaluation. *American Annals of the Deaf* 127:69 – 72.

———. 1984a. *Signed English: A basic guide*. Washington, DC: Gallaudet University Press.

———. 1984b. *The Signed English starter*. Washington, DC: Gallaudet University Press.

———. 1987. *The Signed English schoolbook*. Washington, DC: Gallaudet University Press.

Chafe, W. 1970. *The structure and meaning of language*. Chicago: University of Chicago Press.

Chomsky, N. 1986. *Knowledge of language*. New York: Praeger Press.

Corbett, E., and Jensema, C. 1981. Teachers of the deaf. Washington, DC: Gallaudet University Press.

Corson, H. 1973. Comparing deaf children of oral deaf parents and deaf children using manual communication with deaf children of hearing parents on academic, social, and communicative functioning. Doctoral dissertation, University of Cincinnati, Cincinnati, Ohio.

Cummins, J. 1979. Linguistic interdependence and the educational development of bilingual children. *Review of Educational Research* 49:222 – 251.

———. 1984. *Bilingualism and special education: Issues in assessment and pedagogy*. San Diego: College Hill Press.

———. 1986. Empowering minority students: A framework for intervention. *Harvard Educational Review* 56:18 – 36.

DeVilliers, P. 1987. English language acquisition in the hearing impaired. Paper presented at Boystown Conference on Language and Deafness, Boystown Center for Communication Disorders, Omaha.

Erting, C. 1982. Deafness, communication, and social identity: An anthropological analysis of interaction among parents, teachers and deaf children in a preschool. Doctoral dissertation, American University, Washington, DC.

Erting, C. 1985. Sociocultural dimensions of deaf education: Belief systems and communicative interaction. *Sign Language Studies* 47:111 – 125.

Fischer, S. 1975. Influences on word order change in ASL. In *Word order and word order change*, ed. C. Li. Austin: University of Texas Press.

Flood, J., and Salus, P. 1984. *Language and the language arts*. Englewood Cliffs, NJ: Prentice Hall.

Frishberg, N. 1975. Arbitrariness and iconicity: Historical change in American Sign Language. *Language* 51:676 – 710.

Gee, J., and Goodhart, W. 1986. Nativization, variability, and style shifting in the sign language development of deaf children of hearing parents. Paper presented at the Conference on Theoretical Issues in Sign Language Research, June, University of Rochester, NY.

Gee, J., and Kegl, J. 1983. ASL structure: Towards the foundation of a theory of case. Paper presented at a Special Session on Sign Language, Annual Boston University Conference on Language Development, October.

———. 1984. Semantic perspicuity in American Sign Language. *Discourse Processes* 6.

Goodhart, W. 1984. Morphological complexity, ASL, and the acquisition of sign language in deaf children. Doctoral dissertation, Boston University, Boston.

Greenwald, J. 1984. Bilingual programming for deaf students. Working Paper #2, Center for the Study of Communication and Deafness, Boston University, Boston.

Greenwald, J., Hoffmeister, R., and Kourbetis, V. 1985. Model for assessing communicative competence in deaf students: A team approach. Paper presented at the International Congress on Education of the Deaf, August, Manchester, England.

Groce, N. 1987. *Everyone here spoke sign language*. Cambridge, MA: Harvard University Press.

Gustason, G., Pfetzing, D., and Zawolkow, E. 1972. *Signing Exact English*. Los Angeles: Modern Signs Press.

Hoffmeister, R. 1978. The development of demonstrative pronouns, locatives and personal pronouns in the acquisition of American Sign Language in deaf children of deaf parents. Doctoral dissertation, University of Minnesota, Minneapolis.

———. 1979. The development of possessive pronouns by deaf children of deaf parents. *Communication and Cognition* (Special issue on sign language research).

———. 1980. The influential POINT. In *Proceedings of the National Symposium on Sign Language and Sign Language Teaching*. Silver Spring, MD: National Association of the Deaf.

———. 1982. The acquisition of language abilities by deaf children. In *Communication in two societies*, ed. H. Hoeman and R. Wilbur. Washington, DC: Gallaudet University.

———. 1984. The acquisition of discrete elements in the signed language of deaf children. Working Paper #11, Center for the Study of Communication and Deafness, Boston University, Boston.

———. 1985. Families with deaf parents: A functional perspective. In *Handicapped families: Functional perspectives*, ed. K. Thurman. New York: Academic Press.

———. 1987a. The acquisition of pronominal anaphora in ASL by deaf children. In *Studies in the acquisition of anaphora: Defining the constraints*. Vol. II, ed. B. Lust. Boston: Reidel Publishing Co.

———. 1987b. Educational alternatives: Options, Choices, and questions. Working Paper #10, Center for the Study of Communication and Deafness, Boston University, Boston.

———. 1988a. Central role of communication in the family. Working Paper #12, Center for the Study of Communication and Deafness, Boston University, Boston.

———. 1988b. "Cognitive assessment of deaf preschoolers." In *Assessment of developmentally disabled children*, ed. T. Wachs, and R. Scheehan. New York: Plenum Publishing Corp.

———. 1988c. Historical perspectives in education of the deaf. Working Paper #6, Center for the Study of Communication and Deafness, Boston University, Boston.

———. 1989a. Deafness, literacy, and education. Invited Address, The Northeast Regional Conference of Superintendents of Schools for the Deaf, Princeton, NJ.

———. 1989b. Language power and its impact on deaf children in families and schools. Presented at the Annual Statewide Conference on Deafness and Education, Trenton, NJ.

———. In press. *Acquisition of sign language: Theoretical and educational implications*. New York: Springer-Verlag.

Hoffmeister, R., and Bahan, B. 1989a. Do birds fly? Paper presented at the Applied Linguistics Colloquia, Boston University, February, Boston.

———. 1989b. A house is not a home: Linguistic issues in ASL. A paper presented at the Canadian Hearing Society, Invited Colloguia, Toronto.

Hoffmeister, R., and Gee, J., eds. 1984. *Discourse Processes: A Multidisciplinary Journal* (Special edition on ASL discourse).

Hoffmeister, R., and Goodhart, W. 1978. The semantic and syntactic analysis of the sign language behavior of a deaf child of hearing parents. Paper presented at MIT Sign Language Symposium, Cambridge, Massachusetts.

Hoffmeister, R., and Moores, D. 1980. Expression of abstract concepts by deaf children. In *Proceedings of the 49th Biennial Convention of American Instructors of the Deaf*. ed. G. Propp. Silver Spring, MD: CAID.

Hoffmeister, R., and Moores, D. 1987. Code switching in deaf adults. *American Annals of the Deaf* 132: 31–34.

Hoffmeister, R., Moores, D., and Ellenberger, R. 1975. Some procedural guidelines for the study of the acquisition of Sign Language. *Sign Language Studies* 7:121–137.

Hoffmeister, R., and Shettle, C. 1983. Adaptations in communication made by deaf signers to different audience types. *Discourse Processes* 6:258–274.

Hoffmeister, R., and Wilbur, R. 1980. The acquisition of American Sign Language: A review. In *Current perspectives on sign language*, ed. H. Lane and F. Grosjean. Hillsdale, NJ: Lawrence Erlbaum Associates.

Johnson, R., Liddell, S., and Erting, C. 1989. Unblocking the curriculum: Principles for achieving access in deaf education. Gallaudet Research Institute Working Paper 89-3, Gallaudet University, Washington, DC.

Kantor, R., and Hoffmeister, R. 1983. The development of classifiers in deaf children and its implications for the classroom. In *Selected papers: Convention of American Instructors of the Deaf*, ed. E. Solano, J. Egleston-Dodd, and E. Costello. Silver Spring, MD: CAID.

Kegl, J., and Wilbur, R. 1976. When does structure stop and style begin? Syntax, morphology and phonology vs. stylistic variation in American Sign Language. In *Papers from the 12th Regional Meeting of the Chicago Linguistics Society*, ed. S. Hufwene, C. Walker, and S. Streeven. Chicago.

Klima, E., and Bellugi, U. 1979. *The signs of language*. Cambridge, MA: Harvard University Press.

Kourbetis, V. 1987. Deaf children of deaf parents and deaf children of hearing parents in Greece: A comparative study. Doctoral dissertation, Boston University, Boston.

Kourbetis, V., and Hoffmeister, R. 1986. Greek Sign Language: A preliminary review. Working Paper. Center for the Study of Communication and Deafness, Boston University, Boston.

———. 1987. The Greek Deaf community. Working Paper. Center for the Study of Communication and Deafness, Boston University, Boston.

Labov, W. 1975. The logic of non-standard English. In *Language in the inner city*, ed. W. Labov. Philadelphia: University of Pennsylvania Press.

Lacy, R. 1975. Putting some of the syntax back into semantics. Paper presented at the Linguistic Society of America Annual Meeting, New York.

Lamb, L., and Wilcox, P. 1988. Acceptance of ASL at the University of New Mexico: A history of a process. *Sign Language Studies* 59.

Lane, H. 1984. *When the mind hears*. New York: Random House.

Lapp, D., and Flood, J. 1978. *Teaching reading to every child*. New York: Macmillan Publishing Co.

Liddell, S. 1977. An investigation into the syntactic structure of American Sign Language. Doctoral dissertation, University of California, San Diego.

———. 1978. An introduction to relative clauses in ASL. In *Understanding language through sign language research*, ed. P. Siple. New York: Academic Press.

———. 1980. *American Sign Language syntax*. The Hague: Mouton.

Liddell, S. and Johnson, R. 1986. American Sign Language compound formation processes, lexicalization, and phonological remnants. *Natural Language and Linguistic Theory* 4:445–513.

Luetke-Stahlman, B. 1982. A philosophy for assessing the language proficiency of hearing impaired students to promote English literacy skills. *American Annals of the Deaf* 127:844–851.

———. 1984. Replicating single-subject assessment of language in deaf elementary-age children. *American Annals of the Deaf* 129:40–44.

———. 1986. Building a language base in hearing-impaired students. *American Annals of the Deaf* 131:220–228.

———. 1988. Documenting syntactically and semantically incomplete bimodal input to hearing-impaired subjects. *American Annals of the Deaf* 133:230–234.

Macdonald, B. 1982. Aspects of the American Sign Language predicate system. Doctoral dissertation, University of Buffalo, Buffalo, NY.

Marmor, G., and Pettito, L. 1979. Simultaneous communication in the classroom: How well is English grammar represented? *Sign Language Studies* 23:99–130.

Mather, S. 1987. Eye gaze and communication in a deaf classroom. *Sign Language Studies* 54:11–30.

Meadow, K. 1980. *Deafness and child development*. Berkeley: University of California Press.

Menyuk, P. 1988. *Language acquisition*. Englewood Cliffs, NJ: Prentice Hall.

Moores, D., Kluwin, T., Johnson, R., Ewoldt, C., Cox, P., Blennerhassett, L., Kelley, L., Sweet, K., and Fields, L. 1989. *Predictive factors of literacy in deaf adolescents with deaf parents and deaf adolescents in total communication programs*. Final report to NINCDS. Center for Research in Education and Human Development, Gallaudet University, Washington, DC.

Moores, D. 1987. *Educating the deaf: Psychology, principles, and practices*. Boston: Houghton Mifflin.

Mounty, J. 1986. Nativization and the acquisition of American Sign Language. Doctoral dissertation, Boston University, Boston.

Padden, C. 1983. Interaction of morphology and syntax in American Sign Language. Doctoral dissertation, University of California, San Diego.

Padden, C. ,and Humphries, T. 1988. *Deaf in America: Voices from a culture*. Cambridge, MA: Harvard University Press.

Pattison, R. 1982. *On literacy*. New York: Oxford University Press.

Poplack, S. 1979. *Sometimes I'll start a sentence in Spanish y termino en Espanol: Toward a typology of code-switching*. Center for Puerto Rican Studies, New York.

Quigley, S., and Paul, P. 1984. *Language and deafness*. San Diego: College Hill Press.

Raffin, M. 1976. The acquisition of inflectional morphemes by deaf children using Seeing Essential English. Doctoral dissertation, University of Iowa, Iowa City.

Reagan, T. 1987. The deaf as a linguistic minority. *Harvard Educational Review*.

Rodda, M., and Grove, C. 1987. *Language, cognition and deafness*. Hillsdale, NJ: Lawrence Erlbaum Associates.

Schick, B. 1987. The acquisition of complex classifier predicates in American Sign Language. Doctoral dissertation, Purdue University, West Lafayette, IN.

Siple, P., ed. 1978. *Understanding language through sign language research*. New York: Academic Press.

Stokoe, W. 1960. Sign language structure: An outline of the visual communication system of the American deaf. *Studies in Linguistics* 8.

———. 1970. Sign language diglossia. *Studies in linguistics* 8.

———. 1972. Classification and description of sign languages. In *Current Trends in Linguistics 12*, ed. T. Soeboel. The Hague: Mouton.

Supalla, S. 1986. Manually Coded English: The modality question in signed language development. Master's thesis, University of Illinois, Urbana-Champaign.

———. 1988. Paper presented to the American Society of Parents of Deaf Children, July, Indianapolis, IN.

———. In press. Manually Coded English: The modality question in signed language development. In *Theoretical issues in sign language research*. ed. P. Siple.

Supalla, T. 1978. The morphology of verbs of motion and location in American Sign Language. In *National Symposium on Sign Language Research and Teaching*, ed. F. Caccamisee. Silver Spring, MD: National Association of the Deaf.

———. 1982. Structure and acquisition of verbs of motion and location in American Sign Language. Doctoral dissertation, University of California, San Diego.

———. 1985. The classifier system in American Sign Language. In *Noun classification and categorization*, ed. C. Craig. Philadelphia: John Benjamins.

———. 1986. Serial verbs in ASL. Paper presented at the Conference on Theoretical Issues in Sign Language Research, August, Rochester, NY.

Supalla, T., and Newport, E. 1978. How many seats in a chair? The derivation of nouns and verbs in American Sign Language. In *Understanding language through sign language research*, ed. P. Siple. New York: Academic Press.

Wells, G. 1985. Preschool literacy-related activities and success in school. In *Literacy, language, and learning*, ed. D. Olson, N. Torrance, A. Hildyard.

Cambridge, England: Cambridge University Press.
———. 1989. Early literacy and schooling. Paper presented at the Symposium on Language, Literacy, and Deafness, March, Newport, RI.

Wilbur, R. 1987. *American Sign Language: Linguistic and applied dimensions.* San Diego: College Hill Press.

Wilcox, S., and Corwin, K. 1988. Special Edition on University Acceptance of ASL. *Sign Language Studies* 55.

Woodward, J. 1973. Implication lects on the deaf diglossic continuum. Doctoral dissertation, Georgetown University, Washington, DC.
———. 1982. *How you gonna get to heaven if you can't talk to Jesus?* Silver Spring, MD: T. J. Publishers.

Woodward, J., and Allen, T. 1987. Classroom use of ASL by teachers. *Sign Language Studies* 54:1–10.
———. 1988. Classroom use of artificial sign systems by teachers. *Sign Language Studies* 61:405–418.

CHAPTER 6 ▰

Signing Exact English

Gerilee Gustason

There were three basic reasons for the development of Manually Coded English systems in general and Signing Exact English (SEE) in particular.

1. Dissatisfaction with educational achievement levels of deaf children,
2. Increased knowledge of normal language development in hearing children and the importance of the first few years of life in this process, and
3. Dissatisfaction with the ambiguous input of speechreading alone.

Regarding educational achievement, research studies from the beginning of the century indicated that American programs for the deaf were not doing very well at teaching English to deaf students. Various studies indicated that

1. Deaf children wrote short and simple sentences, those of a 17-year-old deaf student being comparable to those of a hearing child in third grade (Heider and Heider 1940);
2. Deaf students' use of clauses differed from that of hearing children, being simpler and more rule-bound (Reay 1946);
3. Deaf students' vocabulary tended to be considerably smaller than that of their hearing peers (Ibid.);
4. Deaf students' grasp of the morphological and syntactical rules of English was weak and without a clear pattern of development, in contrast to that of hearing children (Cooper 1965);
5. Deaf students used fewer adverbs, auxiliaries, and conjunctions than did hearing children (Simmons 1962);
6. About half the language errors made by deaf students were errors of omission of necessary words (Myklebust 1965);
7. Lexical, or dictionary, meanings were easier for deaf students than structural meanings (e.g., a chair as something to sit on versus to chair a meeting) (Hart and Rosenstein 1964).

Reading achievement and language scores had hovered around the level attained by fourth- and fifth-grade hearing children for more than fifty years. In the 1960s, it was reported that, in studies covering 93 percent of deaf students in the

United States aged sixteen and older, some 30 percent were functionally illiterate—or unable to read and write well enough to get along in life. Sixty percent were reading at grade level 5.3 or below, the average reading level was at grade 3.4, and the average total gain in reading for students between the ages of ten and a half and sixteen and a half was less than one year (Boatner 1965; McClure 1966; Wrightstone, Aranow, and Moskowitz 1963).

Responding in part to this dismal picture of achievement, the Secretary of Health, Education, and Welfare appointed a committee in the early 1960s to conduct a national study on education of the deaf. This committee's 1965 report, the Babbidge report, stated that

> The American people have no reason to be satisfied with their limited success in educating deaf children and preparing them for full participation in our society . . . the basic explanation lies in our failure to launch an aggressive assault on some of the basic problems of language learning of the deaf.

At the same time, studies of the intelligence of deaf people indicated the same distribution of intelligence as for hearing people (Vernon 1969).

This dissatisfaction with the results of efforts to teach deaf children English was surfacing at the same time as research reports on normal language development in hearing children. Key points emerging from this research indicated that

1. Hearing children master a great deal of the structure of English, including basic sentence patterns and inflections, by age three;
2. Between two and three years of age, a great jump is made, including the acquisition of prepositions, demonstratives, auxiliaries, articles, conjunctions, possessive and personal pronouns, the past-tense suffix, the plural suffix, and the possessive suffix;
3. The language of hearing children is fairly stable after age six; and

4. Language habits are difficult to change after puberty (Braine 1963; Brown and Bellugi 1964; Cazden 1968; Weir 1962; Labov 1965; Penfield 1964; Moskowitz 1978).

At that time, in the mid-1960s, there were few preschool programs for deaf children or parent education programs for the parents of deaf infants. Many deaf children entered school at the age of five or six with little or no vocabulary, having missed the critical learning years when language is normally acquired.

Finally, physical studies of children's development indicated that children's eyes do not fully accommodate until about age eight. Small differences in form may be ignored by the children until that time (Mussen 1963). That is why, for instance, books for toddlers use large print and big pictures. In addition, research on speechreading indicated that 40 to 60 percent of the sounds of English looked like other sounds on the lips. For instance, *15* and *50* look alike, as do *17* and *70*, or *8, 9,* and *10*. *Pan, ban,* and *man* look the same. Many word endings are not visible (e.g., *interest, interesting, interests,* and *interested* are nearly impossible to distinguish) and, since some involve hard-to-hear sounds, this is a problem for hard-of-hearing as well as deaf children. Many of the best speechreaders use their knowledge of English to fill in the gaps. According to one researcher, many bright and otherwise capable deaf children caught only 5 percent of what was said through speechreading. Much of the focus was on key words, and structure words (such as *the*) and word endings were often ignored (Vernon 1968; Lowell 1957–1958; Hart and Rosenstein 1964).

Accordingly, it is not surprising that many college-age deaf students who did not see or hear English word endings, but for years had studied the rules of English grammar that said one should use *-ing* when speaking of the present and *-ed* when speaking of the past, created sentences such as:

I am interesting in TV. (I am watching it now.)

The movie was interested. (I saw it yesterday.)

Hard-of-hearing students display similar problems, although their hearing may be good enough for them to catch key words and function adequately in conversation.

THE ESTABLISHMENT OF THE SEE GROUP

Manually Coded English systems developed out of the frustration with problems just described. The first system to appear was Seeing Essential English, later called SEE I. David Anthony, a deaf teacher of the deaf, had created the concept of SEE when he worked in Michigan with mentally retarded deaf adults. Mr. Anthony brought the concept with him to southern California and introduced it in a day class program in Anaheim. As other teachers and educational interpreters became involved with the concept, the need for its development was realized.

In January 1969, a group of deaf adults, parents, teachers, and interpreters met in Hollywood to discuss working together on such development. During the next few months guidelines were written, the Seeing Essential English name selected, and a working committee of five elected. Sign classes in SEE I were taught by four of the five individuals: David Anthony, Donna Pfetzing (the mother of a deaf daughter and an educational interpreter), Esther Zawolkow (the daughter of deaf parents, an interpreter certified by the Registry of Interpreters for the Deaf, and a leading educational interpreter at the high school level), and me (a deaf teacher of the deaf). The fifth member of the steering committee, Marjoriebelle Holcomb, aided Mr. Anthony in some of these classes. The working committee was selected because the original group grew larger and larger as more teachers, parents, deaf people, and interpreters became involved, and it be-

came unwieldy. Interest had also spread to northern California and other parts of the United States. Copies of papers were prepared with written descriptions of the newly developed signs, and these papers were used in sign classes and mailed to interested individuals (see figure 1).

In an attempt to make the development of new signs linguistically sound, a panel of linguists was convened with the assistance of the University of Redlands in California. This panel included Dr. William Stokoe, a pioneer researcher on American Sign Language (ASL). Information was sought in an open session concerning how to define the morphology of a signed word and the extent to which English words could and should be broken up to best represent their English morphemes (e.g., should the word *butterfly*, which has a sign equivalent in ASL, be kept as a single sign or signed as BUTTER + FLY? or as BUT + ER + FLY?) It must be kept in mind that at this time research on ASL had only just begun, and very little information was available yet on its grammar, morphology, structure, or principles. Accordingly, it probably should not be surprising that the outcome of this panel discussion was a consensus among the linguists that they could not really provide helpful advice on developing an English sign system and that the developers needed to "go by gut feelings."

In the fall of 1970, a split occurred. Mr. Anthony stopped teaching and spent a year preparing a complete book of SEE signs, working independently of the original group. The original committee was left with the responsibility for teaching the SEE sign classes and became more deeply involved than before in correspondence with interested parties, explanatory lectures, and parent education. No materials other than the previously copied papers were available yet, and more such material was produced to aid in instruction and information sharing, since attempting to describe a sign over the telephone was somewhat difficult.

ART

Left open B hand, palm right, fingers point outward.

Right A hand, palm left, thumb uppermost.

With right hand draw a wavy line downwards across the palm of the left hand.

ALLOW

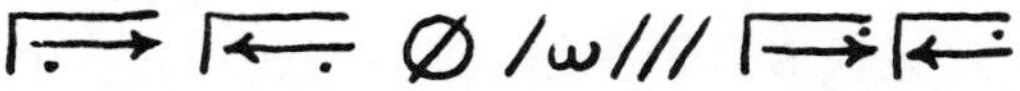

Both open B hands, palm to palm but not touching in front of you, pointing down.

Twist to point upward.

(cf. let, permit)

ASK

Both open B hands, palms facing each other, fingers pointing forward.

Touch hands together and arch toward chest.

BAR

Left 1 hand, palm in, fingertip pointing right.

Right B hand, palm out, fingertips up.

Place heel of right hand on top of left wrist and slide along hand and off to the right.

(cf. row, line)

BASE

Left open B hand, palm down, fingers pointing right.

Right B hand, palm left, fingers pointing outward.

With right hand make small circular motion under left hand.

BASIC: base + ic

BED

Two open B hands, palms together.

Place hands on right cheek, fingers pointing upwards; rest head on the back of the left hand.

BEEF

Left B hand, palm in, fingertips pointing right.

Right 9 hand, palm down.

Grasp the flesh between the thumb and forefinger with right hand, as in the traditional sign for "meat."

(cf. ham, pork)

BIG

Both B hands, palm out, fingertips upward.

Touch sides of index fingers, move outward in a slight upward arc.

(cf. great, large)

Figure 1. Description of signs created for Seeing Essential English.

In the early summer of 1971, Mr. Anthony finished a two-volume book, *Seeing Essential English*. The original committee had awaited this book for use in teaching, but they found many of its signs unacceptable and presented in a format they felt was difficult to decipher. The chief reason for this disagreement was the degree of dependence by Mr. Anthony on the "root-word" concept; for example, he considered *gene* the root for *general* and *generous*, and *secret* the root for *secretary*. The others in the original group felt this was an excessive breaking up of English words and too radical a departure from the traditional signs of ASL. While they accepted the sign for *gene*, they did not feel that *general* or *generous* were related to this word, nor did they feel that *secretary* was related to *secret*.

Meanwhile, the inadequacy of the copied descriptions and the difficulty of sharing information concerning newly developed signs over a geographical separation of hundreds of miles, coupled with a disagreement over the clearest and easiest way to depict a sign in print, led to a further split of the original group. Most members of the group were in favor of pictures and written descriptions of signs. Dennis Wampler, of northern California, had been interested in the SEE work for over a year. He believed that exact correctness of sign production from a printed page was possible only with a symbol system such as that developed by Dr. Stokoe in his work with ASL. This system utilized symbols for handshape, position, and movement. While the original group had attempted to use, with Dr. Stokoe's permission, an adapted form of these symbols, they had found most parents unable to cope effectively with symbols. Mr. Anthony's book included similar symbols paired with a written description, but Mr. Wampler felt so strongly about the value of such a symbol system that he decided to publish on his own. In the summer of 1971, he printed a morpheme list under the name *Linguistics of Visual English* (see figure 2).

While agreeing to the value of such a symbol system in studying sign language linguistically, the remaining members of the original group found it impractical for use in teaching sign classes. Accordingly, work progressed on a picture-plus-written-description book of basic signs.

At the same time, the committee had been approached during early 1971 by the National Association of the Deaf (NAD) concerning the possibility of developing drawings for 300 basic new signs, including verb inflections (-*ing*, -*ed*, etc.) and pronouns (*he*, *she*, etc.), and these drawings had been made. Upon the publication of *Seeing Essential English*, and the discovery that it would not fill the need the committee felt to exist, the committee requested the 300 drawings back from the NAD. An artist, Carolyn Norris, was en-

listed, approximately 1200 more drawings were done, and a basic volume was readied for publication. The NAD was not at that time interested in publishing an entire volume of SEE signs, so Ms. Zawolkow, Ms. Pfetzing, Dr. Norris, and I formed a partnership to underwrite the first publication of *Signing Exact English*, in the spring of 1972. Signing Exact English is now known as SEE II. The SEE acronym was kept because it was felt that the general thrust of the work was already being labelled as SEE.

THE ORIGINAL TEN TENETS

When the SEE group was formed in early 1969, the following ten basic tenets were accepted by the entire group:

1. *Acquiring good English is a tremendously difficult task for a child born deaf.* The information on the educational achievement of deaf students was most relevant to this tenet.

2. *The most important factor in acquiring good English is an understanding of its syntax or structure.* Word order is important (e.g., *The man beat the boy* and *The boy beat the man* contain the same words, but their meanings are different because of word order). Also, word endings are important (e.g., an *interested* man is different from an *interesting* man). As the number of words in a sentence increases, the complexity of their relationship may increase and so may the need to understand grammar and syntax to properly interpret the meaning of the sentence.

3. *Normal input must precede normal output. Aural input being blocked, visual input must be used.* For a hearing child, constant repetition of a language in his or her environment, rather than formal lessons, constitutes the base of his or her native language learning. Since a deaf child cannot hear such language, he or she must see it.

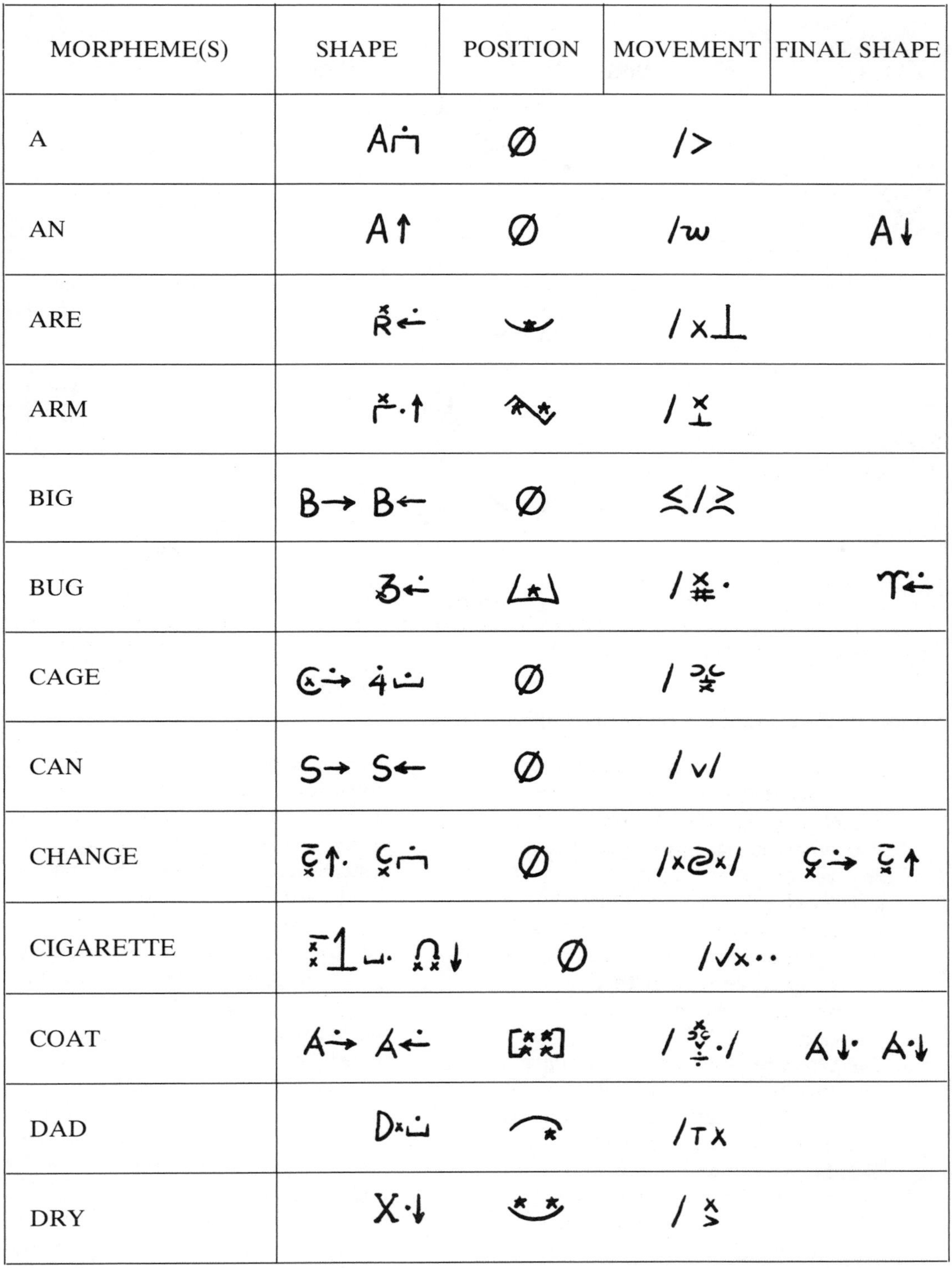

MORPHEME(S)	SHAPE	POSITION	MOVEMENT	FINAL SHAPE
A				
AN				
ARE				
ARM				
BIG				
BUG				
CAGE				
CAN				
CHANGE				
CIGARETTE				
COAT				
DAD				
DRY				

Figure 2. The symbols developed for Linguistics of Visual English.

-EST
A-hands together; right A
moves up

-ED
(ALT. 1)
Palm of hand flips back toward
shoulder
(past tense)

-ED
(ALT. 2)
For regular past tense (-ed),
make a palm-out D at the end of
the sign

-ING
Palm-in, I-hand twists in slight
downward arc to right, ending
palm-out

-MENT
Side of M slides down left fingers
and palm

UN-
U-hands, palm-down, cross at
wrists; separate sideways
(See "NOT")

Figure 3. **Word affixes used in Manual English systems.**

4. *The visual cues of speechreading are too small and ambiguous to make normal, natural language learning possible.* Research on this has already been cited.

5. *Sign language is easier to see than speechreading or fingerspelling.* Since the focus was on very young children, the perception of gross movements as contrasted with the small movements of the lips or fingers was stressed.

6. *The feeling for structure is more important than the ability to spell the word in question immediately.* It was pointed out that the hearing child learns words as a whole, such as *cat* instead of the letters *C-A-T*. Verb tenses, articles, and auxiliaries are spoken before they can be spelled. It was felt that if a deaf child knew when to use a sign for *the*, or for word endings, she or he would be

more able to use a printed or spelled substitute in a sentence.

7. *The patterns or structure of English may easily be added to sign language.* The traditional sign TO BE has had at least twelve different translations— *is, am, are, was, were, been, being, exist, real, true, sure, be*. No signs existed in ASL for many structural English words, such as *the*. Tenses were indicated by the use of a time word, such as *yesterday*, and the words *go*, *went*, and *gone* had the same sign.

8. *It is easier to sign all parts of a sentence than to sign some and spell others.* Signs and fingerspelling had been around for quite some time, but few individuals would sign INTEREST and spell *i-n-g* or *e-d*. In addition, the inclusion of spelled items in a signed sentence was easy to overlook, es-

FRUIT
Finger and thumbtip of F on cheek;
twist wrist
(See "APPLE")

THE
(Alt. 1)
Palm-down Y drops slightly

THE
(Alt. 2)
Palm-in T; twist to palm-out

Figure 4. **Examples of new signs created for SEE II.**

pecially when the spelled words were not content words but structure words such as *the, so,* and *to.*

9. *Any specific sign should mean one and only one thing.* Although ASL did not distinguish among *have, has,* and *had,* there were at least three different signs for *have,* depending on whether the meaning was possession, completion, or a finished act. Differences in signs among English synonyms such as *pretty, beauty, beautiful,* and *lovely* often depend in ASL on a difference in size or emphasis of sign. Deaf students had demonstrated problems with multiple-meaning words such as *run.* Accordingly, the SEE group felt that a visual representation of English needed to reflect English word usage, not ASL usage. The traditional signs of ASL were fine, it was felt, for the communication of concepts. However, the students using these signs were often unable to translate them to appropriate English. Accordingly, this tenet "froze" signs to represent only one English word each.

10. *English should be signed as it is spoken. This is especially true of idioms.* English is a highly idiomatic language, and many deaf students had demonstrated difficulty with such idioms.

The SEE group felt that signing English literally would naturally expose the students to idioms, such as "dry up," "stop horsing around," "pipe down," "knock it off," and "blow my mind." Meaning would come through usage and exposure, just as a hearing child learns language.

THE PRINCIPLES OF SIGNING EXACT ENGLISH

Generally speaking, Manual English systems have three basic types of additions to the traditional signs of ASL, other than following English word order. Because the grammar of ASL is not the grammar of English, the use of English word order is common to all Manual English systems. In addition, these systems employ (a) the addition of word endings, tenses, and affixes (e.g., *-est, -ed, -ing, -ment, un-,* etc.), (b) the creation of new signs for English words not represented in ASL by single signs (e.g., *fruit* [signed in ASL as "APPLE-ORANGE-BANANA-ETC."] and *the*); and (c) the use of initials with base signs to distinguish English synonyms (e.g., maintaining the basic ASL sign for BEAUTY, using the P handshape in the same movement for PRETTY, and the L handshape for LOVELY) (see figures 3, 4, and 5).

Beyond this, SEE divides English words

FACE
Index finger circles face

BEAUTY
Circle face with 5-hand closing to 0
BEAUTIFUL (BEAUTY + /-FUL)
(See "FACE")

LOVELY
Palm-in L circles face
(See "FACE")

PRETTY
Middle fingertip of P circles face
(See "FACE")

Figure 5. Initialized signs created for SEE II.

into three groups—basic words, complex words, and compound words.

Basic Words. Those words from which no letter can be taken away and still leave a whole word (e.g., *girl*, *run*, or *happy*) are called basic words. In order to represent as exactly as possible what is said in English, including the use of multiple-meaning words, a "two-out-of-three" rule is followed in determining whether or not to use one sign for words: Is the word *spelled* the same? Does the word *sound* the same? Does the word *mean* the same thing?

If any two of the three elements are the same in a given English word, only one sign is used. If only one element is the same, a different sign is used. For example, *right*, *rite*, and *write* are signed differently because, although they sound the same, spelling and meaning are different.

To *wind* a watch is signed differently from the *wind* is blowing because only spelling is the same, while sound and meaning are different. However, to *bear* a burden, to *bear* a child, and to meet a *bear* are all signed with the same basic sign for the word *bear* because spelling and sound are the same and only meaning differs. Similarly, only one sign for *run* is used whether the meaning is John is *running*, the water is *running*, your nose is *running*, the motor is *running*, or the man is *running* for office.

The placement or movement of the sign may vary to aid in conveying meaning, but the basic sign is the same for such multiple-meaning words, to indicate what English word was used. The main reason for this was to represent on the hands what was said in English, so the students learned how a concept was represented in English. It should be remembered that deaf students in past research had exhibited difficulty with multiple-meaning English words, such as *chair* or *run*. By representing the English word and adding meaning through context, experience, explanation, mime, or any other means, the student would theoretically end up with both the English word and the concept it represented in a given sentence.

Complex Words. When an affix is added to a basic word it creates a complex word (e.g., *girls, talking,* or *unhappy*). With such words, the affix is added in sign to the basic sign. The addition represents the spoken/written affix, not the word class; for instance, *-s* may represent the plural (*girls*) or the third person singular verb (he *walks*); *-ing* may be used with verbs (he is *walking*) or with adjectives (it was an *interesting* lecture). Because English has many words with multiple affixes, the signing of every affix on a complex word may become cumbersome—as in *anti-dis-establishment-ar-ian-ism*. When multiple affixes are used, SEE drops middle affixes if there is no resulting confusion as to which English word is represented. An introduction to the word for the first time might include all the markers for instruction, but in normal communication middle markers could be dropped. For instance:

Exam is a basic sign.
Exams is signed EXAM + S.
Examine is signed EXAM + INE.
Examines is signed EXAM + INE + S, as dropping the *-ine* could result in confusion between *exams* and *examines*.
Examination is signed EXAM + TION, as dropping the *-ine* does not cause confusion as to which word is represented.
Examinations is signed EXAM + TION + S, to differentiate from *exams* and *examines*.

Compound Words. Two or more basic words together form a compound word. A compound word is signed as the component basic words only if the meanings of the basic words are retained in the compound (e.g., *blackbird, chalkboard,* or *underline*). If the meanings of the basic words are not retained, the word is considered to be a basic word itself. *Understand*, for instance, has no relation to the meaning of the words *under* or *stand*, and *understand* is considered a basic word. Similarly, *forget* is not related to the meaning of *for* or *get*, so *forget* is treated as a basic word with one sign.

When an inflection, such as past tense, is added to a basic sign, the resulting word is no longer a basic word. Accordingly, adding the past tense marker to SEE to produce SAW is appropriate for "I *saw* you yesterday," but it would not be the same sign for the basic word *saw* in "I will *saw* some wood." Similarly, in "I *left* town yesterday," LEFT is signed LEAVE + past tense (*-ed*), while in "turn *left* at the corner," LEFT is a different sign and is a basic word itself.

Inventing

When a sign already exists in ASL that is clear and unambiguous and translates to only one English word, that sign is retained in SEE. This is true not only of basic signs/words such as GIRL, TREE, THINK, and the like, but of complex words such as CARELESS, CAN'T, or MISUNDERSTAND. Some signers prefer to sign these words as their component English parts (e.g., *mis-* + *understand*).

When the first letter is added to a basic sign to create English synonyms, the uninitialized basic sign is retained wherever possible for the most commonly used English word. For instance, the basic uninitialized sign is retained for MAKE, while initials are added for CREATE, PRODUCE, etc.

When several ASL signs exist for one English word, such as *right* or *bear*, SEE determines whether any of the signs have other English words. For instance, the ASL sign RIGHT is different in "you are *right*" than in "turn *right* at the corner." The ASL sign in the first example, meaning *correct*, is also translatable as *correct*, while the ASL sign in the second example, which indicates direction, has no other English translation. Accordingly, in SEE, the ASL sign for the direction RIGHT is retained for the English multiple-meaning word *right*, while the ASL sign for *right*, meaning *correct*, is used for the English word *correct*. In SEE, a longer movement may be used for RIGHT when direction is meant and a shorter movement when the meaning is *correct*, but the basic sign is the same. When there are multiple signs, as with *bear*, SEE attempts to select the most neutral sign rather than one that visually represents the concept of one meaning, or to combine several meanings into one sign. The SEE sign for *bear* is a combination of the ASL sign for the animal and the ASL sign for *carry*. Such combination signs may be signed creatively in SEE to retain the basic sign while suggesting meaning (see figure 6).

When selecting signs, SEE suggests that five steps be followed.

1. Seek an existing sign. Consult sign books, Deaf adults, expert signers. Do not invent a sign if one already exists.
2. Modify an existing sign. This may mean the addition of the first letter to a basic sign.
3. Consider fingerspelling. If the word is seldom used, it may not be necessary to invent a sign.
4. When inventing a sign, follow the principles of ASL. These include keeping the sign in normal signing space (usually from top of head to waist), having both hands the same shape if both hands move, and keeping small differences in signs to those made near the center of vision, such as the mouth area.
5. Consider the meaning of the word, including all multiple meanings, and look for obvious characteristics or similar words that already have signs that could be modified.

Inclusion of Features of ASL

As noted previously, SEE retains clear and unambiguous signs from ASL that have only one English translation. In addition, SEE users are encouraged to incorporate as many of the following principles from ASL into their signing as possible.

Negation.   A phrase can become negative in ASL without signing *not* or other negative by shaking the head. This headshake is important to use with negatives in SEE.

Questioning.   Raising the eyebrows and tilting the head slightly indicates that a yes-no question is being asked (e.g., Do you want some cake?). Another facial expression often used is frowning slightly when asking a question with a WH word (*who, what, when, where, how*, and *why*; e.g., What did you say?).

Placement.   The location of the sign for the thing or the act being described adds additional meaning. For example, signing BOW near the hair conveys a different meaning than signing BOW near the neck (for a bow tie). Similarly, the placement of the sign PAIN indicates where the pain is located (e.g., near the neck, near the side, near the head, etc.).

Directionality.   The signs for action verbs are made in the direction of the receiver of the action. For example, signing GIVE away from yourself when you are the giver or toward yourself when you are the receiver.

Emphasis.   An emphasized word can be signed a bit larger and stronger and by leaning forward slightly with an appropriate expression.

Modification.   Signs can be made larger or smaller, or faster or slower, to fit what is meant. For example, in the sentence, He lives in a big house, BIG may be signed with a large movement to show a really big house or with a very small movement to show a very small house and that you are being sarcastic. SLOW may be signed at a normal rate, or very slowly if you want to emphasize just how slow the action is.

Reduplication.   Sometimes signs may be

LAST IN LINE.

LOLLIPOPS CAN
LAST ALL DAY.

REMEMBER LAST WEEK?

A DUCK LOVES WATER.

DUCK THAT BALL!

THE BEAR IS BIG.

BEAR YOUR LOAD.

BEAR YOUR PAIN.

Figure 6. Slight variations of SEE signs can convey different meanings.

repeated to show plurality. *Books* may be signed BOOK-BOOK-S, or *trees* may be signed moving the sign TREE to represent several trees before adding -*s*. A sign may also be repeated to show continuing action; for example, to convey the meaning of He studies every day, *study* would be signed STUDY-STUDY-STUDY-S. The sign STUDY would also be repeated and made

with more emphasis to show difficulty, as in He is studying very hard.

Sight-line. The direction of the sign and the signer's gaze should be in the direction meant by the sentence. For example, Look out the window, should be signed (and the signer should look) in the direction of the window; Look at the plane, should be signed upward (if that is where the plane is). Look at the floor, should be signed downward, and so on.

Translation/comparison. When the deaf student knows ASL, it is very helpful to add the ASL translation of an idiom or concept following the English. For instance, Your nose is running, can be signed in SEE and followed by the ASL sign for that concept. Run up the flag, can be signed in SEE and followed by the miming of pulling the rope on the flag; and I have a run in my stocking, can be followed by the ASL sign for a run in a stocking. This, of course, implies that both the student and the signer know ASL. Also, a teacher who knows both SEE and ASL can in this way present a student with the opportunity to learn how concepts are represented in both English and ASL.

SUPPORT MATERIALS AND SERVICES FOR SEE

The SEE text has undergone several revisions over the years. Two supplements have been published since the original text was published in 1972. Some of the signs in the original edition changed over time, partly as a result of use and experience with the signs in the field and the modification of unwieldy signs, and partly as a result of more and more information becoming available from the research on ASL. For instance, in the first edition, the sign for *mushroom* consisted of a dominant hand M handshape rubbing the back of a base hand R handshape. This not only gave no indication of the concept of a mushroom, but violated the ASL principle of having the same handshape on both hands or the nonmoving hand having a neutral (1, A, S, B, C, 5, or 0) handshape. Accordingly, the sign was modified so the bent dominant hand capped a base flat-0 hand, representing the mushroom shape.

Similarly, some signs became more simplified. The original sign WAS consisted of a W handshape at the lips (where the traditional sign for TO BE originated), changing to an S going backwards over the shoulder to indicate the past. This was modified by usage into a W handshape in front of the shoulder moving backwards without changing into the S.

Such changes, of course, were met with complaints from people who had purchased and were using the original edition. However, they were made, although some people who learned to sign from the first edition have retained the original signs.

Through the years, additional materials were developed by a variety of individuals, all of whom worked with deaf children in some way or were related to them. The basic text of *Signing Exact English*, which in the 1980 edition included over 3750 words and affixes, is organized in dictionary format. An increasing number of support materials are also available. Three kits of five-by-eight-inch flashcards are available (Censoplano, Gustason, and Zawolkow 1981). Kit A includes 406 vocabulary items organized in categories of foods, clothing, people, etc. Each card presents a picture of an object on one side and its sign on the other. Kit B presents the same vocabulary as in Kit A with the sign on one side and the printed word on the other. Kit C consists of the 220 words from the Dolch basic vocabulary list (the most common words in print in English—*a, the, an,* etc.), with the sign on one side and the printed word on the other. These materials have been used not only in preschools for deaf children but in homes, with individuals who have no language, with non-English-speaking families learning English along with signs, with hearing children who are autistic or aphasic, and with others.

In addition, several storybooks for children are available, with more in preparation. Some of the books are *Jean's Christmas Stocking, In Our House, I Was So Mad, The Little Green Monster, Popsicles Are Cold,* and *At Grandma's House* (all available from Modern Signs Press, Inc., Los Alamitos, CA). A fingerspelling coloring book for children and a coloring book of numbers are also available. A collection of signed songs for children, *Music in Motion* (Wojcio, Gustason, and Zawolkow 1983), includes words, signs, and music. There is a SEE poster of the Pledge of Allegiance. Some of the most basic uninitialized vocabulary from SEE has been translated into Spanish for Spanish-speaking families of children in school programs using SEE. This book is called *Signos para Ingles Exacto* (Gustason and Zawolkow 1982). A manual for teachers of sign classes teaching SEE to teachers, parents, or other sign class students, called *Teaching and Learning Signing Exact English: An Idea Book* (Gustason 1983), is available. This manual includes background information on SEE, two beginning-level curricula, worksheets on basic/complex/compound words, practice sentences for the use of affixes, and practice sentences for sign families (e.g., *make/create/produce*). Some sample items for tests of knowledge of SEE, and sample projects for college classes, are included. A videotaped series of fourteen lessons is available in Beta, VHS, or ¾″ U-matic format for one of the beginning-level curricula. A newsletter, *SEE What's Happening* (available from Modern Signs Press, Los Alamitos, CA), is published quarterly, with articles by teachers, administrators, parents, deaf students, educational interpreters, and others using SEE.

Two videotapes are available from Modern Signs Press (Los Alamitos, CA) concerning the use of SEE. One, *Sign What You Say*, is a set of interviews with seven students, ranging in age from nine to seventeen, to show how students who grew up with SEE were communicating in English, speech, and signs. The second tape, *Mothers Look at Total Communication*, is an interview with two mothers of deaf children as they talk about their discovery of their children's deafness, their decision to use signs, and their experience with SEE.

A book of collected articles about total communication in general and SEE in particular, called *Using Signing Exact English in Total Communication*, was published in 1980. This book is now out of print but was updated and republished under the title *Signing English: Exact or Not?* (Gustason 1988). More materials are constantly being added.

In addition, workshops on SEE-related topics are given on request to school programs or parent organizations. These include basic information on SEE, workshops to improve signing skills, including the use of ASL features while signing SEE, and information on evaluation of signing skills.

Recently, an expressive skills evaluation was developed to provide feedback to signers on their use of SEE vocabulary, their clarity, fluency, rhythm, rate, expressiveness, and use of ASL principles.

A nonprofit membership organization, The SEE Center for the Advancement of Deaf Children, was established in the fall of 1984 and provides information not only on SEE but on deafness, resources for parents of deaf children, evaluations and workshops for SEE skills, and other services. The SEE Center is located in Los Alamitos, California, between Los Angeles and Orange counties.

COMMON CONCERNS, PROBLEMS, AND MISCONCEPTIONS

As interest in both SEE and ASL grew, critics expressed concern that the developers of SEE were ignorant of ASL and/or wanted to do away with it. This was very far from the truth, though. One of the developers, Ms. Zawolkow, is the daughter of deaf parents and she had grown up using ASL. I, myself, although deaf, am not a native signer. I had, however, become familiar with ASL during my years as a dormitory supervisor and a teacher in a residential school and as a professor at Gallaudet University, and during my interaction with other deaf adults over the years.

Ms. Pfetzing, who was not an ASL signer, died in 1976, and further developmental work rested with Ms. Zawolkow and me. We were careful not to invent signs when a viable sign already existed and had only one English translation; we followed ASL principles in inventing signs as more knowledge of these principles became available through research; and we urged SEE users to incorporate ASL principles such as placement and directionality. In addition, we encouraged the use of English-as-a-Second-Language methods with older deaf students who already knew ASL, but were enrolled in programs that used SEE.

Over the years we have identified eleven basic problems common to users of the new system.

Excessive Breaking-up of Words. This was sometimes done as a joke and taken seriously, and was sometimes due to ignorance of ASL and English morphemes. For instance, *understand* was sometimes signed as UNDER + STAND, or *always* as ALL + WAY + S, or *ahead* as A + HEAD.

Overinitialization. While using the first letter is a common way to handle synonyms, some people got carried away and began to add the first letter to almost everything. Examples of unneeded initialization include RED and PLEASE.

Ignoring Local Variants of Signs. The signs in the SEE book were meant as suggestions, not gospel. They were not meant to take precedence over clear, unambiguous, local signs. For instance, *football* has a number of different sign variants in different parts of the country, and which one should be used depends on common usage in the locality. Many individuals, however, taught themselves to sign from the SEE book and were not in contact with the local Deaf community to learn local usage.

Irresponsible Creation of Signs. When a parent or teacher began using SEE or other Manual English systems, it was difficult not to invent signs when none were listed in the book for vocabulary the parent or

teacher needed. However, most such individuals had no background in ASL and did not always search for already existing signs in other books. Accordingly, it was possible to (a) have too many signs for the same word in the same school, (b) invent signs for words that already had existing signs, and (c) invent signs that already existed but meant something else or were in some way offensive.

Improper Stress or Separation of Word Endings. Sometimes word endings, such as *-ing* or *-ed*, were stressed by individuals who were trying to remember to make the sign, creating a situation in which more stress or importance seemed to be given to the ending than to the basic word sign itself. The SEE book added instructions on how to make the word ending flow from the basic word sign.

Use of SEE in an Inappropriate Situation. It was never intended, nor was it appropriate, to use SEE to interpret for a group of Deaf adults who did not understand SEE. However, some parents and teachers who had learned SEE used it in perhaps inappropriate situations because they had not yet learned how to use anything else.

Failure to Build an Awareness of and a Positive Attitude Toward All Forms of Sign on the Continuum. This has been a very real problem. Some individuals who were willing to learn and use Signed English were afraid that ASL would be a negative influence on children's English skills. Far more common, however, were negative attitudes toward SEE in teachers of ASL, which were then instilled in their students. This created a polarization that was destructive and unnecessary. The SEE teacher's manual stresses the importance of building positive attitudes toward all forms of communication and the awareness that there is a time, place, and advantage for everything. Negative attitudes instilled toward other forms can only do harm.

Colorless Signing. In our society, expressiveness is not highly valued when it means facial and body movement and gestures. It is common for hearing persons learning to sign to do so in a "monotone." Sign classes need to incorporate exercises in expressiveness and usage of ASL principles in Signed English.

Too Fast a Signing Rate with Young Children. Some individuals talk and sign at a very fast rate. Because it is physically possible to speak approximately twice as fast as one can sign, this sometimes leads to the dropping of signs. In any case, a very fast rate is hard for young children to perceive. Long sentences, a rapid delivery, and other adult techniques are not appropriate with babies.

Omissions. As just noted, the difference in signing and speaking rates contributes to a tendency (especially among beginners) to drop signs. *Look at the list* may be signed LOOK LIST. Research is now indicating, however, that signing every word is possible, and it may be a question of conscious decision and training.

Lack of Consistency Within a Program. While some people believe that children's flexibility and the need to expose them to variations in sign vocabulary mean it is permissible for different persons to sign differently, unnecessary confusion and delayed language development may result if five teachers in the same school use five different signs for the same word. The deaf child, even in the best of circumstances, has much more limited input than the hearing child, and probably would benefit from consistency of input. Spoken vocabulary and signs vary in different parts of the country (e.g., a sandwich may be called a *grinder*, a *poor boy*, a *submarine*, a *hoagie*, a *hero*, etc.). However, they do not vary that appreciably in a given locality.

Some comments have been made in recent years about ASL being the native language of all deaf children. The developers of SEE hold that the native language of

any child is that to which he or she is exposed in the home and school during his or her early language-learning years, and that the native language of many hearing parents of deaf children in the United States is English. SEE gives these parents a means of exposing their child to their own native language, in a modality (visual) he or she can take in. ASL, like any other language, may also be learned at home from parents who use it. The development of skill in any language depends on the degree of exposure to it and the opportunity to practice it in meaningful, everyday settings.

RESEARCH RESULTS

Extent of Usage

The rapid spread of Manual English systems in the 1970s following their introduction in 1971 and 1972 was phenomenal. Prior to the 1970s, most elementary school programs and day school and public school classes were oral. The rapid shift to Total Communication (TC) in general and Manual English systems in particular was documented in 1976 (Jordan, Gustason, and Rosen), and the results were reconfirmed in 1979. At that time, two-thirds of all classes for the deaf in the United States were using some form of manual communication, and by 1978, 67 percent of preschool programs and 62 percent of elementary school programs using signs reported the use of a Manual English book as their primary reference. In 1978, *Signing Exact English* was the most frequently reported such text at all levels.

In 1985, a national survey indicated that the majority of school programs using signs were not specific as to sign system but sought teachers skilled in the generic TC approach (41 percent of programs surveyed). Those identifying a specific sign system (31 percent) tended to choose SEE (Parkins and Whitesell 1985).

In addition, SEE is used in other countries around the world, such as the Philippines, Singapore, and South Africa. Work has been done with people from other countries (i.e., Scotland, Burkina Faso, Australia, Israel, and Iran) to help them follow appropriate procedures when developing similar sign systems, and to share information on the process with those already making such attempts.

Usage by Parents and Teachers

Because of the different production rates possible for speech and signs, the problem of omission has been documented for some time (Moores 1970–1974; Kluwin 1981a, 1981b; Marmor and Pettito 1979; Swisher 1985). However, recent research indicates that it is possible for parents and teachers to sign SEE and speak English with few omissions (Luetke-Stahlman 1988a, b, c, d). Wodlinger-Cohen (1986) reported three teachers with an average of 88 percent completely signed utterances, ranging from 95 percent complete by a teacher of five-year-olds, through 91 percent by a teacher of 10-year-olds, to 81 percent by a teacher of fourteen-year-olds. She suggested that the teachers of the older students drop word endings, and some structure words, such as THE, as the students develop increased skill in English and do not need complete input. While Wodlinger-Cohen reported an overall rate of 35 percent completely signed utterances by the six mothers in her study, Leutke-Stahlman (1988d) reported that such percentages can be improved. She noted that on first examination the parents in her study were using short utterances and dropping signs, with an average of 48 percent accuracy in completely signed utterances. However, with minimal intervention, these parents improved to an average of 73 percent completely signed longer utterances. Luetke-Stahlman, in an unpublished report, indicated that her study of four teachers and four parents, most with fewer than three years of signing experience, were

signing 90 percent to 100 percent of what they said.

In addition, researchers have noted that deaf persons with already well-established sign and speech skills are able to use both simultaneously with no detrimental effects on either (Fischer, et al. 1986). Other researchers have noted that experienced deaf signers using Manually Coded English make use of certain techniques to save time—for instance, signing THE near the head when the next sign is HAT, near the waist then the next sign is BOAT, etc. (Gaustad and Kluwin 1986).

Effect of Usage on Children

A major question is whether signing everything is worth the effort—whether deaf children are capable of learning and using such a signed English system and whether their reading and writing skills are improved by it.

Older studies had looked at the English skills of deaf children of deaf parents as compared to deaf children of hearing parents who did not sign. Brasel and Quigley (1977) compared four groups of parents: deaf parents who signed English, deaf parents who used ASL, hearing parents who used the oral method and worked intensively with their children, and hearing parents of oral deaf children who did not work intensively with their children. Brasel and Quigley reported the highest English scores with deaf children of deaf parents who used English. Babb (1979) studied deaf children of hearing parents who used SEE at home and found the students equal to Brasel and Quigley's group of children of deaf parents signing English, although the children in Babb's study were three to eleven years old when the SEE books were first published. In a study of SEE I classes, some researchers reported that the key factor associated with higher English skills in the students was teacher consistency in SEE usage (Gilman, Davis, and Raffin 1980; Raffin, Davis, and Gilman 1978).

One study of mine, in 1979, used the

Test of Syntactic Abilities in a study of five programs around the United States using SEE. Although the SEE book had only been available since 1972, I found that seven-to-nine-year-old deaf students were scoring, at 56.4 percent correct, above the standardization sample norms for ten- to eighteen-year-old deaf students (53 percent). Students aged ten to twelve scored 63.4 percent correct, while students aged thirteen to fifteen, who were already six to eight years old when the SEE book came out, scored 58.1 percent.

Looking at the children's ability to learn and use a manual English system, Wodlinger-Cohen (1986) found that the children were able to learn the system, and that they adjusted their use of signs and speech based on the speech and sign language abilities or preferences of their communication partners—their mothers, their teachers, or other children. Gaustad (1986) reported on the long-term effects of such instruction on deaf students aged five to seven. She reported that the length of time students had been in an early intervention program using Manually Coded English had an influence on their spontaneous language production, and that the students with longer time in such a program were more like hearing children in overall English scores, types of errors, and grammaticalness of productions. She described the differences based on that criterion as "remarkable." Mayberry and Wodlinger-Cohen (1987) reported that reading skills of deaf students in their study were not related to speech skills, but to the students' ability to understand signing in either English or ASL. Students with two hearing parents who signed did better than students with only one parent, or no parent, who signed, although not as well as students with deaf parents. Mayberry and Wodlinger-Cohen pointed to the importance of parental involvement in communication in providing a rich language environment.

Finally, in a comprehensive study of English literacy skills in nearly 200 deaf students using a variety of communication modes (oral, ASL, PSE, Signed/Manual English, SEE I, and SEE II), Luetke-Stahlman (1988b) reported that the students in SEE II programs scored significantly higher more frequently than any other group when comparing white students with unaided severe and profound losses. No group of such students scored significantly higher than the SEE II students on any test. In a long-term study of one program using SEE II, Moeller (1988) reported that nine of twelve students tested were reading at or above grade level for hearing students of the same age; one student who was not was an eleventh grader reading at ninth-grade level. This compares extremely favorably with the reported average reading level of third to fourth grade for deaf high school graduates. Luetke-Stahlman (1988d) indicated, moreover, that SEE II students are able to comprehend ASL/PSE stories on videotape.

In sum, research is beginning to appear reporting that parents and teachers *can* and *do* use SEE clearly and consistently, and children *are* developing good English skills, as well as an ability to understand ASL/PSE.

REFERENCES

Anthony, D. 1971. *Seeing Essential English Manual: Books 1 and 2.* Anaheim, CA: Anaheim Union High School District.

Babb, R. 1979. A study of the academic achievement and language acquisition levels of deaf children of hearing parents in an educational environment using Signing Exact English as the primary mode of manual communication. Doctoral dissertation, University of Illinois, Urbana.

Babbidge, H. D. 1965. *Education of the deaf: A report to the secretary of Health, Education, and Welfare by his Advisory Committee on the Education of the Deaf.* Washington, DC: U.S. Dept. of Health, Education, and Welfare.

Boatner, E. B. 1965. The need of a realistic approach to the education of the deaf. Paper presented to a joint convention of the California Association of Parents of Deaf and Hard-of-Hearing Children, California Association of Teachers of the Deaf and Hard-of-Hearing, and the California Association of the Deaf.

Bornstein, H., and Saulnier, K. 1981. Signed English: A brief follow-up to the first evaluation. *American Annals of the Deaf* 126:69–72.

Bornstein, H., Saulnier, K., and Hamilton, L. 1980. Signed English: A first evaluation. *American Annals of the Deaf* 125:467–481.

Braine, M. D. S. 1963. The ontogeny of English phrase structure: The first phase. *Language* 39:1–13.

Brasel, K., and Quigley, S. 1977. The influence of certain language and communication environments in early childhood on the development of language in deaf individuals. *Journal of Speech and Hearing Research* 20:95–107.

Brown, R., and Bellugi, U. 1964. Three processes in the child's acquisition of syntax. *Harvard Educational Review* 39:133–152.

Cazden, C. B. 1968. The acquisition of noun and verb inflections. *Child Development* 39:433–448.

Censoplano, S., Gustason, G., and Zawolkow, E. 1981. *Signing Exact English vocabulary development kits.* Los Alamitos, CA: Modern Signs Press.

Center for Assessment and Demographic Studies, Annual Report 1982–83. Gallaudet University, Washington, DC.

Cooper, R. L. 1965. The ability of deaf and hearing children to apply morphological rules. Doctoral dissertation, Columbia University, New York.

Crandall, K. 1978. Inflectional morphemes in the manual English of young hearing impaired children and their mothers. *Journal of Speech and Hearing Research* 21:372–386.

Fischer, S. D., Metz, D., Brown, P., and Caccamise, F. 1990. The effects of bimodal communication on the intelligibility of sign and speech. In *Theoretical Issues in Sign Language Research, Vol. 1: Linguistics,* ed. S. Fischer and P. Siple. Chicago: University of Chicago Press.

Gaustad, M. G. 1986. Longitudinal effects of manual English instruction on deaf children's morphological skills. *Applied Psycholinquistics* 7:101–128.

Gaustad, M. G., and Kluwin, T. N. 1986. Integrating ASL and English: Experienced signers' modifications of manually coded English. Paper presented at the 11th Annual Boston University Conference on Language Development, Boston.

Gilman, L., Davis, J., and Raffin, M. 1980. Use of common morphemes by hearing impaired children exposed to a system of Manual English. *Journal of Auditory Research* 20:57–69.

Gustason, G. 1981. Does Signing Exact English work? *Teaching English to the Deaf* (Winter).

Gustason, G. 1983. *Teaching and learning Signing Exact English: An idea book.* Los Alamitos, CA: Modern Signs Press.

Gustason, G., ed. 1988. *Signing English: Exact or Not?* Los Alamitos, CA: Modern Signs Press.

Gustason, G., and Zawolkow, E., comps. 1982. *Signos para el Ingles exacto* (trans. M. Cargill and L. Brown). Los Alamitos, CA: Modern Signs Press.

Hart, B. O., and Rosenstein, J. 1964. Examining the language behavior of deaf children. *Volta Review* 66:679–682.

Heider, F., and Heider, G. 1940. Comparison of sentence structure of deaf and hearing children. *Psychological Monographs* 52:42–103.

Jordan, I. K., Gustason, G., and Rosen, R. 1976. Current communication trends at programs for the deaf. *American Annals of the Deaf* 121:527–532.

———. 1979. An update on communication trends at programs for the deaf. *American Annals of the Deaf* 124.

Kluwin, T. 1981a. The grammaticality of manual representations of English in classroom settings. *American Annals of the Deaf* 126:417–421.

———. 1981b. A rationale for modifying classroom signing systems. *Sign Language Studies* 31:174–187.

Labov, W. 1965. Linguistic research on the nonstandard English of Negro children. *Yearbook, New York Society for the Experimental Study of Education,* 1110–1117.

Lowell, E. L. 1957–1958. John Tracy Clinic Research Papers III, V, VI, & VII. Los Angeles: John Tracy Clinic.

Luetke-Stahlman, B. 1987. Educational ramifications of using various instructional inputs to hearing impaired students. Paper presented at the Convention of American Instructors of the Deaf, Santa Fe, New Mexico.

———. 1988a. The benefit of oral English-only as compared with signed input to hearing-impaired students. *The Volta Review* 90:349–361.

———. 1988b. A description of the form and content of four sign systems as used in classrooms of hearing impaired students in the United States. Paper submitted to *American Annals of the Deaf.*

———. 1988c. SEE II in the classroom: how well is English grammar represented? In *Signing English: Exact or not?* ed. G. Gustason. Los Alamitos, CA: Modern-Signs Press.

———. 1988d. A series of studies investigating SEE II use. In *Signing English: Exact or not?* ed. G. Gustason. Los Alamitos, CA: Modern Signs Press.

Marmor, G., and Pettito, L. 1979. Simultaneous communication in the classroom: How well is English grammar represented? *Sign Language Studies* 23:99–136.

Mayberry, R., and Wodlinger-Cohen, R. 1987. After the revolution: Educational practice and the deaf child's communication skills. In *They grow in silence,* 2nd ed., ed. E. Mindel and M. Vernon. San Diego: College Hill Press.

McClure, W. J. 1966. Current problems and trends in the education of the deaf. *The Deaf American* 18:8–14.

Moeller, M. P., et al. 1988. A long-term study of a SEE II program. Paper presented at the convention of the American Speech Language Hearing Association, Boston.

Moeller, M. P., and Luetke-Stahlman, B. 1988. Parents' use of SEE II: A descriptive analysis. *Journal of Speech and Hearing Research.*

Moores, D. F. 1970–1974. *Research Reports 27, 39, 57, 81: Evaluation of programs for hearing impaired children, 1970–71, 71–72, 72–73, 73–74.* University of Minnesota Center in Education of Handicapped Children, Minneapolis, MN.

Moskowitz, B. A. 1978. The acquisition of language. *Scientific American* (December):92–108.

Mussen, P. 1963. *The development of children.* Englewood Cliffs, NJ: Prentice Hall.

Myklebust, H. R. 1965. *Development and disorders of written language: Volume 1, Picture Story Language Test.* New York: Grune and Stratton.

Parkins, S., and Whitesell, K. 1985. Evaluating the manual communication skills of prospective teachers and currently employed teachers in two hundred and fifty-four schools/programs for hearing impaired children in the United States. Unpublished survey conducted for the North Carolina Council for the Hearing Impaired.

Penfield, W. 1964. The uncommitted cortex: The child's changing brain. *The Atlantic Monthly* (July):77–81.

Raffin, M., Davis, J., and Gilman, L. 1978. Comprehension of inflectional morphemes by deaf children exposed to a visual English sign system. *Journal of Speech and Hearing Research* 21:387–400.

Reay, E. E. 1946. A comparison between deaf and hearing children in regard to the use of verbs and nouns in compositions describing a short motion picture story. *American Annals of the Deaf* 91:331–349.

Schlesinger, H. S. 1978. The acquisition of bimodal language. In *Sign Language of the Deaf.* New York: Academic Press.

Schlesinger, H. S. 1978. The acquisition of signed and spoken language. In *Deaf Children: Developmental Perspectives.* New York: Academic Press.

Simmons, A. A. 1962. A comparison of the type-token ratio of spoken and written language of deaf and hearing children. *Volta Review* 64:417–421.

Swisher, M. W. 1985. Characteristics of hearing mothers' manually coded English. In *SLR '83: Proceedings of the III International Symposium on Sign Language Research,* eds. W. Stokoe and V. Volterra. Silver Spring, MD: Linstok Press.

Swisher, M. V., and Thompson, M. 1985. Mothers learning simultaneous communication: The dimensions of the task. *American Annals of the Deaf* 130:212–217.

Vernon, M. 1968. Fifty years of research on the intelligence of the deaf and hard of hearing: A survey of the literature and discussion of implications. *Journal of Rehabilitation of the Deaf* 1:1–11.

———. 1969. Sociological and psychological factors associated with hearing loss. *Journal of Speech and Hearing Research* 12:541–563.

Wampler, D. 1971. *Linguistics of Visual English: An introduction.* Santa Rosa, CA: Linguistics of Visual English.

Weir, R. 1962. *Language in the crib.* The Hague: Mouton.

Wodlinger-Cohen, R. 1986. The manual representation of speech by deaf children, their mothers, and their teachers. Paper presented at the Conference on Theoretical Issues in Sign Language Research, Rochester, NY.

Wojcio, M., Gustason, G., and Zawolkow, E. 1983. *Music in motion.* Los Alamitos, CA: Modern Signs Press.

Woodward, J., Allen, T., and Schildroth, A. 1985. Teachers and deaf students: An ethnography of classroom communication. In *Proceedings of First Annual Pacific Linguistics Conference,* eds. S. Delaney & R. Tomlin. Eugene: University of Oregon Press.

Wrightstone, J. M., Aranow, M. S., and Muskowitz, S. 1963. Developing test norms for the deaf child. *American Annals of the Deaf* 108:311–316.

CHAPTER 7

Signed English

Harry Bornstein

In 1971 I thought that existing Manual English systems, primarily the several SEE systems, were unnecessarily complex, attempted to represent sound and spelling for no valid purpose, and did not offer age-appropriate signs and teaching materials to students, parents, and teachers. Consequently, our working group, Lillian B. Hamilton, Barbara Kannapell, and Ralph R. Miller, Sr., started the Signed English project. A few years later Barbara Kannapell took on another assignment and Karen L. Saulnier joined the core group. Lillian B. Hamilton retired in 1980, followed by Ralph R. Miller, Sr., in 1984. Currently, Karen L. Saulnier and I continue as the core workers on the project. Many other educators at Gallaudet University, as well as a number of artists and authors, have also participated in the effort. Their contributions are acknowledged on the particular works that they helped prepare.

Signed English is intended to be a reasonable manual parallel to spoken English. It is an educational tool meant to be used with speech and serve as an aid to com-

municating with deaf children. Signed English uses two kinds of gestures or signs: sign words and sign markers. Each sign word stands for the meaning of a separate entry in a standard English dictionary. Sign words are signed in the same order as the words would appear in an English sentence. Sign markers are added to these basic signs when the speaker wants to show, for example, that he or she is talking about more than one thing or that something has happened in the past. The fourteen sign markers were developed and/or chosen to represent the most frequently used word-form changes in English. In Signed English, a speaker uses either a sign word alone or a sign word and one sign marker to represent a given English word. When this does not represent the intended word, the speaker should fingerspell that word.

A technique such as Signed English serves two general purposes. First, it can serve as a relatively complete model of English for a child who needs to learn that language. Second, it can be used as a vehicle to communicate information between individuals. The basic premise of this theory of use is that the first purpose is more important to a child in the earliest years of life and becomes less important as the child grows older, when comfortable transmission of information becomes more important. It is expected that at that time a child will be more able to receive and process information from sound and speechreading. It should be clear that these are relative terms; *less important* is not to be equated with *unimportant* (Bornstein 1982).

Karen Saulnier and I believed that the principal initial problem of deaf children is the absence of language stimulation and the language deprivation that results from it during the most formative language-learning period of a child's life (i.e., from one to five years of age). This is where the problem begins, and the simple fact is that this is where most deaf children fall behind, *never* catching up. More than 90 percent of these children are known to be deaf by one year of age. Further, more than two-thirds of them can acquire some information from sound. It simply makes good sense to employ additional capabilities (e.g., the hands, arms, and eyes) to enhance the probability that children will better acquire the English language. And there's the rub. Ninety-seven percent of their families do not use manual communication in any organized, systematic way. They must learn it, and they should learn it fast and well if they want to do the most good for their children.

One further aspect of the problem bears heavily on the design of a manual system. *It is not a tidy world.* Different children have different needs. As just one example, table 5 in chapter 3 reveals that 29 percent of these children have a variety of additional handicaps. Further, children's needs change as they get older. They may become more able to process some information from sound and the appearance of the lips and to fill in missing information from their own internalized knowledge of English. Also, as Allen and Karchmer demonstrate

so clearly in chapter 3, a variety of educational settings and conditions exist. Some are deemed desirable; others have to be tolerated.

Parents and teachers have different goals, capabilities, language skills, motivations, and economic circumstances. Along these lines, the reader should know that it is possible to find some parents who have the determination, intelligence, and energy to learn any system, no matter how complex, and to use it to advantage. Most probably, these are relatively few in number and are not the principal targets of this system. Indeed, the primary concern of the designers of Signed English has been directed in the opposite direction—toward the larger number of families who might find a manual system too difficult to learn and use. Hence, we wanted to develop an educational tool that was, on one hand, a reasonable approximation of spoken English and, on the other, something that could be learned and used by the largest possible group of people.

To this end, the system was designed to be *simple and flexible*, accompanied by teaching aids that were age-appropriate and/or designed for specific users.

SYSTEM SIMPLICITY

No metalanguage other than the dual classification of signs (i.e., sign words and markers) is employed in Signed English. No grammatical or linguisitic terms are used. A working description of Signed English, adequate for the beginning adult, can be depicted on a single page. This includes a picture of the fourteen markers (see figure 1). In addition, each teaching aid is self-contained, so that it can be used without recourse to other materials or explanations.

SYSTEM FLEXIBILITY

A system such as Signed English should be modified when used in the real world.

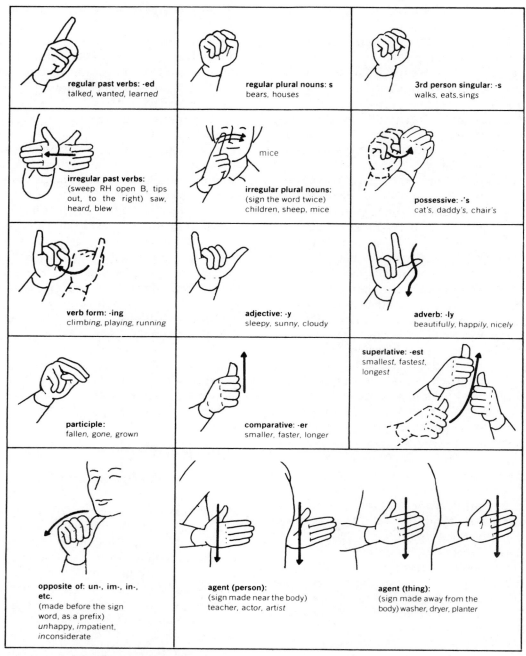

Figure 1. Signed English sign markers.

Note. Reprinted by permission of the publisher, from H. Bornstein, K. Saulnier, and L. Hamilton, eds., *The Comprehensive Signed English Dictionary* (1983): ii. Washington, DC: Gallaudet University Press.

The reasons for this are explained in the following section.

Parental English Language Desires and/or Limitations

For those parents who have difficulty learning the full set of fourteen markers, it is suggested that smaller sets of sign markers may be easier to learn and use. If this practice is followed, of course, less manual information will be presented to the child. That loss must be balanced against possible favorable effects on parental motivation to use the system. We think that it is a better practice to present a more manageable task to parents and, if they do well, enrich the system later, rather than overwhelm them with complexity. Judgments of this kind are best left to teachers and counselors who know the parents and child rather than to remote system designers.

For these parents the first set of markers is reduced to seven—the irregular past for both regular and irregular past-tense verbs, the irregular plural for both regular and irregular plural nouns, the *-ing* verb form, the third person singular *-s*, the adverbial *-ly*, the adjectival *-y*, and the possessive *-'s*. When seven markers still appear to be too many, four markers are suggested— the possessive *-'s*, the irregular past for both regular and irregular past-tense verbs, the irregular plural for both regular and irregular plural nouns, and the *-ing* verb form. The markers can be eliminated completely if they appear to interfere with the parent's ability to function.

It is important to note that there are some parents who, at best, will learn only a small number of sign words and, probably, no sign markers. Usually these are parents with little education and, often because of dire economic circumstances, little time for their children. In such situations, if the child gets little or no information from sound or speechreading, even a few signs will be helpful. Parenthetically, this is another reason evaluation of sign system success is so complex. The proper base for comparison in this situation is not average language development or achievement. The proper comparison base is nothing. Are ten signs better than nothing?

Another situation must still be addressed. Some parents may wish to use signs only as a temporary expedient. In that event, children are usually expected to learn quickly to process sound and speechreading. If that happens, signs may be discontinued without loss. Here again, such a decision is best made by parents and professionals on the scene.

The Child's Language-Learning Potential

As indicated in chapter 9, a large number of children manifest severe language-learning disabilities for reasons other than loss of hearing. For such children, sign markers in addition to the English function words may simply be too difficult and need not be presented. Indeed, a key-word approach may be all that can be used.

Regional Variation in Signs and Sign Usage

There is considerable regional variation in sign forms used throughout the United States (Shroyer and Shroyer 1984). It was not deemed practical to try to include most of these variants in Signed English educational materials. Consequently, when a given sign was selected to represent a word such as *dog*, or *walk*, that sign was usually the one most commonly used in the greater Washington, D.C. area. Sometimes, two signs appeared to be acceptable. The practice followed, therefore, to designate the "simpler" sign as preferred and, in these cases, offer the second as an alternative. In those locales where still different signs are used, it is suggested that the local sign be viewed as an acceptable alternative. In short, treat them as synonyms. We do not know a better solution to this problem.

AGE APPROPRIATENESS OF SIGNED ENGLISH MATERIALS

Vocabulary

As noted earlier, the original principal and continuing concerns of the Signed English system are directed at the very young child. Since most parents do not use complex language with young children, the principal tools and the initial vocabulary were designed to meet their language needs. The word lists were gleaned from preschool and parent logs. Gaps in vocabulary are bound to happen, but we felt that these gaps would appear as the children became older. Older children are better able to use the manual alphabet to represent infrequent words or infrequent sign-word-and-marker combinations. However, the system is continually accumulating new signs for older children.

Teaching Materials

The original materials were designed to appeal to children and to foster language interaction between adult (parent and/or teacher) and child. Consequently, the first publication was not a dictionary or textbook, but a full-color rendition of *Little Red Riding Hood* (Washington, DC: Gallaudet University Press). Given the large number of children's sign books that have appeared since that publication, the idea of a child's sign book may be the most lasting contribution of Signed English. In any event, there are now beginning books, growing-up books, posters, flash cards, coloring books, a songbook and record, and books of poems, as well as fairy tales and other stories—about fifty titles in all.

As the work progressed, other materials were developed for older children and special users. The dictionary has grown from the *Basic Preschool Dictionary* to *The Signed English Dictionary for Preschool and Elementary Levels* to *The Comprehensive Signed English Dictionary* (Washington, DC: Gallaudet University Press, 1983); from 980 to 2,200 to 3,100 words. A revision and further enlargement of the dictionary is planned. In addition, two topically organized texts for parents and teachers are available—*The Signed English Starter* (Washington, DC: Gallaudet University Press, 1984) and *The Signed English Schoolbook* (Washington, DC: Gallaudet University Press, 1987). The latter is largely a replacement for three smaller out-of-print works—*Signed English for the Classroom*, *Signed English for the Residence Hall*, and *Signs for Instructional Purposes*.

The teaching aids can be used at home or in the classroom. They are organized into three different language levels. Level I exposes the child to basic vocabulary, phrases, and simple sentences that relate to the child's daily experiences and activities. Level II concentrates on the description of high-interest-level topics and activities. Level III covers classic fairy tales that contain more complicated plots and more sophisticated vocabulary. It also deals with linguistic and conceptual material of a more advanced nature. In addition to varied language levels, the subject matter of these aids has been developed to serve needs beyond those related to language development.

The beginning books are small and sturdy enough to be given to the smallest child. With beginning books, the child can look at, point to, and describe important parts of his or her environment.

The growing-up books are efficient tools for acquainting the child with the larger world. The carefully developed descriptions in the growing-up books are designed to increase a child's understanding of and ability to cope with his or her environment.

The stories in the Signed English series deal with some aspects of our heritage that should be familiar to all children. While these stories were designed to be read to children, they are also useful as skits and plays. The poetry and songbooks in the series offer both parent and child an opportunity to practice signing parallel to spoken English rhythm. This rhythm is important to English and often precedes specific vocabulary acquisition.

THE PURPOSE OF SIGNED ENGLISH

As chapters 3 and 4 clearly reveal, usage of manual systems varies widely in both systematic and nonsystematic ways in the United States. In a society in which educational practices are largely determined locally, there appears to be little that can be done to equalize opportunities to learn and practice Signed English or any other form of manual communication; nor is it likely that performance standards for parents, teachers, or other professionals can be legislated. At best, system designers can try to describe what appear to be reasonable expectations and appropriate practices. Finally, a way to measure and monitor those expectations can be proposed. The essence of these appropriate practices is embodied in a theory of use prepared some years ago (Bornstein 1982). It suggests how the Signed English system is to be modified when used with older children. I believe that the contents of that theory, which follow, are applicable today.

The Basic Problem

Some differences between the speech of young children and that of adults, especially those who are deaf, are obvious. Adults speak more rapidly than very young children, use more complex sentence structures, and employ a larger vocabulary. In the face of such facts, it would seem that the most complete version of Signed English, using all fourteen sign markers and a sign or fingerspelling for every spoken word, would be appropriate for adolescents and young adults. Actually, Signed English follows exactly the opposite reasoning. A leaner or reduced version of Signed English appears to be more appropriate for adolescents and adults, while the more complete version should be used with the youngest children, actually from birth, if the hearing impairment is known at that time. Keep in mind that the patterns at this level, while complete, remain relatively simple.

There are several reasons for this recommendation. First, assuming that adolescents and older children already have some internalized English language patterns, it is usually more important for parents and teachers to communicate information rather than to serve as language models. Second, signs, on the average, take longer to execute than words take to speak. Faced with dealing with faster rates of speech and more complex sentences, it is likely that the user of a manual system will delete elements, substitute pantomime, incorporate signs and sign constructions from ASL, and/or make random or systematic errors (Reich and Bick 1976; Marmor and Pettito 1979; Kluwin 1981; Strong and Charlson 1987). It is simply more comfortable for users of Signed English to use a leaner version than the more complete one. The problem, therefore, is to marry comfort to purpose. The solution results from a closer examination of the notion of meaning as represented by sign words and sign markers. Through this, a manual system can take advantage of the great amount of redundancy in meaning that exists in the English language. And, of course, the reader will remember that two other sources of redundant information, sound and lip movements, are also operative.

Some Ideas About Meaning

It is possible to view both sign words and sign markers as falling into one of two classes: (a) those whose meaning can be readily inferred from other elements in the sentence (or paragraph), even when they are missing or absent, and (b) those that cannot be inferred when they are missing. An example of the latter can be found in the sentence, A dog has four legs. If *dog* is missing or deleted, it cannot be readily inferred from the rest of the sentence. There is no way for the viewer to know the meaning of that missing word except by guessing or inferring from other parts of the message or context, if such exist. If this sentence were embedded in a larger message where *dog* was clearly stated, *dog* could also be viewed as being readily inferred.

More importantly, elements in this sentence fall into our first class. They can be deleted and still be readily inferred from other elements in the sentence. If the plural marker is deleted from *legs*, the viewer still knows that there is more than one leg, if he or she knows the meaning of *four*. Thus he or she can readily infer that the plural -*s* should be there if *four* is also present in the sentence. This suggests that a deaf child may never need to see the plural marker, recognize the appropriate shape of the lips, hear the -*s* sound, or be able to recognize the letter -*s* on the printed page, to understand that a dog has more than one leg. However, it is hard to imagine intelligible speech, literate writing, or the ability to read material of any complexity without full comprehension of the plural marker.

Now to return to the original sentence, A dog has four legs, for other problems of meaning that I believe are commonly overlooked in teaching language to the deaf. It has long been a common observation that deaf students have problems with articles (Greenberg and Withers 1964). The example sentence contains an indefinite article, *a*. If it were deleted, or if the definite article were inadvertently substituted for it, the sentence would still most often be comprehended because all the important meaning can be readily inferred from the rest of the sentence. In most instances, articles are simply words that convey less information than other parts of a sentence. In some cases, of course, the article offers a great deal of information. Another way of stating this argument is to postulate that the "density" of information contained in sign words varies. Some are "dense" in meaning; others, such as articles and some prepositions, are often "thin" in meaning.

It is now appropriate to discuss the basic problem of how to move from a complete system to a leaner one in a purposeful and coherent manner. Two other ways of stating the problem would be: How does a parent or teacher change from a language model to a communicator? and How does one move from Manual English to Pidgin Sign English (PSE)? The principal tools to effect this movement are *deletion* and *substitution*.

Deletion. When moving from a complete modeling of English, the user of Signed English should systematically delete those sign words and markers whose meaning could be readily inferred from the rest of the sentence, or whose meaning is thin after the child has demonstrated mastery of those elements of English *in any modality* (i.e., speech [by actual sound and/or appropriate lip formation], sign, reading, or writing).

At this time, there are no data to support an adequate proof of mastery; however, a strict criterion would seem most appropriate. Mastery should be demonstrated for an extended period of time, perhaps for as long as two years, before the teacher deletes sign words and/or markers from the signs he or she uses to parallel speech. Further, I suspect that regular, periodic reintroduction of the deleted signs and words is probably required to maintain mastery. It may well be that this point in the language development of some children will come only after they begin to read with some facility. Therefore, all the sign words and markers may provide the best transition to the printed word. Earlier plans to prepare transitional Signed English readers have not developed because of a lack of resources.

Before attempting to categorize the fourteen sign markers as to whether they can or cannot be readily inferred when deleted, one should note that native users of English can very easily construct sentences that fall into both categories. For example, the sentences He is the larger boy, and He is the larger of the two boys, illustrate that the meaning of the comparative *-er* is not readily inferred in the first sentence, but is in the second sentence. However, the first sentence is much more likely to be used by and with deaf children. It is with this likelihood that our system was designed to deal, not the almost infinite variety of language expression that highly educated native users of English employ.

Table 1 is an intuitively derived table offered as a guide for systematic deletion of sign markers after demonstrated mastery. As the layout suggests, the five markers in the far left column could be the first markers deleted after demonstration of mastery, especially as rate of communication and sentence complexity increase. However, since the adverbials and adjectivals have a relatively low frequency of use and appear to be mastered much later in the course of language development, these markers may need to be used regularly throughout adolescence. Practically speaking, therefore, the third person singular and the plurals should be the first to disappear from the manual system.

The past forms in the second column appear in English with great frequency. They are especially redundant throughout a long message such as a story. Hence, they can often be deleted with little loss of meaning. The participle and progressive *-ing* both appear in English with auxiliaries. The progressive is used very frequently, while the participle is used less so. It would seem that if the auxiliaries are expressed, so should the markers be. However, it is possible that these forms, without the auxiliaries, may be sufficient. Often these forms can be inferred from other sentences. Finally, the last column lists those five markers that are usually not readily inferred from the rest of the sentence (i.e., comparative, superlative, opposite, agent, and possessive). These markers usually need to be expressed or their individual meanings would be lost. Fortunately, they are used in a relatively small proportion of sentences.

After having provided a general model for deleting markers, we turn to sign words. Which of these could be deleted with relatively little loss of meaning? Some of the highly frequent function words of English may be the most likely candidates. Found among the 100 most frequently used words in English (Carroll, Davies, and Richman 1971) are the articles and other determiners (*the, a, an, this, that, these, those*), the forms of the verb *to be* (*is, are, was, were*), the forms of the verb *to have* (*has, had, have*), the modals (*will, would, can, could, should*), the prepositions (*to, in, of, for, on, as, with, like, after*), and the conjunctions (*if, and, or, but, then*).

Current users of simultaneous commu-

Table 1. Guide for Signed English Marker Deletion

Readily Inferred Meaning Within a Sentence	Readily Inferred Meaning Within and Between Sentences	Readily Inferred From Auxiliary or Verb "To Be"	Not Readily Inferred
third person singular plurals (regular and irregular)	participle "ing"	participle "ing"	comparative superlative
adverbial	past (regular and irregular)		opposite
adjectival			agent possessive

Note. Reprinted by permission of the publisher, from H. Bornstein, "Towards a Theory of Use for Signed English: From Birth through Adulthood," *American Annals of the Deaf* 127(1982):28.

nication with adults usually make the following adjustments:

1. The articles are almost always deleted, while most of the other determiners are frequently represented.
2. The several forms of the verbs *to be* and *to have* are often represented by a single sign or deleted entirely. Since a single sign does not save any time, there is little justification for using one *to be* or one *to have* sign.
3. Some of the prepositions occasionally are used.
4. Conjunctions almost always seem to be used.

In general, many communicators (teachers) make an effort to include most of these function words if they regard them as necessary for comprehension of the message. This was probably the general practice at secondary and postsecondary institutions long before the appearance, or reappearance, of Manual English systems.

These judgments about what is necessary for comprehension may be based more on the teacher's mastery of English forms than on the student's. Most of the eliminated words, such as the articles, are thin in meaning (i.e., they provide largely redundant meaning or information). If students attend to each and every sign word and can fill in the gaps from their linguistic competence, they should be able to comprehend the message perfectly. Many cannot fill in the gaps, however, so teachers at secondary and postsecondary levels use other devices or strategies. Some simplify their own English when they simultaneously sign and speak; for example, they use simpler sentence forms and easier words), or they substitute a sign for a group of words, and/or they inflect sign words, as is done in ASL (e.g., spreading the hands farther apart to show a larger group or circle). It seems that, except for the most simplified discourse, the student must demonstrate mastery in some modality before these very important function words should be deleted.

Substitution. The second principal method of reducing the sign load on the communicator is the substitution or use of one sign to represent two or more English words. Substitution can occur before and after a demonstration of mastery.

Signs that could be substituted before mastery include (a) a small group of colorful and appealing single signs, each of which represents more than one English word, such as those included in the Signed English dictionary (e.g., *Santa Claus, chewing gum, French fries, guinea pig, hot dog,* and *ice cream*); (b) a small group of double verbs, such as *back up, line up, hand in, hang up, go on,* and *lie down*; and (c) a small group of signs that can be used to represent common English phrases frequently used with very young children (e.g., *you're welcome, a little bit, stand still,* and *it doesn't matter*).

The important point about substitution before mastery is that the teacher knows exactly which signs have been used before mastery has been achieved and devises an explicit strategy to teach children that these signs represent more than one English word. Perhaps the most appropriate time for this might be when the teacher is matching or pairing signs with their printed English counterparts or in speech instruction. It would probably not confuse students if they were taught that a special group of signs could represent more than one word as long as this group was designated a small proportion of the whole and given special attention as such.

The second form of substitution would come after clear and explicit demonstration of mastery. This form includes (a) sign idioms (i.e., single signs that conceptually represent several synonymous English expressions), and (b) the variety of ways of inflecting signs in ASL that are incorporated as part of the basic sign rather than following the essentially sequential character of spoken English. For example, one can sign *one, two,* or *three weeks* by changing the number of fingers drawn across the palm, rather than using a different sign for *one, two,* or *three* followed by the sign for *week*. The number of such substitutions is probably much larger than before mastery and, normally, would be employed with older children, adolescents, and adults. Again, such substitutions are desirable only if the students have demonstrated their mastery of the basic forms.

EDUCATIONAL IMPLICATIONS

In effect, a richer, more complete form of Signed English is most appropriate at the youngest ages, while a leaner, reduced system is most effective with adolescents and adults. However, strict demonstrations of mastery in some communication modality should obtain. What are the educational implications of these suggestions? First, a much larger proportion of the resources devoted to educating deaf children should be assigned to teaching parents how to sign English more effectively during the child's preschool years. A larger effort does not mean a one-night-a-week course. Ideally, the course should be given several times a week, with individual tutoring, especially for the parent who will spend the most time with the child. Like it or not, school starts for the deaf child at home at year one. A full manual model should work best at an early age.

Second, the receptive and expressive skills each child has mastered should be evaluated carefully and regularly. Expensive equipment is not required to monitor the English competence of every child in a school. A simple description system can be devised and regularly updated. This is very important at the secondary level, where classes are larger and instructors have many different classes. Teachers can simply be given a monthly description of the language capabilities of the students in each of their classes. If teachers choose to delete sign words or employ some of the substitutions noted earlier, they will have a better guide than their own comfort

and mastery of the English language on which to base this choice.

Third, Signed English is an educational tool, not a new religion. It should be adapted to meet the needs of children, parents, and teachers, but these adaptations should be purposeful and public. For example, almost all parents want their children to speak, to be able to use any residual hearing effectively, and to be able to speechread. As a child demonstrates his or her mastery of English words and word forms in these modalities, the manual parallels can be withdrawn or eliminated entirely from ordinary discourse. This is especially true for the hard-of-hearing child. Manual English can be reemployed whenever the teacher believes it will facilitate learning or understanding.

Fourth, because it is more comfortable to use a manual system with simpler English patterns, it is doubtful that any manual system will, by itself, be sufficient to yield an English level adequate for high school or college. Here it is almost certain that more effective reading and writing will be the vehicles by which deaf children reach this level of competence.

Finally, these have been theoretical formulations. Some deletions and substitutions may be more useful than others. There may well be an optimum sequence of events that would facilitate English-language development. The suggested length of time for demonstration of mastery may be too long or too short. Periodic reintroduction of sign words and markers should be better specified. If objective information on these suggestions could be gathered and documented, it would be possible to provide guides for teachers and schools that would better enable them to carry out one of their central tasks; that is, teaching English to deaf students.

RESEARCH AND EVALUATION

It is apparent from the very existence of this book that there is continuing concern that the methods of communication used with deaf children unduly limit their English-language development. Preoccupation with the "preferred" or "best" method is unending, largely unchanging, and, as Stedt and Moores amply demonstrate in this volume, centuries old. Some of the controversy stems from a misunderstanding of the very nature of simultaneous communication and, hence, inappropriate or inefficient use of the technique. Some stems from the evidence usually obtained by severely limited research procedures (i.e., tiny, unrepresentative chunks of students, teachers, and/or schools with limited language samples analyzed). And, finally, it persists because there is probably no best method for all deaf students in all settings and circumstances.

In earlier phases of the work with Signed English, attempts were made to evaluate the effects of using Signed English (Bornstein, Saulnier, and Hamilton 1980; Bornstein and Saulnier 1981). The children observed were an unselected sample from the state of Maryland—the Western hills, the Eastern shore, inner city Baltimore, and Prince George's County. These children seemed to show substantial progress, but there were no real standards of comparison other than the intuitive judgments of their teachers. Moreover, there was almost no way to know if they were a representative sample of deaf children. Consequently, it became increasingly clear that a radically different approach to research and evaluation must be made. I have conceptualized just such an approach, but it necessarily includes all methods of communication used with all deaf children. Therefore, it seems best to present it in the final chapter of this volume, which is a closing statement on manual communication in United States education.

REFERENCES

Bellugi, U., and Fischer, S. 1972. A comparison of sign language and spoken language: Rate and grammatical mechanisms. *Cognition* 1:173–200.

Bornstein, H. 1974. Signed English: A manual approach to English language development. *Journal of Speech and Hearing Disabilities* 38:330–343.

———. 1978. Sign language in the education of the deaf. In *Sign language of the deaf: Psychological, linguistics, and social perspectives*, ed. I. Schlesinger and L. Namir. New York: Academic Press.

———. 1979. Systems of sign. In *Hearing and hearing impairment*, ed. L. Bradford and W. Hardy. New York: Academic Press.

———. 1982. Towards a theory of use for Signed English. *American Annals of the Deaf* 127:26–31.

Bornstein, H., and Pickett, J. 1976. Time coordination of spoken and signed English. Gallaudet University, Washington, DC. Typescript.

Bornstein, H., and Saulnier, K. 1981. Signed English: A brief follow-up. *American Annals of the Deaf* 126:69–72.

Bornstein, H., Saulnier, K., and Hamilton, L. 1980. Signed English: A first evaluation. *American Annals of the Deaf*, 125:467–481.

Carroll, J. B., Davies, P., and Richman, B. 1971. *The American heritage word frequency book*. Boston: Houghton Mifflin.

Greenberg, B., and Withers, S. 1964. *Better English usage*. Indianapolis: Bobbs-Merrill.

Kluwin, T. 1981. The grammaticality of manual representation in classroom settings. *American Annals of the Deaf* 126:417–421.

Marmor, G., and Pettito, L. 1979. Simultaneous communication in the classroom: How grammatical is it? *Sign Language Studies* 23:99–136.

Reich, P., and Bick, M. 1976. An empirical investigation of some claims made in support of visible English. *American Annals of the Deaf* 121:573–577.

Shroyer, E. H., and Shroyer, S. P. 1984. *Signs across America*. Washington, DC: Gallaudet University Press.

Stokoe, W. 1975. Face-to-face interaction: Sign to language. In *Organization of behavior: Face to face interaction*, ed. A. Kendon and M. Key. The Hague: Mouton.

Strong, M., and Charlson, E. S. 1987. Simultaneous communication: Are teachers attempting an impossible task? *American Annals of the Deaf* 132:376–382.

CHAPTER 8

Cued Speech

Elizabeth L. Kipila, Barbara Williams-Scott

Cued Speech is a phonemically based hand supplement to speechreading. It is based on the sounds that orthographic letters represent, not the letters themselves. Cued Speech is comprised of eight handshapes that represent groups of consonant sounds, and four positions about the face that represent groups of vowel sounds. Combinations of these hand configurations and placements show the exact pronunciation of words in connected speech by making them clearly visible and understandable to the recipient. Cued Speech allows the deaf person to "see-hear" precisely every spoken syllable that the hearing person hears, even the sounds that cannot be heard or speechread (Williams-Scott and Kipila 1987).

Cornett developed Cued Speech in 1966 after learning that many persons born deaf never become able to read well enough to enjoy reading or able to look up a word in the dictionary and learn its meaning. He had supposed that deaf people were bookworms, using reading as their "one clear window on the world" to gain new vocabulary and information not received through mass media (e.g., movies, radio, and TV), as hearing people do (Cornett 1984). After a few months of study, Cornett became convinced that the underlying cause of the reading problem faced by so many deaf people was their lack of a clear way to learn spoken language—without which speech, speechreading, and reading skills cannot be easily learned. He concluded that a convenient way to visually represent any spoken language accurately (with a manual supplement), in real time, was needed. The result was Cued Speech.

Cornett initially made Cued Speech a phonetic system. After studying the phonemes of English as separated into visually contrastive sets (Woodward and Barber 1960), he decided to make it phonemic instead. He found that grouping by place or manner of speech production caused speechreading problems. By assigning homophenous vowels to different placements, and look-alike constants to different handshapes, he solved the problem of the ambiguity of speechreading alone. Cornett used the frequency tables of Denes (1963) to assign phoneme groups to hand

139

positions and configurations in an effort to minimize energy usage and facilitate movement when consonant clusters occur (Cornett 1967). The underlying premise of Cued Speech is that when the speech articulators (e.g., lips, tongue, and teeth) look the same, the handshape or hand placement is different; when the handshape or hand placement is the same, the articulators are different.

Based on the pronounciation of isolated sounds or syllables in words, Cued Speech is, therefore, a combination of speechreading with handshapes and/or hand placements. One cues according to sound, by phonemes, not by spelling. There are twenty-six letters in the English alphabet and approximately forty-three phonemes in the English language. These phonemes are the sounds that the letters can make, either alone or in combination. For example, the first letter of the alphabet, *a*, has five possible pronunciations.

/ah/ as in father,	/ae/ as in face,	/a/ as in fat
/aw/ as in fall,	/u/ as in about	

In Cued Speech, these distinctions are shown by placement of the hand while cueing and speaking, as each of these vowels has a different cueing position or movement.

The following words are all spelled similarly, with the ending *ough* in common, but they are cued according to their different pronunciations.

rough (cued /ruf/),	dough (cued /doe/),	cough (cued /kawf/),
bough (cued /bou/),	through (cued /thrue/)	

HOW CUED SPEECH WORKS

The following two charts show how the Cued Speech system is organized. Vowels (figure 1) are shown by placement of the hand and consonants (figure 2) by handshape. Because speechreading is 50 percent of the system, the Cued Speech recipient (cuereader) watches the mouth and sees the handshape and its position at the same time through peripheral vision.

When a syllable is spoken and cued, one of the eight handshapes is placed at one of the four vowel positions. For example, the sound made by the letter *m* is cued with handshape #5. The vowel sound of long *ee* (as in the word *me*) is cued at the corner of the mouth. To cue the syllable *mee*, handshape #5 is placed at the edge of the mouth precisely when saying *me*.

The following sets of words are visually equivalent on the lips: *come, cup, cub, gum; met, bet, pet; mat, bat, pat*. Because each group uses the same vowel sound, each set of words is placed in the same vowel position when cueing, but they all have different handshape cues for the different consonant sounds involved.

The following words are all cued exactly the same: *him, hit, ham, hat, sit, Sam, sat*. This is possible because they are visually contrastive on the lips. The vowels are distinguishable because *i* is made with a flat opening of the mouth and *a* with a wider opening. The consonants are distinguishable because the mouth is slightly open for *h*, the teeth are together for *s*, the lips are together for *m*, and the mouth is slightly opened with a visible flash of the tongue on the alveolar ridge for *t*.

The deaf cuereader must use context to extract the meaning of words that "sound" alike, just as hearing people do. For example, the syllable *tee* is cued by placing the #5 handshape at the mouth, regardless of whether we mean the *tea* we drink, the name of the letter *t*, the golf *tee*, or the expression of anger when one is *tee'd off*. When the deaf cuereader cannot extrapolate the concept of the spoken syllable, it must be explained through cueing more spoken English sentences, just as one would explain it to a hearing person. Thus, the concept of any new word or phrase is learned through usage.

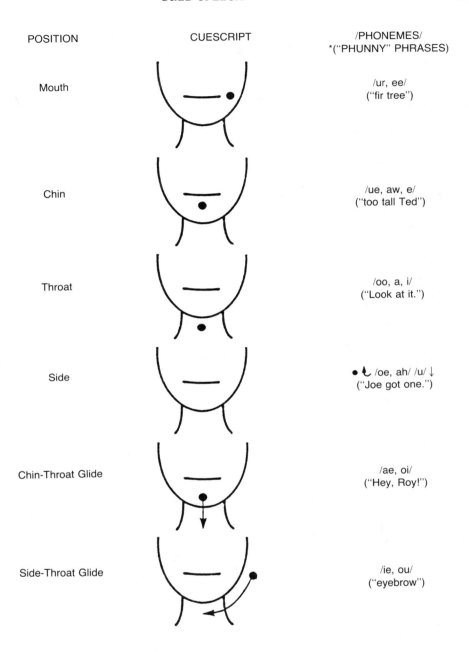

Figure 1. Vowel code and cuescript chart.

Note: Vowels alone are cued with open handshape.

Consider the words *red, read* (past tense), and *right* used in the following sentence: He read, "Turn right, right after the red light." The concepts must be derived from the meaning in the sentence. Colloquial language and the many idioms of English are easily shown by cueing because it reflects precisely what is spoken as it is spoken. The cuereader who has internalized the system through natural, repeated exposure can receive and comprehend the cues as rapidly as they are presented. The

Handshape	Cuescript	Handshape Code Number	/Phonemes/ *("Phunny" Phrases)
		1	/d, zh, p/ ("déjà pu")
		2	/tH, k, v, z/ ("the caves")
		3	/h, r, s/ ("horse")
		4	/b, hw, n/ ("By when?")
		5	/m, f, t/ ("miffed")
		6	/w, l, sh/ ("Welsh")
		7	/j, g, th/ ("joggeth")
		8	/ch, y, ng/ ("Chai Yung")

Figure 2. Consonant code and cuescript chart.

cueing patterns for common words and phrases become recognized as the words and phrases themselves.

Consider the analogy of wordshapes. When one draws a square around short lower-case letters and a rectangle around tall lower-case letters, the words become patterned shapes. The wordshape of *hat* and *but* are alike, although their meanings are different. The wordshape alone is almost meaningless. Cues alone represent only isolated or consecutive phonemes and are ambiguous. With speechreading added, cues depict the spoken words themselves, as they are pronounced. Cued Speech is not a signed system (symbolizing concepts) or fingerspelling, but *a manual adjunct to speechreading that clarifies whatever spoken language is being presented.*

Cueing shows the duration and rhythm of speech. When a singer warms up with "mi-mi-mi-mi-miiiiiiiii," the movement of the hand repeats for each *mee* syllable spoken, and the final hold in the *ee* vowel position shows how long we sing that vowel. Rhythm is shown when cueing a nursery rhyme, such as "Hickory dickory dock, the mouse ran up the clock . . ."The words are cued in real time as they are recited: *hikuri dikuri dahk, tHu mous ranup tHu klahk*. If one turns off the sound (i.e., doesn't use voice), the rhythm is still seen via the cues, much as a hearing person recognizes the beat when it is tapped out on a table top.

Cueing also shows rhyming, as words that sound alike are cued in the same vowel position. *Bed, red, head, dead,* and *said* all have the vowel sound *e* (short *e*) and are all cued at the chin position. Because they all end with the same consonant sound *d*, they all end with the index finger in handshape #1.

Certain basic rules concerning the mechanics of cueing, such as placement of consonant clusters without a vowel, words beginning with a vowel, phonemes in isolation, and liaisons are consistent throughout the system. There are no vocabulary words or syntax rules to memorize because cueing is a communication mode and tool and not a language in itself. Once the groupings are learned, anything that can be said can be cued. Live instruction is highly recommended for the initial learner, to ensure proper expressive cueing posture and synchronization and for the learner to accurately internalize these rules.

Cued Speech is a finite system, with the basics learnable in twenty hours of direct instruction. It has been the authors' experience that proficiency and fluency come within six months, and, within one year of concerted practice, a dedicated cuer should be able to cue at a natural speech rate without hesitation. Once the cues are automatic, the goal is maintenance of accuracy and clarity as speed increases.

CUED SPEECH AS A COMMUNICATION SYSTEM FOR DEAF CHILDREN

Cued Speech was developed to improve the reading skills of deaf individuals and allow the development of reading skills by deaf children to be comparable to that of their hearing peers. It has generally been agreed that very young deaf children, even infants, understand cues at a normal speech rate. Parents and teachers report that a child as young as three years of age (hearing or deaf) can cue expressively and be understood, with the system becoming internalized through use. The young deaf child does not analyze the phonemes in spoken (cued) words any more than does a young hearing child. Phonics workbooks and TV shows like "Sesame Street" are meaningful and fun to a Cued Speech child, allowing for the enjoyment of rhyming words and games to discover words that begin and/or end alike.

Clinical experience and observation have shown that Cued Speech can be useful in the continuous teaching of speech and in auditory development, preparing the deaf child with the precise language being listened for in auditory training sessions and the expected rhythm, stress, and duration of natural speech. Cueing also offers the proper pronunciation in real time of the speech for which one is striving. It serves as a helpful reminder of acquired speech targets, with the physical motor act of cueing offering a quick reference to proper pronunciation, without regard to spelling. When a deaf child produces an incorrect sound, cueing facilitates the clinician's rapid feedback. Continuous training and ongoing practice can then enhance the skills of listening and production.

Children who use Cued Speech as their mode of communication can read cues in conjunction with mouthshapes and the movements of speech articulators, even when the cuer's voice is not present (Nicholls 1979). When amplification is added to cues and speechreading, the cuereader learns to associate the stimulated sound(s) with the appropriate pronunciation and prosody. Through speech therapy and auditory training, the deaf child can acquire targeted listening goals with the aid of Cued Speech and eventually apply those developed skills as the use of residual hearing is learned and utilized.

When young deaf children cue expressively while speaking, the cues, in addition to lip movements and formations, are used as an aid in understanding the child whose speech skills are not yet established. This was demonstrated by Kipila (1985), who analyzed the cued spoken language of a profoundly deaf child, aged five years, four months.

The child in this analysis could not produce a clear difference between the vowels *ue* and *oo*. When the words *look* and *Luke* were said and cued, they sounded the same. In the child's cues, however, the difference was easily discernible, as *look* was always cued at the throat vowel position and *Luke* at the chin vowel position. Plural endings were also a pronunciation problem, with clear *s* and *z* phonemes not produced and sometimes not heard at all. Again, with the use of cues, linguistic credit could be given for the correct plurals for *books*, *boats*, and *lights*, as each of these

words ended with handshape #3, the *s* phoneme, and for *wars*, *fries*, and *brothers*, which ended with handshape #2, the *z* phoneme.

As is true for many young language learners, the child tended to invent words. For example, when the child was asked what *radar discs* were, the cued response was "outer space—outer lights." Later, upon seeing a hydroplane, the child referred to it as a "boat airplane." These and other items initiated by the child, such as "Star Wars," "a fighter wing," "ketchup," and "hot-air balloon," would have been difficult to decode without the aid of the cues. The child's cued utterances were understood and responded to appropriately when speech was heard and the cues and lip and mouth formations were watched.

While some deaf children cue when speaking, others use speech alone for communication. Originally, Cued Speech was seen as a receptive language tool only, but now even preschoolers are encouraged to cue while speaking. A Cued Speech child's reaction to being misunderstood is to say it again with cues! Baby cues are accepted for cuers under five years of age (when gross movements and exaggerated placements, such as chest for throat, occur), until their fingers become dextrous enough to deliver the distinctions necessary for a complete, clear, cued message.

For families whose established home language is spoken English (parents with normal hearing), Cued Speech fits into this mode of communication by providing a clarified form of the native tongue. Hearing siblings learn the system easily and rapidly and apply their cueing skills with little reticence. Cueing allows all family members to communicate any topic in detail; if it can be sounded out, it can be cued (*Fathers Who Cue* 1982).

Families who have chosen oral and/or Total Communication (TC) approaches often make the transition to Cued Speech. This change need not be confusing to the deaf child if approached honestly, with explanation and demonstration of how cueing helps with pronunciation and/or seeing words clearly on the lips. It should be pointed out how the hand placements help with the flat vowels, for example, that are difficult to hear and/or see, or how the hand changes for words that look alike, such as *pop, bob, mom, mob,* or *bomb.* Cues should not be confused with signs, gestures, or fingerspelling, since they have nothing in common with them.

EDUCATIONAL IMPLICATIONS OF CUED SPEECH

Cued Speech can be an independent educational program or a supplement to aural/oral or TC programs. In a Cued Speech program, cueing is used as the communication system. As a supplement to an aural/oral program, cueing is used for speech reinforcement when working on specific speech targets, for pronunciation of proper names, and as an aid in learning to spell; it readily clarifies those sounds and words that are not audible or speechreadable.

Cueing as an integral part of an established TC program may have several goals, including (1) to increase the students' receptive and expressive vocabulary with cueing implemented for English vocabulary for which there are no standard signs (e.g., bubbles, fossil, brontosaurus, tympanic membrane); (2) to clarify the fine nuances in English when one sign can represent many synonymous words (e.g., fast, quick, rapid; formal, fancy, sophisticated); (3) to increase speechreading skills (e.g., crane, crate, grain, great); and (4) to increase the speech abilities of students through the use of cues in speech therapy (Otero 1986).

In some TC programs sign language interpreters are trained in Cued Speech and are expected to use the system for spelling tests and the sample sentences that commonly accompany those tests (Williams-Scott and Kipila 1987). Sign interpreters who cue use the system for English

vocabulary reinforcement and in foreign language classes.

Cued Speech and Other Populations

Cued Speech has been used as a language and speech tool for hearing children. Schilp (1986) reported that an eight-year-old, normally hearing boy was exposed to two months of intensive articulation therapy (sixteen sessions) using Cued Speech to help him visualize *s* and *z* production and to motivate him to correct his errors. This was done after he had failed to make significant progress in correcting his *s* and *z* misarticulations in three years of traditional articulation therapy. The student "made rapid improvement because of his interest in learning a new skill and his willingness to practice at home. At the end of two months he was able to articulate *s* and *z* at criterion level and therapy was terminated" (Schilp 1986). In an earlier (1985) study Schilp found that Cued Speech could be used to control the rate of speech of dysfluent children in an attempt to eliminate their dysfluencies.

Although no formal studies have been reported, clinical and educational experience demonstrates that deaf children with learning disabilities or vision impairment benefit from instruction through Cued Speech. Schools exist that have self-contained classes for such children, who are mainstreamed for socialization or carefully selected academic subjects.

Children and adults with acquired hearing loss also benefit from Cued Speech (Turner 1984, 1986, 1988). As spoken English is the first language, learning to cue in one's native tongue need not be laborious, as is often the case when learning the vocabulary and syntax of a new language at a later age. These individuals already know the sounds of spoken English and can be instructed in Cued Speech from the speechreading aspect to see how the supplement of hand cues can clarify homophenous or obscure words. Senior citizens, however, do best when learning Cued

Speech with a partner. Phonics is often a totally new phenomenon, and it is difficult to break the habit of spelling. Practice is a fundamental necessity to expediting learning of the system, and it is extremely helpful to have someone to cue with in a relaxed atmosphere.

Speech pathologists and audiologists who teach speechreading classes report that they have formed small groups of adults who have shown an interest in Cued Speech. Cueing is viewed as an additional technique to utilize when speechreading alone is inadequate. For example, in the metropolitan Washington, D.C. area, the Adult Cuers' group meets bimonthly to practice speechreading and Cued Speech (*Adult Cuers* 1985).

Research

A profoundly deaf person can be taught spoken language through the cues of Cued Speech, which appear to fill the gap of the missing auditory signal. The brain receives a cued signal representing an auditory/visual input, and the cues become the unheard phonemes necessary for encoding spoken language and for decoding language when learning to read. While formal research on Cued Speech is limited, several important studies have been completed (Kaplan 1974; Ling and Clarke 1975; Clarke and Ling 1976; Chilson 1979; Nicholls 1979; Nicholls-Musgrave 1985; Walworth 1986; Wandel 1990).

Ling and Clarke (1975) tested twelve severely deaf subjects (aged seven to eleven years with one year of experience with cues) and found that significantly more cued than noncued material was correctly identified. They pointed out, however, that after only one year of experience with cues, the overall performance was poor. In a follow-up study (Clarke and Ling 1976) using the same subjects, scores were again significantly superior when the material was presented with cues, with greater improvement after a second year of exposure to cueing.

Nicholls (1979) studied eighteen profoundly deaf children, aged nine to sixteen years, who were in a program in which Cued Speech had been the primary means of communication for eleven years. Under the conditions of speechreading with cues, and audition coupled with speechreading and cues, the mean scores on syllables and sentences were 95 percent or better. Mean scores of 30 percent were obtained on syllables and key words in sentences for the speechreading-alone condition.

Nicholls-Musgrave (1985) tested twenty subjects, aged ten to eighteen years, who had been in a Cued Speech program for at least four years. These profoundly deaf subjects were found to have developed a high level of skill in comprehending conversational discourse when material was cued, comparable to that of an age-matched group of normal-hearing subjects.

Cued Speech Interpreting

Through a Cued Speech interpreter, the mainstreamed deaf child has full access to spoken English subject matter, as well as peer communication and environmental sound effects. Cued Speech can be used with any spoken language and has been adapted to almost fifty languages and dialects. For deaf students taking a foreign language, a Cued Speech interpreter allows access to that language's exact spoken form, as foreign language classes are generally taught through conversation.

It should be noted that, for simplicity, the generic term *interpreter* is utilized in this chapter when referring to transmission of a spoken/audible message through a cueing facilitator. Technically, when remaining in the same language, this person functions as a transliterator. In most cases, *a Cued Speech transliterator facilitates communication from spoken English to (a cued form of) spoken English.*

In a mainstream educational setting, a major goal of the deaf student/client's placement is to offer the least restrictive environment for learning. The interpreter should always be alert to anything audible—spoken or unspoken, within or outside the classroom—in order to provide the client with equal opportunity to process the same auditory information (incidental or direct) from which hearing people draw inferences and make judgments.

The Cued Speech interpreter uses onomatopoeia to describe nonverbal sounds (e.g., crunch, splat, clank). The skilled interpreter also indicates speech differences among speakers, such as dialects, accents, hesitancies, and errors.

A qualified Cued Speech interpreter is a crucial link in the deaf student's education. The demand for qualified Cued Speech interpreters is growing in public schools, from kindergarten through college level. The National Cued Speech Association has developed a certification process for Cued Speech interpreters. Training programs at varying levels, which provide instruction and evaluation, as well as the opportunity to apply the trainees' newly acquired skills, are offered each summer at Gallaudet University.

Cued Speech and Mainstreaming

In public school systems throughout the United States, deaf children are mainstreamed in their home schools, with their hearing peers, through the services of interpreters, including Cued Speech interpreters. These children still need a support program for the speech and auditory training needs that are unique to deafness. Information on the fundamentals of auditory training, the function and limits of hearing aids, visual materials that aid in speech production, awareness of physical changes in the speech mechanism that hearing people take for granted, or voice characteristics of deaf speech, is often not available to regular classroom teachers.

Cued Speech is not a panacea for all aspects of deafness. A regular classroom curriculum is appropriate, however, for those deaf children who can attain and maintain academic levels equal to those of their hearing peers through the use of Cued Speech. The school staff should have expectations of these deaf students equal to those they have of the hearing children. In this way, Cued Speech can help endow deaf children with the naturally developed spoken English skills necessary to achieve and maintain grade-level performance.

CUED SPEECH USAGE

In 1986–1987, Gallaudet University conducted a one-year study of the use of Cued Speech in the United States. This study had three goals.

1. To establish a database of Cued Speech users in the United States,
2. To survey families who use Cued Speech as a mode of communication with their deaf children, and
3. To set up a pilot study on the spoken English-language competency of deaf children who use Cued Speech.

Responses were received from more than 3,400 parents, professionals, relatives, and friends of deaf individuals, with 54.1 percent indicating that they had learned to cue. More than 300 families returned follow-up questionnaires. An analysis of 271 questionnaires (representing 280 deaf children) showed that 83.2 percent of these families still cue (Williams-Scott 1987).

The well-informed Cued Speech parent often has to work diligently to get experienced teachers of the deaf (who are inexperienced with Cued Speech) to listen to up-to-date facts about cueing. There are not many reference books with an adequate description of Cued Speech and its applications, and many professionals lack current information or knowledge about it. A listing of Cued Speech contacts in the United States and several foreign countries is published yearly by the Cued Speech Team at Gallaudet University and is available on written request. The 1990 listing includes more than 125 administrators, audiologists, speech/language pathologists, teachers, parents, and/or Cued Speech transliterators who are knowledgeable about Cued Speech and willing to share personal experiences and/or teach Cued Speech. The National Cued Speech Association, founded in 1983, is a nonprofit organization that provides services and information about Cued Speech, as does the National Centre for Cued Speech. (See figure 3 for additional sources of information on Cued Speech.)

The Cued Speech Team at Gallaudet University offers graduate and undergraduate courses on Cued Speech each semester, as well as special programs each summer teaching cueing and training Cued Speech interpreters. Cued Speech is offered as an adjunct system, when deemed appropriate for speech therapy sessions, by a clinically certified speech pathologist

working with Gallaudet students and/or staff. A quarterly newsletter, *Cued Speech News*, is published by the team and is an excellent source of up-to-date information on Cued Speech in the United States and abroad. A list of current Cued Speech materials is also available on request.

Autocuer

In 1969, Cornett began work on the development of a speech-analyzing speech-reading aid based on the principles of Cued Speech. This project centered on the creation of a pair of computerized eyeglasses called an Autocuer. According to Cornett,

> The Autocuer is designed to provide to the deaf wearer the equivalent of the cues of manually Cued Speech, operating automat-

ENGLAND
  The National Centre for Cued Speech
  June Dixon-Millar, Director
  29/30 Watling St.
  Canterbury, CTI 2UD
  United Kingdom
  0227-45057

FRANCE
  A.L.P.C.
  21-23 rue des 4 Freres Peignot
  Paris, France 75015
  (1) 65 79 16 06

THE NETHERLANDS
  VISI-C, Miriam Bruggemann-Winter
  Emmalaan 9, 3481 VB Harmelen
  The Netherlands
  03483-1881

UNITED STATES
  California
    West Coast Cued Speech Programs
    Joan Rupert, Director
    348 Cernon St., Suite D
    Vacaville, CA 95688
    (707) 448-4060 (V/TDD)

District of Columbia
  Cued Speech Team
  Audiology & Speech-Language Pathology
  Gallaudet University, MTB 217
  800 Florida Avenue, NE
  Washington, DC 20002
  (202) 651-5330 (V/TDD)

Louisiana
  Gulf Coast Cued Speech Services
  M. Carolyn Jones, Ph.D.
  332 Audubon St.
  New Orleans, LA 70118
  (504) 861-8913

North Carolina
  Cued Speech Center, Inc.
  Mary Elsie Daisey, Ex. Dir.
  P.O. Box 31345
  Raleigh, NC 27622
  (919) 828-1218 (V/TDD)

Ohio
  North Coast Cued Speech Services
  Pamela H. Beck, Director
  23970 Hermitage Road
  Shaker Heights, OH 44122
  (216) 292-6213
  National Cued Speech Association
  Pamela H. Beck, President
  23970 Hermitage Road
  Shaker Heights, OH 44122
  (216) 292-6213

Figure 3.   Sources of information on Cued Speech.

ically from the sound of the speaker's voice. The cues are seen as a virtual image in the air, a few feet in front of the wearer. By positioning his/her head the wearer can place the images of the cues on the speaker's face, near the lips (1988).

If the Autocuer becomes a reality, it may be useful to adults in social or public situations and to children when communicating with a speaker who does not cue. A comparison of the efficiency of manual cueing and the Autocuer output will be needed when a field-test model becomes available.

Research Needs

The lack of available Cued Speech research is due in part to the inability of researchers to obtain sufficient numbers of subjects. Cued Speech families or programs tend not to be clustered, and there is difficulty in properly matching subjects for background, hearing loss, cueing experience, etc. In any case, studies need to be conducted in a number of areas, including those discussed below.

1. The visual and auditory aspects of cueing: How is cueing processed visually or phonologically? Do cuereaders depend more on the cues or on the lips?
2. Expressive cueing: Children as young as two-and-one-half years of age expressively use cues. Can the performance of these children help establish a criterion for recommending Cued Speech? At what age can a deaf (or hearing) child internalize the system receptively or expressively?
3. The psychological factors of accepting one's deafness: Do cueing children meet other deaf children? Are they exposed to deaf adult role models?
4. Appropriate use of cueing: Is Cued Speech appropriate for deaf children from families who use ASL at home or for deaf children enrolled in residential schools?
5. Longitudinal studies: Information is needed on cueing students and their families throughout the deaf children's school careers.
6. Comparison of Cued Speech and Signed English systems.
7. The feasibility and significance of truly bilingual education: Can students use both ASL and English via Cued Speech?

In relation to this last research topic, we believe that all deaf children need to be bilingual. They deserve to know both the language of the Deaf culture and the language of the hearing culture. This is now possible through the use of ASL and English through Cued Speech. For this to happen in the educational setting, teachers would need to conduct their classes, as well as conversations, in both languages. Deaf teachers would be needed who have ASL as their native tongue, and who are also skilled in spoken (via Cued Speech) and written English. Hearing teachers would be needed who are fluent in Cued Speech, but who are also knowledgeable about and/or conversant in ASL. Students in such a program would come from homes where either ASL (deaf parents) or Cued Speech (hearing parents) is used.

The primary goal of such a program would be to achieve bilingualism in deaf children in an organized manner, in an educational setting. Much thought must go into the balancing of such a curriculum. Just as hearing children in regular schools learn and study the grammar of English, deaf students would be exposed to the grammars of both languages through use and structured assignments. To learn and utilize two languages in their purest forms seems to be the most logical way for deaf children to master both ASL and English. Choice of identity or communication form would never be forced on the students outside of class. It is hoped that the graduates of such a bilingual program would emerge with the skills necessary to float freely between the Deaf and hearing communities.

SUMMARY

Cued Speech is a practical communication system/tool that clarifies the ambiguities of speechreading, and it has a variety of applications to deaf and/or hearing individuals. (Cued Speech is not a language, nor is it a method or philosophy.) Anecdotal evidence and limited research indicate that the system works for a variety of populations. Cooperation among researchers, Cued Speech users, and proponents of other methodologies is necessary to set up studies and collect data on the efficacy of Cued Speech.

REFERENCES

Adult cuers. 1985. Washington, DC: Cued Speech Office, Gallaudet University.

Beaupre, W. J. 1984. *Gaining Cued Speech proficiency (A manual for parents, teachers, and clinicians).* Washington, DC: Gallaudet University.

Chilson, R. F. 1979. The effect of Cued Speech instruction on speechreading ability. Master's thesis, Department of Communicative Disorders, University of Rhode Island, Kingston.

Clarke, B., and Ling, D. 1976. The effects of using Cued Speech: A follow-up study. *Volta Review* 78: 23–34.

Cornett, R. O. 1967. Cued Speech. *American Annals of the Deaf* 112:3–13.

———. 1984. Foreword. In *Gaining Cued Speech proficiency (A manual for parents, teachers, and clinicians)* iii–vi, W. J. Beaupre. Washington, DC: Gallaudet University.

———. 1988. *The Autocuer.* Washington, DC: Cued Speech Office, Gallaudet University.

Denes, P. B. 1963. On the statistics of spoken English. *Journal of the Acoustical Society of America* 36(6): 892–904.

Fathers who cue. 1982. Washington, DC: Cued Speech Office, Gallaudet University.

Furth, H. 1966. A comparison of reading test norms of deaf and hearing children. *American Annals of the Deaf* 111:461–462.

Hamill, P. 1982. Reflections on Cued Speech in a hearing class. *Cued Speech News* 15:6.

Kaplan, H. 1974. The effects of Cued Speech on the speechreading ability of the deaf. Doctoral dissertation, Department of Hearing and Speech Science, University of Maryland, College Park.

Kipila, B. 1985. Analysis of an oral language sample from a prelingually deaf child's Cued Speech: A case study. *Cued Speech Annual* 1:46–59.

Kipila, E., and Williams-Scott, B. 1988. Cued Speech and speechreading. In *New reflections on speechreading,* ed. C. L. DeFilippo and D. G. Sims. *Volta Review* 90:179–189.

Ling, D., and Clarke, B. 1975. Cued Speech: An evaluative study. *American Annals of the Deaf* 120: 480–488.

Nicholls, G. H. 1979. *Cued Speech and the reception of spoken language.* Washington, DC: Gallaudet College.

Nicholls-Musgrave, G. H. 1985. Discourse comprehension by hearing-impaired children who use Cued Speech. Doctoral dissertation, School of Human Communication Disorders, McGill University, Montreal.

Otero, J. 1986. School successfully incorporates Cued Speech into total communication program. *Cued Speech News* 19:3–5.

Research Triangle Institute. 1984. Autocuer field tests begin. *Hypotenuse* September-October:2–5.

Riley, A. 1980. Normalizing the deaf child. *North American Montessori Teachers' Association Quarterly* 6:10–15.

Schilp, C. E. 1984. Cued Speech helps hearing children. *Cued Speech News* 17:1, 4–6.

———. 1986. The use of Cued Speech to correct misarticulation of /s/ and /z/ sounds in an 8-year-old boy with normal hearing. *Language, Speech and Hearing Services in Schools* 17:270–275.

Today's hearing-impaired children and youth: A demographic and academic profile. 1985, Winter. *Gallaudet Research Institute Newsletter.*

Turner, A. 1984. Cued Speech as a tool for older users. *Shhh,* January/February:5–6.

———. 1986. The teaching of Cued Speech to hearing-impaired adults. *Cued Speech Annual* 2:34–41.

———. 1988. Cued Speech: An aid to speechreading. *Shhh:*8–9.

Walworth, M. 1986. Short-term memory encoding in deaf children who use Cued Speech. Washington, DC: Gallaudet University.

Wandel, J. 1990. Use of internal speech in reading by hearing and hearing-impaired students in oral, total communication, and Cued Speech programs. Doctoral dissertation, Teacher's College, Columbia University, New York.

Williams-Scott, B., ed. 1987. Gallaudet presidential award grant report on Cued Speech research. *Cued Speech News* 20:1, 3, 5.

Williams-Scott, B., and Kipila, E. 1987. Cued Speech: A professional point of view. In *Choices in deafness: A parents guide,* ed. S. Schwartz, 23–31. Kensington, MD: Woodbine House.

Woodward, M. F., and Barber, C. G. 1960. Phoneme perception in lipreading. *Journal of Speech and Hearing Research* 3:212–220.

CHAPTER 9

Manual Communication With Those Who Can Hear

George R. Karlan

It is widely recognized that the process of communication and interaction between two individuals occurs whether or not clear and intelligible speech is present. Infants who have not yet developed language (Bates et al. 1979; Bruner 1977; Fogel 1982; Kaye 1977), prelinguistic children and adolescents who demonstrate severe intellectual impairments (Cirrin and Rowland 1985; Lobato, Barrera, and Feldman 1981), and those who have severe language disabilities resulting from congenital disorders such as cerebral palsy or progressive neurological disorders such as muscular dystrophy (Beukelman and Yorkston 1982; Calculator and Luchko 1983; Kratt 1985; Light, Collier, and Parnes 1985a, 1985b) communicate with those who are important to them. Communication, in this context, refers to the exchange of meaning or information between two individuals; in effect, it is the process of getting another person to share your thoughts (Sanders 1976), with the goal being the sharing of attention to some common occurrence (Sa-

meroff and Harris-Fiese 1988). To effectively get another person to share your thoughts in order to establish a shared objective, there are three requirements that must be met: the two individuals must share a common set of values or experiences, they must share a common set of symbols or "tokens" for representing these values and experiences, and they must share some agreement or conventions for the manner in which these symbols or tokens may be combined to form messages (Sanders 1976).

The first of these requirements, commonality of experience, is achieved by a significant number of children and adolescents, though in varying degrees, through their interactions with the worlds of objects and people. This "totality of experience-derived knowledge and skill" (Schiefelbusch 1988, xiv) enables the competent speaker to communicate effectively and appropriately when interacting with another person. This experience-derived knowledge is recognized to form the basis for an individual's communicative competence. Those children and adolescents who demonstrate severe intellectual impairments may share with adults only a small portion of common experience concerning the properties of objects and the ways in which people behave when one interacts with them, resulting in only limited communicative competence. Yet this is usually sufficient to permit them to communicate discomfort or protest to an adult or to get basic needs or wants met by an adult, although, admittedly, not efficiently and not without errors during the transaction.

This is done typically without benefit of formal linguistic symbols (spoken words), through the media of gesture, facial expression, or motor movements. These gestures, expressions, or movements are sometimes conventional within a culture and sometimes highly idiosyncratic and "agreed upon," or understood, only by the two persons interacting through their shared experiences. Children and adolescents with cerebral palsy or muscular dystrophy may share a much larger and more varied set of experiences with their communicative partners. Their severe language disabilities do not arise primarily from significant constraints on their communicative competence, although some constraint may be imposed by their physical limitations; for example, they may take only a passive or respondent role when communicating, as they do in most other physical situations. Constraints on their communicative interactions arise largely from their inability to effectively form the spoken or printed symbols used when communicating through spoken or written language.

The common purpose, then, for using manual communication with those who can hear has been to facilitate the development of communication, that is, to augment or supplement existing communicative abilities when spoken language has either failed to develop or has developed but is in some way limited in its effectiveness as a medium for the process of communicating and

interacting with others. The "failure" of spoken language to develop does not imply here a total absence of vocal ability (i.e., the ability to make sounds or use sound to communicate a need); it simply means that a child has not developed a functioning system of spoken words and rules for combining words to control and affect his or her surroundings. Thus, manual communication systems generally have been used to meet the second of the three requirements, namely that the partners share a common set of conventional and arbitrary symbols by which they can represent their experiences, values, and the real, possible, or imaginary aspects of their world when communicating (Kuczaj 1988).

POPULATIONS WITH WHOM MANUAL COMMUNICATION SYSTEMS HAVE BEEN USED

In order to fully discuss the hearing populations with whom manual communication has been used it is necessary also to distinguish among the manual communication systems or approaches that have been used. These may be broadly categorized as either manual communication systems or gestures (Fristoe and Lloyd 1979a, b). Gestures refer to relatively concrete movements that, in some way, represent an action or object, whose meaning is usually easily guessed (Pennington, Karlan, and Lloyd 1986). Gestures will typically involve more total body movement than do manual signs. Gestures tend not to have the linguistic constraints of manual sign systems, but they often have many cultural constraints (i.e., many gestures are culture-specific). It is important to remember that gestures are part of the communicative repertoire of both normal speakers and those with severe communication impairments.

Manual sign systems, in contrast to gestures, are more conventionalized and conform to certain language rules (Lloyd and Karlan 1984; Pennington, Karlan, and Lloyd 1986). Those true natural sign languages having their own grammatical rules (e.g., American Sign Language [ASL] or British Sign Language [BSL]), do not parallel spoken English and, therefore, do not translate directly into spoken languages (Bellugi and Klima 1975; Wilbur 1976, 1979). When ASL and BSL have been used with individuals having intellectual impairments, they have usually been used in English word order. The use of sign order that closely parallels spoken English may be referred to as Manually Coded English (MCE) (Pennington, Karlan, and Lloyd 1986). A variation on this approach would be the use of manual signs to support spoken English, wherein only the key words or major meanings of a sentence are signed.

Intellectually Impaired Individuals

For much of the history of communication training with individuals who demonstrated moderate to severe intellectual impairment resulting from mental retardation, the focus was on teaching oral speech and language (Ibid.). In the 1960s and 1970s, manual communication began to be more extensively introduced as an approach to communication training with hearing but intellectually impaired individuals, especially with those who had demonstrated little or no progress in oral language-based training. In many instances, people receiving manual communication-based training were residents of institutions and exhibited multiple disabilities (Bricker and Bricker 1970; Creedon 1973; Fristoe and Lloyd 1979a, b; Hall and Talkington 1970; Hoffmeister and Farmer 1972; Kiernan 1977; Kopchick and Lloyd 1976; Lloyd and Karlan 1984; McDade, Simpson, and Booth 1980; Topper 1975; Walker 1973). In general, the social behavior and communication abilities of many of these people were found to improve when manual communication was used, but language gains varied among the individuals involved. A number of different gesture and manual sign systems have been employed within the general realm of manual communication-based training.

Gestures. Examples of gesture systems used with individuals who demonstrate severe communicative impairments include generally understood gestures (Hamre-Nietupski, et al. 1977; Karlan and Fiocca 1982), mime (Balick, Spiegel, and Green 1976; Levett 1969, 1971) and Amer-Ind, which is based on American Indian Hand Talk (Daniloff and Shafer 1981; Lloyd and Daniloff 1983; Skelly 1979; Skelly, et al. 1975; Topper 1975). Generally understood gestures have been defined as simple body movements that convey information (Hamre-Nietupski et al. 1977) and can include arm or hand signals, facial expressions, mime-like imitation of the movement of a referent, pointing, drawing objects or aspects of objects in the air, or shaping the hands into a representation of an object. Because many of these gestures often can be easily guessed or interpreted by people without specialized training, they are thought to provide for a more extensive communicative audience (Doherty, Karlan, and Lloyd 1982; Karlan and Fiocca 1982). Being taught a simultaneous communication approach involving modelling, handshaping, and selection of functionally useful and meaningful items, individuals with intellectual impairments have been trained to use these commonly understood gestures (Hamre-Nietupski et al. 1977; Hobson and Duncan 1979).

Mime, which employs gross motor movements often involving full-body as well as hand and facial movement and facial expression, was used by Levett (1969, 1971) with intellectually impaired individuals who had not achieved success using communication boards and traditional orthography. Students, staff, and, in a follow-up program, parents were trained in the use of mime gestures in natural environments. Levett later introduced a formal manual sign system and suggested that mime might be considered an appropriate transitional approach for the introduction of systematic manual sign language training. Amer-Ind, a modern version of the hand signals used by American Indian tribes to communicate across language barriers, was developed and revised by Skelly et al. (1975) for use with nonspeaking adult patients. Its use has been reported with individuals with severe intellectual impairment (Daniloff and Shafer 1981). Because of the inclusion of many one-handed gestures, its benefits for use with individuals with severe physical impairments has been advocated (Daniloff and Vergara 1984).

Manual Sign Systems. The use of true, natural sign languages (e.g., ASL) having their own grammar, syntax, and morphology, has not been considered appropriate for use with hearing, severely intellectually impaired individuals (Pennington, Karlan, and Lloyd 1986). With these people, ASL signs have been used with English syntax and have been frequently shortened or modified. More appropriate is the MCE approach, in which a contrived or "pedagogical" (or instructional) system of signs is used to represent, in parallel, spoken English. Systems of this sort used with individuals having severe intellectual impairments include Signed English (Bornstein and Hamilton 1978; Bornstein, Saulnier, and Hamilton 1983); Signing Exact English (SEE II) (Gustason, Pfetzing, and Zawolkow 1972), and Seeing Essential English (Anthony 1971).

Autistic or Autistic-Like Individuals

Following an early, and not universally effective, focus on oral speech in communication training for autistic or autistic-like children with intellectual impairment (Carr 1979; Konstantareas, Oxman, and Webster 1978), the use of manual communication was examined and appeared to be successful in many cases (Bonvillian and Nelson 1978; Carr 1979; Cohen 1981; Creedon 1973; Konstantareas, Oxman, and Webster 1978). One difficulty in examining

the use of manual communication systems with autistic and autistic-like children with intellectual impairments is the general lack of information concerning the actual sign system used or any comparative information (Leslie, Layton, and Helmer 1982). In addition, little discussion of modifications to the signs used has been presented (for an exception, see Layton and Helmer 1981). ASL signs plus speech (Cohen 1981), SEE II and ASL signs (Bonvillian and Nelson 1978), and Signed English (Creedon 1973) have been reported as having been used within communication training programs for these populations.

Although the results of communication training programs for individuals with autism and severe intellectual impairments vary, Carr (1979) noted that gains were most apparent in the area of noun use (e.g., labelling objects and requesting food). Increases in the acquisition of vocabulary, production of vocalizations (including unprompted vocal labelling), and reduction in echolalic responses have been reported (Bonvillian and Nelson 1978; Cohen 1981). Studies employing manual communication training with these individuals have also reported collateral changes, including reductions in self-stimulation and increases in social activity (Creedon 1973; Leslie, Layton, and Helmer 1982). Carr (1979) has suggested that facilitation of spoken language through the use of manual communication systems may depend on certain characteristics of the individual with autism. He noted that those who had some rudimentary form of oral speech or vocal ability, even if only echolalia, prior to manual communication training, had a much better prognosis for developing spontaneous spoken language as a result of such training. Mute autistic or autistic-like children, at the outset of training, had a poor prognosis for manual communication training intended to facilitate the development of oral speech skills.

The successful use of manual communication systems with individuals exhibiting autism or autistic-like behavior may be, in part, related to certain information processing characteristics of this group. This group exhibits information-processing deficits with respect to auditory input and may not even respond to noise (Alpert 1980). Whereas visual and motor responses tend to be similar to those of normal children, auditory and vocal skills are more deviant (Bonvillan and Nelson 1978). In fact, these individuals tend to "overselect" the visual modality, relying extensively on visual cues (Konstantareas, Oxman, and Webster 1978). This, together with the fact that they tend to function in a more concrete manner with limited symbolic representation, suggests that the use of visual-motor-based manual sign systems takes advantage of underlying skills that are relatively unimpaired in contrast to those skills required for oral speech (Pennington, Karlan, and Lloyd 1986).

Deaf-Blind and Intellectually Impaired Individuals

It has been estimated that 60 to 75 percent of people diagnosed as deaf-blind are also severely to profoundly impaired intellectually (Jensema 1979). While many may have less severe hearing and/or visual impairment than the term *deaf-blind* would seem to indicate, they are classified thus because of the severity of the problem resulting from the combination of the two conditions. As might be expected, the language abilities of these people are quite limited; communication occurs mostly through gesture and mime, although an oral/sign approach is typically used in teaching (Pennington, Karlan, and Lloyd 1986). The general nature of the communication abilities and deficits is a result of the age of onset, degree of visual and hearing loss, severity of behavioral problems, and presence of additional handicaps (e.g., severe physical impairments) (Griffith, Robinson, and Panagos 1983).

In using manual communication systems with these individuals, teachers adopted methods for expressing standard English, rather than introducing another language, and thus Signed English is often used, but often with a variety of methods, to achieve comprehension of concepts (Jensema 1979). Another "manual" communication system that has also been used with deaf-blind individuals is Tadoma, a method for receiving information through the sense of touch by placing the hand over the face of the speaker with the thumb covering the mouth in order to feel lip, jaw, and tongue movements, and spreading the fingers over the cheek, jaw, and throat to detect vibrations (Chomsky 1986; Jensema 1979; Pennington, Karlan, and Lloyd 1986; Reed, Durlach, and Braida 1982; Vivian 1966). Other manually based communication approaches include Cross Code, a method based on the position of contact on the back of the hand to designate letters of the alphabet when spelling words (Jensema 1979), and Braille Hand Speech, which uses the position of the initial, middle, and ring fingers of both hands to represent the six braille dots (Jensema 1979; Thorley, Watkins, and Binepal 1984).

USING MANUAL COMMUNICATION SYSTEMS WITH INDIVIDUALS WITH SEVERE INTELLECTUAL IMPAIRMENTS OR AUTISM

Communication Development Through the Use of Manual Systems

Before continuing this discussion, it is useful to define specific terms that will appear throughout the discussion.

Speech is the spoken—voiced and articulated—output of the communication system. Language is a conventional set of arbitrary symbols and set of rules for combining these symbols to represent ideas about the world for the purposes of communication. Communication is the transmission of meaning from one individual to another, whatever the means that is used (verbal with and without speech and nonverbal with and without vocal output). Communication implies a process of social interaction. Symbols are spoken, graphic, or manual representations of objects, actions, relationships, etc. While spoken symbols are temporal and are conveyed through the auditory-vocal modality, graphic and manual symbols are spatial or spatial-temporal and are conveyed through the visual modality. Gestures and signs are two related types of manual symbols used in nonspeech, or augmentative and alternative communication (Lloyd and Karlan 1984, 5).

The discussion of why and how the use of nonspeech communication in general, and manual communication in particular, have functioned to facilitate the communication development of those individuals who had previously failed to progress in programs of spoken language training, was initiated by Fristoe and Lloyd (1979b). They proposed sixteen factors or characteristics that could account for these facilitative effects. These factors were later organized into six categories, with general conceptual descriptors added for each category, by L. Lloyd and Karlan (1984).

General Simplification of Input. The first of the six categories pertains to the information presented to the individual. Information, when presented in a nonspeech form, is simplified in context and manner of presentation. Simplification presumably facilitates processing and, hence, understanding of the communication message, and is accomplished in two says:

1. Verbiage (noise) is reduced. When speech and manual symbols are simultaneously presented, irrelevant or parenthetical comments are eliminated from the trainer's speech.
2. Rate is adjustable. When manual symbols are presented simultaneously with speech, the rate of presentation is slowed, allowing more processing time. Because even the most experienced users of sign slow their rate when simultaneously signing and speaking, it is to be expected that trainers who are less experienced

with manual communication will slow their presentation rate even more.

Response Production Advantages. There are four factors that fall within the area of production advantages that relate either to the actual production of a manual sign or to the teaching of expressive communicative responses. In contrast to speech production, the individual's production of the manual symbol or the teaching of expressive responding is facilitated in the following ways:

1. Pressure for speech is removed. With some individuals demonstrating moderate to severe intellectual impairments or autism, especially those capable of some limited and often barely intelligible speech production, communicative partners have exerted great pressure to speak. Because the expected performance exceeds the capacity or readiness to perform, the individual experiences social pressure that becomes detrimental to further development of his or her productive responding abilities. Manual symbols provide an augmentative mode by which messages can be conveyed, and pressure for speech production is relieved, in some cases leading to subsequent improvement.
2. Physical demands are decreased. The motor acts necessary to produce an expressive manual response are far less complex than those required for speech production. While seemingly complex, the motor coordination required for manual sign or gestural production is still far simpler than that required for speech phonation and articulation.
3. Physical manipulation of the productive response is possible. Just as the user's difficulty of response production is decreased when manual communication is used, so too is the trainer's difficulty of physical manipulation of the user's production decreased. It is possible but arduous to

physically guide the individual in producing an oral response. Greater ease for the trainer in actually physically guiding the formation of manual sign or gestural responses undoubtedly adds substantially to the more rapid acquisition of manual communication.

4. Clinician's observation of shaping is facilitated. The fact of manual signs and gestures being in the visual modality may facilitate the trainer's process of judging the closeness of attempts at response production to the target response. Analysis of the characteristics and topography of approximations to the desired production requires much less training and technical background than such an analysis of speech production would require.

Advantages for the Severely Intellectually Impaired. For individuals exhibiting severe intellectual impairments, the use of gestures or manual communication systems has two characteristics that would contribute to the acquisition of improved communication development.

1. Vocabulary is limited and functional. Often as a consequence of trainers' (e.g., teachers and classroom aides) and parents' learning to use and understand manual signs, the vocabulary has been kept small, and the lexical items that have been selected for representation in sign have been made more broadly functional to the person (e.g., *drink, play, no, more*). As a result, conceptual rather than syntactic learning is emphasized.

2. The individual's attention is easier to maintain. Because manual signs are presented with control over spatial placement and temporal duration, evaluation and maintenance of attention to visual input can be accomplished through the assessment of direction of gaze or eye contact. Simple visual evaluation of attention to auditory/oral symbols cannot be done.

Receptive Language/Auditory Processing Advantages. Gestures and manual communication systems affect both auditory processing and language comprehension, which in turn affect the comprehension of communicative messages. The apparent causes for these effects reflect different levels of the comprehension process and include:

1. Simplified language input structure. When gestures or manual signs are presented simultaneously with spoken words, the full syntactic structure of the spoken message is often not represented. These manual symbols often represent only the most semantically relevant or meaningful information in the message, thus highlighting what is critical for comprehension.

2. Minimized auditory short-term memory and/or auditory processing problems. Because they are conveyed via the visual modality, gestures and manual signs bypass the auditory channel and, thus, eliminate any particularly pronounced auditory processing deficits that may exist with individuals having severe intellectual impairments.

Stimulus Processing/Stimulus Association Advantages. Again because of the visual modality, the use of gestures or manual signs in communication creates certain advantages in the processing of visual symbols and the development of associations between visual symbols and their referents.

1. Enhancement of figure-ground differential. The visual mode of gestures and manual signs may help to differentiate the communicative message (the figure) from the general visual environment (the ground) more than auditory symbols can be differentiated from ambient back-ground noise. This would be especially true

for those severely intellectually impaired individuals who are "overselective" to the visual modality.

2. Optimization of stimulus consistency. Visual symbols appear to have greater consistency in representation and production than do auditory/oral symbols. With manual signs or gestures, especially at the slow rates presented to those with intellectual im-

pairments, contextual or coproduction influences are minimal compared with speech, where contextual or coarticulatory influences may greatly affect what the listener perceives as the same or different phonemes.

3. Increased temporal duration. The temporal duration of gestures and manual signs presented to those with intellectual impairments is greater than

Table 1. Symbol System or Set Selection Considerations

Selection Considerations	Gesture Sets or Manual Sign Systems							Speech
	Pointing	Yes/No Gestures	Generally Understood Gestures	Amerind	ASL	Signed English	Manual Alphabet	
Acceptability to users								+
Acceptability to peers								+
Acceptability to others								+
Intelligibility to untrained peers	+	+	+	?	−	−	−	+
Intelligibility to general community	+	+	+	?	−	−	−	+
Correspondence to written English	−	−	−	−	−	?	+	+
Correspondence to spoken English	−	−	−	−	−	+	+	+
Facilitates active participation	+	−	+	+	+	+	+	+
Facilitates face-to-face interaction	?	+	+	+	+	+	+	+
Facilitates optimal communication rate	?	−	?	+	+	+	?	+
Permits communication at a distance	+	+	+	+	+	+	?	+
Representational range of system or set	−	−	−	?	+	+	+	+
Symbol permanency	?	?	?	?	?	?	−	−
Rapid symbol accessibility	+	+	+	+	+	+	+	+
Portability	+	+	+	+	+	+	+	+
Low physical demands	?	+	?	?	−	−	−	−
Low memory demands	+	+	?	?	−	−	−	−
Low cognitive demands	+	+	?	?	−	−	−	−
Low linguistic demands	+	?	+	+	−	−	−	−
Limited training required	+	+	?	?	?	?	−	−
Low cost	+	+	+	+	+	+	+	+

Note. Adapted, by permission of the publishers, from L. Lloyd and G. Karlan, "Nonspeech Communication Symbols and Systems: Where have we been and where are we going?"*Journal of Mental Deficiency Research* 28 (1984): 3–20.

+ system has the particular quality or feature; − system lacks the particular quality or feature; ? system tends toward the particular quality or feature.

that of speech symbols. In addition, this duration can generally be adjusted for even greater duration without altering what the individual perceives to be the form of the stimulus. With people for whom greater time to orient to, perceive, and process stimulus presentations is desirable, the presentation rate and duration of manual symbols can be adjusted easily without loss of relevance or information value of the communicative message.

4. Manual symbols bear a unimodal relationship to visual referents. Spoken symbols are in the auditory modality while the referents with which they must be associated are typically in the visual modality. This creates a crossmodal relationship between symbols and referent. Gestures and manual signs are in the visual modality and thus are unimodal in relation to most referents. Learning that a symbol represents a referent may be easier when both are in the same modality. In addition, temporal characteristics or copresentation of the symbol and the referent are more easily matched when the relationship is unimodal.

Symbolic Representational Advantages. Other aspects of gestures and manual signs that may facilitate communication development are the amount and type of information conveyed within the symbol itself and the use to which it is put. Two possibilities are:

1. Supplemental representation. When used simultaneously with speech, gestures and manual signs supplement the representational input of the speech symbols. With some individuals, this supplementation has led to accelerated development of both speech comprehension and production. The success of this supplementation is possibly the result of a type of representation found within

certain gestures and manual signs themselves.

2. Visual representation. A gesture or manual sign may contain within the symbol itself an actual representation of the referent, some portion of the referent, or something highly associated with the referent. This representational characteristic has been referred to as *iconicity*. The iconicity of manual symbols certainly varies but, where greater iconicity exists, meaning, memory, and/or concept visualization can be facilitated.

The potential of the sixteen factors or characteristics just described to contribute to the communication development of people with severe intellectual impairments or autism has been suggested by existing clinical practice, direct application of research data, or application of basic research findings concerning intellectual impairment. Their exact role and relative contribution continue to be explored through careful empirical investigation.

Selecting a Manual System or Gesture Set

Given the number of gestural approaches, gesture sets, or manual sign system options available, it is not surprising that general considerations for selecting a system for use with an individual or group have received special attention (Carlson 1982; Lloyd and Karlan 1984; Nietupski and Hamre-Nietupski 1979; Yoder 1980). L. L. Lloyd and I, in 1984, summarized these selection considerations as the set of factors listed in table 1. These consideration factors have been used to evaluate a representative set of gestural approaches and manual signs. For general comparative purposes, speech also has been included in the table.

Acceptability. It is reasonable to assume that that which is unacceptable is unlikely to succeed; thus, the first area of consideration is acceptability. However, acceptability to the user, to the user's peers, and to others (e.g., adults and the community) depends on individual judgments of acceptability. Thus, the gesture sets and manual sign systems found in table 1 cannot be judged, a priori, to be acceptable or unacceptable. While important, this factor can only be considered within the context of the individual for whom a program of manually based intervention is being developed.

Intelligibility. With an even greater current emphasis on community-based educational, vocational, and independent-living programs for people with severe or multiple handicaps, the issue of intelligibility of gestures and manual signs to untrained peers and the general community is indeed a critical one. Pointing is clearly a highly intelligible system, though limited in its representational range. Yes/no gestures and generally understood gestures are relatively intelligible to those sharing the cultural context. Amer-Ind gestures, although suggested to be quite guessable or intelligible, have been shown to be only 50 percent guessable by naive viewers (Daniloff and Lloyd 1983). Although some ASL and Signed English signs are guessable, the majority of such signs and of the manual alphabet cannot be guessed by naive individuals (Lloyd and Karlan 1984).

Other Factors. The other factors found in table 1 can be considered together within some generalizations. Correspondence to spoken and written English is achieved only as the representational range (the number and type of ideas that can be symbolically represented) increases and as appropriate grammatical markers are included or represented. Thus, only Signed English and the manual alphabet attain clear advantage. ASL certainly achieves the representational range but, being a natural language, does not achieve correspondence to written or spoken English. However, this increased representational range occurs with concomitant increases in motoric, cognitive, linguistic, and mnemonic demands. Regarding effects on the interaction process, most of the gesture sets and systems facilitate active participation (initiation and maintenance of control by the gesture or sign user), optimal communication rate, and communication at a distance, with the exceptions noted. They also permit communication of messages over some distance between communicator and partner; the exception of the manual alphabet largely rests with the problem of discriminating differences among the letters when viewing from a distance. Such factors as symbol permanency, rapid accessibility, portability, and low cost are included, not to illuminate differences among the gesture sets and manual sign systems, but to indicate their advantages in comparison to aided symbol sets and systems such as pictures, rebuses, printed words, or Blissymbolics (for more information see Lloyd and Karlan 1984, or Vanderheiden and Lloyd 1986).

In summary, what these selection factors reveal is not superiority of one gesture set or manual system or another. Rather, they indicate that decisions can be made only when consideration is given to the constellation of needs and abilities of the individual for whom the program is intended. Thus, relative to the needs of the individual, the abilities of the individual, and the goals of the intervention program, these selection factors can be applied and a set or system selected. It is important to keep in mind that changes in these needs and abilities, either as a result of the intervention or any other factor, will necessitate reevaluation of the selection decision and may necessitate selection of a new approach or addition of a second one (Yorkston and Karlan 1986).

Selecting an Initial Lexicon

Selection of a manual communication system for use in an intervention program is merely an initial step in the process of implementation. One cannot teach someone the entire set of Amer-Ind gestures or

ASL or Signed English signs at one time nor would this assure that the individual knew how to communicate using them. A critical step in planning a manually based intervention program, especially for persons with severe intellectual impairments, is the selection of a lexicon for use in the initial intervention program. The issues discussed in this section will be restricted to those concerning selection of initial lexical items (i.e., content of the lexicon). The forms, or actual gestures and manual signs, of the symbols used to represent this lexicon will be addressed separately.

Data on normal language development suggest that children acquire approximately fifty single words before they begin to use multiple-word utterances or strings of words (Nelson 1973). When examining these initial lexical items, one must consider both the conceptual or semantic content expressed by the words and the communicative function of the message being expressed (Karlan and Lloyd 1983). Conceptually or semantically, a single word such as *no* can be used to reject something offered but unwanted, to indicate that something in motion has just stopped, or to indicate that something has just disappeared or no longer exists. In terms of communicative function, a single word such as *ball* might serve as an answer to a question, a request for the ball, a command to do something with it ("Ball!"—"Okay, I'll throw it"), or a request for information ("Ball?"—"Yes, that's a ball"). The communicative importance of these initial lexical items for a person with severe communicative or intellectual deficits must not be overlooked; the span of time between the acquisition of single-symbol utterances (whether spoken or signed) and of multiple-symbol phrases will be much greater than is generally true for the normally developing child. Therefore, individuals with these impairments will rely on the initial lexicon of single items much longer within their communicative interactions.

Two basic strategies have been used to identify an initial lexicon for individuals with severe or multiple impairments: a behavioral remedial strategy and a developmental strategy (Ibid.). The first strategy, based on behavioral-remedial logic (Guess, Sailor, and Baer 1977), uses student preferences, frequency of occurrence data, functional utility across situations, and basic human needs to identify the desired lexical items (Nietupski and Hamre-Nietupski 1979). Implementation of this strategy requires that an actual inventory of the individual's environment be undertaken, including systematic recording of student preferences for objects, actions, people, places, etc., and an activity-based inventory to determine the relative frequency of activities, their potential lexical content, and the potential frequency of use of lexical items within given activities (Karlan and Lloyd 1983). L. L. Lloyd and I have suggested that this approach may be limited by existing context constraints, that is, opportunity to use a lexical item, and hence its observed frequency of use, may be restricted because of other intervening factors (e.g., physical limitations, time constraints, or convenience to caregiver).

A second strategy, based on models of the sequence of normal communication development (Holland 1975), identifies items through representation of those content categories found within the lexica of normally developing children (Lahey and Bloom 1977). Holland was concerned that intervention be efficient and parsimonious in that the acquired language skills be of use to the individual in his or her natural environment. Thus, she recommended that (a) a child's language be used as a model, (b) the chosen words have importance to the child, (c) emphasis be placed on functional communication, and (d) the focus be placed on referents that are present and/or events that are happening (i.e., the here and now, not the was or will be). To these recommendations Lahey and Bloom added that (a) the ease with which the referent can be demonstrated in the teaching context (e.g., *hug* or *kiss* rather than *love*, be considered); (b) the number of different nonlinguistic contexts (i.e., settings or activities) and linguistic contexts (i.e., semantic combinations) within which an item can be used be considered; and (c) the lexical items be organized according to the ideas or content they express (e.g., rejection, recurrence, attribution, and action).

Application of these recommendations results not only in identification of items to be included in the initial lexicon but also in classes of items to be specifically excluded. Referents involving internal states (e.g., *love, hate, sad*) are excluded in favor of referents representing their more easily demonstrated behavioral manifestations (e.g., *hug, kiss, mad, cry*). A referent relating to affirmation need not be included; it functions only as a response to a direct question and can be represented by a headshake. However, negation can serve several communicative functions and is used in combination with other lexical items (e.g., *no want* or *no more*); thus, a specific lexical item for negation (e.g., *no*) would be included, rather than merely the negative headshake. Personal pronouns and color items are not included in the initial lexicon; this is based on their absence from normal development until multiple-item utterances have appeared. Finally, children first learn the marked member of polar opposite attributes (e.g., *big, hot, dirty*) before the unmarked, or less salient, member of the polar opposite (e.g., *little, cold, clean*), and refer to the unmarked case by the use of *no* + attribute (e.g., "no hot"). Thus, Lahey and Bloom suggested that, in order to avoid confusion by introducing two lexical items (e.g., *hot* and *cold*) for what may in fact be one concept (e.g., *heat*), the unmarked members be excluded from the initial lexicon.

Based on these recommendations, Fristoe and Lloyd (1980) compiled an initial manual sign lexicon for use with individuals who have severe communication impairments (see table 2). This was accomplished by first determining the most frequently appearing items in manual sign

dictionaries developed for use with severely intellectually impaired individuals who are learning to communicate in manual sign. These items were then evaluated using Holland's and Lahey and Bloom's criteria. L. L. Lloyd and I subsequently questioned whether a lexicon based on secondary data (i.e., frequency-of-occurrence data in manual sign dictionaries and data from normal development) would be useful to persons with severe communicative and intellectual impairments (Karlan and Lloyd 1983). For the purpose of resolving this question, we subjected the suggested lexicon to social validation.

Social validation involves assessing the usefulness and acceptability of intervention programs (Kazdin 1977; Wolf 1978). Of concern here is the question of whether behaviors, skills, or items selected for intervention or teaching are important to the individual in the natural environment. The process of social validation can be approached through either social comparison or subjective evaluation. Social comparison techniques use the behavior exhibited by or skill level of nonhandicapped peers as the standard of comparison. Subjective evaluation, the technique we used, relies on evaluation by individuals (important others) who have contact with the person for whom the intervention is intended. For their validation, we used fifty-seven teachers and speech therapists in Illinois, Indiana, and California who worked with elementary-aged children having severe intellectual impairments, and forty-three parents, teachers, teaching assistants, speech therapists, vocational trainers, group home trainers and staff, and institutional direct care staff in Illinois and Indiana who had contact with adolescent or adult individuals with severe intellectual impairments, as evaluators.

The judges rated each of eighty-four possible lexical items as being *essential* (1.0), *useful* (2.0), *could be useful* (3.0), or *of no value* (4.0). Table 3 lists the items that fell into the first three categories for the two different age levels; none of the items was

Table 2. Organization of a First Lexicon by Content and Form

Content Categories	Form		Substantive Signs
	Relational Signs		
	Signs That Are Not Object-Specific	Signs Relating to Many Objects	
Rejection	negative		
Nonexistence or disappearance	negative, all gone		
Cessation of action	negative, stop		
Prohibition of action	negative		
Recurrence of objects and actions on objects	more		
Noting the existence of or identifying objects	this/that/those		
Actions on objects		bring, drink, eat, get, give, help, kiss, look, make, open, play, throw, wash	
Actions involved in locating objects or self		fall, go, put, sit, stand, run, walk, up, down	
Attributes or descriptions of objects		bad, big, broken, dirty, good, happy, heavy, hot, open	
Persons and animals associated with objects (as in possession)			baby, big, bird, cat, dog, father, girl, hat, mother, you, and name signs
Other objects named			apple, ball, bathroom/toilet/potty, book, candy, car, chair/sit, coat, comb, cookie, cup, door, drink, eat/food, house, milk, pants, school, shirt, shoe(s), sock, spoon, TV, table, water

Note. Adapted, by permission of the publisher, from G. R. Karlan and L. L. Lloyd, "Considerations in the Planning of Communication Intervention: I. Selecting a Lexicon," *Journal of the Association for the Severely Handicapped* 8 (1983):13–25.

listed as being of no value. Because the rating system assigned higher values to lower ratings (essential = 1.0 but of no value = 4.0), the following items had a median value that placed them in the useful category but with a substantial percentage of respondents rating them as essential (the percentages of ranking them as essential and useful are listed in parentheses, respectively): ELEMENTARY—*all gone/used up/finished* (46.6, 50.0), *cold* (45.6, 40.4), *spoon* (44.8, 44.8). ADOLESCENT/ ADULT—*all gone/used up/finished* (40.0, 55.0), *angry/mad* (55.0, 35.0), *bad* (47.5, 42.5), *chair/ sit* (48.7, 43.6), *father/daddy* (47.5, 42.5), *mother/mommy* (52.5, 32.5), *pants* (42.5, 52.5), *sock* (47.5, 45.0).

L. L. Lloyd and I (1983) questioned whether the initial lexicon compiled by Fristoe and Lloyd (1980) was age-appro-

Table 3. Social Validation of Proposed Initial Lexical Items

Elementary		Adolescent/Adult	
Essential Vocabulary (Median Ratings = 1.0–1.5)			
bathroom/toilet/potty	name sign (I, me, my)	angry/mad/bathroom/	look/watch
bed/sleep	no	toilet/potty	milk
coat	stop	bed/sleep	more
drink	water	clean	name sign (I, me, my)
eat/food		coat	no
father/daddy		cold	open
go		come	sad
good		drink	shirt
happy		eat/food	shoes
help		go	stop
hot		good	walk
look/watch		happy	wash
milk		help	water
more		hot	work
mother/mommy		in	you
Useful Vocabulary (Median Rating = 1.6–2.5)			
afraid	hat	afraid	have/possess
all/gone/used	house	all gone/used	heavy
up/finished	in	up/finished	house
angry/mad	make	angry/mad	make
bad	now	bad	map
ball	on	ball	money
big	open	big	Mother/Mommy
book	pants	book	now
boy	play	boy	on
break/broken	run	break/broken	pants
candy	sad	candy	play
car	school	car	pat
chair/sit	shirt	chair/sit	run
clean	shoes	comb	school
cold	sock	cookie	sock
comb	spoon	cry	spoon
come	stand	cup	stand
cookie	table	dirty	table
cry	TV	do	TV
cup	throw	down	this/that/those
dirty	under	fall	throw
door	up	Father/Daddy	under
down	wash	get	up
fall	what	girl	what
get	who	give	who
girl	you	hat	woman
Could Be Useful Vocabulary (Median Ratings = 2.6–3.5)			
apple	heavy	apple	
baby	kiss	baby	
bird	man	bird	
cat	money	cat	
do	pt	dog	
dog	this/that/those	kiss	
have/possess	woman		

Note. Adapted, by permission of the publisher, from G. R. Karlan and L. L. Lloyd, "Considerations in the Planning of Communication Intervention: I. Selecting a Lexicon," *Journal of the Association for the Severely Handicapped* 8 (1983):13–25.

priate given that it was based on normal child development and dictionaries that were developed without specific attention to age. To investigate this, we conducted a systematic survey with adolescent/adult-oriented respondents. Prior to rating the Fristoe-Lloyd lexicon, we interviewed the respondents and asked them to provide all items they believed to be important for inclusion in an initial lexicon for adolescents or adults with severe handicaps. We questioned them first without using any other prompts, then questioned them again using twelve content category prompts (e.g., persons, places, things, relations, actions, and emotions). The survey revealed 106 lexical items that were named by at least 25 percent of the respondents, with thirty-six of these being named by at least 50 percent. There was substantial overlap with the proposed Fristoe-Lloyd lexicon; fifty-two of their eighty-three items were named by at least 50 percent of the sample.

As might be expected, additions to the lexicon tended to concern independent living and community mobility (e.g., *work*, *bus*, *home*, *store*, *doctor/doctor's office*, and *nurse*), the importance of personal hygiene (e.g., *soap*, *shampoo*, *toothbrush*, *toothpaste*, *deodorant*), and vocational and recreational activities (e.g., *money*, *coffee*, *hamburger*, *workshop/work area*, *breaktime*, *restaurant*, and *bowling*). It is very likely that, given the current initiatives in the area of community-based educational, vocational, and residential programs for those with severe physical and/or intellectual impairments, another validation would reflect even more emphasis on lexical items related to these areas.

As L. L. Lloyd and I noted, (Ibid.), the compatibility of the functional-remedial strategy with the developmental strategy is also demonstrated by these survey results. Table 4 presents the lexical items (forms) suggested by at least 25 percent of the respondents, organized according to the content and form categories suggested by Lahey and Bloom (1977). This organization reveals that there are a substantial number of substantive items (i.e., items referring to concrete things or places). However, it also reveals a more than adequate number of relational items; thus, this functionally based lexicon meets the developmental requirements for communicative and linguistic utility and generality (Karlan and Lloyd 1983).

In summary, the goal of developing an initial lexicon is to provide the individual with a single-word (or manual sign) vocabulary that is useful both for communication within his or her immediate environment and for furthering the acquisition of communication itself. However, planning the content of an initial lexicon is but one step in the process of implementing a program of manual sign communication intervention. Decisions must be made as to what to teach first, second, third, and so forth. These decisions can be affected by characteristics of the manual signs that represent these lexical items. Such characteristics can affect the rate at which the manual signs are acquired and used or result in errors or confusion in recall and use of learned manual signs.

Characteristics Affecting the Learning of Manual Signs

Characteristics that affect the acquisition of manual sign use by individuals with intellectual impairments fall into two basic areas: representational level, or iconicity, of the manual sign, and physical and motoric characteristics of the manual sign (Fristoe and Lloyd 1980; Reichle, Williams, and Ryan 1981). Iconicity refers to the representational abstractness, or the degree to which a sign or gesture, or any aspect of the sign or gesture, is defined by, resembles, or suggests its referent (Brown 1978; Lloyd and Fristoe 1978). Physical characteristics refer to the motoric components or physical features that must be used to produce or define a manual sign (Doherty 1985; Kohl 1981; Dennis, et al. 1982) and are analogous to the phonological components of a spoken word.

Table 4. Organization of an Adolescent/Adult Lexicon by Content and Form

Content Categories	Form		
	Relational Signs		Substantive Signs
	Signs That Are Not Object-Specific	Signs Relating to Many Objects	
Rejection	no		
Nonexistence or disappearance	no, bye/ goodbye		
Cessation of action	no, stop, done/ finished		
Prohibition of action	no		
Recurrence of objects or actions on objects	more		
Noting the existence of identifying objects		hello/hi	
Actions on objects		eat, (work), drink, help, wash, want, play, bath, come	
Actions involved in locating objects or self		go, walk, in, bye/goodbye, on, under, run, outside, sit, out, stand/stand up	
Attributes or descriptions of objects		happy, sad, sick, hurt, hot, (cold), sleepy, tired, (clean), like, (color words)	
Persons and animals associated with objects (as in possession)		dad/father, mom/mother, teacher, doctor, name, sister, brother, friend(s), peers	
Other objects and places named			bathroom, bus, home, soap, toothbrush, ball, shoe(s), store, doctor's office, milk, bed, pop/Coke, school, nurse, car, cookie, toilet, book, coat, (money), pants, shirt, brush, candy, comb

Note. Adapted, by permission of the publishers, from G. R. Karlan and L. L. Lloyd, "Considerations in the Planning of Communication Intervention: I. Selecting a Lexicon," *Journal of the Association for the Severely Handicapped* 8 (1983):13–25.

Iconicity. Two types of iconicity have been identified based on the procedures for determining symbol iconicity: *transparency* and *translucency*. Transparency refers to the guessability of meaning of the sign when the referent is not present or known (Bellugi and Klima 1975; Brown 1978; Lloyd and Fristoe 1978). Transparency is not a characteristic of the manual sign system as a whole but derives from the specific guessability of the chosen manual signs. It has been shown, for example, that a sample of 100 manual signs used with persons with severe intellectual impairments is, on the whole, more transparent than a sample of 100 signs selected at random from the entire manual sign system (Lloyd and Fristoe 1978). Translucency refers to the semantic, conceptual, or linguistic relationship between a sign and its referent; such a relationship is apparent when the referent is known but may not be apparent from merely seeing the sign alone (Bellugi and Klima 1975; Brown 1978). One must then establish translucency values, or judgments concerning the perceived degree of relationship between the manual sign and its referent (Goossens' 1984; Griffith 1980; Griffith and Robinson 1981; Griffith, Robinson, and Panagos 1983; Karlan and Lloyd 1988a, b; Luftig, Page, and Lloyd 1983; p. 1985).

The influence of iconicity on the acquisition of manual sign production or comprehension has been directly investigated by a number of researchers. Unfortunately, interpretation of their findings is complicated by the fact that different methods for initially determining manual sign iconicity were used. Using procedures that established the translucency of the manual signs but favored more transparent or guessable signs, Konstantareas, Oxman, and Webster (1978) found that iconicity facilitated the acquisition of production of verb and adjective signs by autistic children. It did not, however, affect the acquisition of manual signs representing nouns. Based on translucency ratings, it has been demonstrated that learning to comprehend manual signs is easier for moderately and severely intellectually impaired students when the signs are more iconic (Goossens' 1984; Griffith and Robinson 1981). With dichotomous sets of high translucency (at least 5.5 on a 7-point scale) and low translucency (≤2.5), iconicity has been shown to have a significant facilita-

tive effect on acquisition of manual sign production by students with moderate or severe intellectual impairments. Interestingly, while it has been demonstrated overall that iconicity can influence the acquisition of manual sign comprehension or production, what has not been examined is the influence iconicity might have on the retention or long-term recall by these individuals.

Motoric Characteristics.   Seven basic motoric or physical features or dimensions have been identified that might affect the learning of manual signs by individuals with moderate or severe impairments (Doherty 1985; Karlan and Lloyd 1988a; Kohl 1981; Dennis, et al. 1982).

1. Handedness: the number of hands used in forming the sign:
2. Symmetry: whether or not the hands do the same thing, that is, whether the hands are symmetrical or assymmetrical in their configuration and movement;
3. Proximity or Production Mode: whether or not the hands touch each other or some part of the body (touch vs. nontouch);
4. Repetition: whether or not there is repetition or reduplication of movement within the sign (repetitive vs. nonrepetitive);
5. Visibility: whether the sign is visible to the signer when it is formed or invisible within the direct line of regard;
6. Complexity: whether one or two (or more) distinct movements are made in producing the sign;
7. Fluidity: whether there is transitional movement between the different handshapes required to produce the sign when more than one handshape is used (transition) or just one handshape is used (one move).

Doherty (1985) extensively reviewed the research literature concerning the effects of these motor characteristics on the acquisition of manual signing by individuals both with and without intellectual or hearing handicaps. The remainder of this discussion will focus on the findings and conclusions relating to those persons having moderate or severe intellectual impairments.

The question of the effect of handedness on the acquisition of manual signing cannot be addressed without also considering symmetry of configuration or movement. Thus, one must not simply consider one- versus two-handed signs, but also whether the two hands are symmetrical or asymmetrical in their configuration or movement. Doherty (1985) suggested that there is a possible continuum of complexity from one-handed to two-handed symmetrical to two-handed asymmetrical manual signs. Observational reports (Bonvillian and Nelson 1978) and empirical research (Kohl 1981) support the conclusion that symmetrical signs are more easily acquired than those that are asymmetrical, although little is known about whether this effect persists during recall or retention (Doherty 1985). The data are unclear as to whether one-handed signs are indeed easier to learn than the two-handed symmetrical or asymmetrical types. Informal reports have supported this conclusion (Grinnel, Detamore, and Lippke 1976), but others have observed that children with severe intellectual impairments spontaneously change one-handed signs to two-handed ones during acquisition (Doherty 1985; Stremel-Campbell, Cantrell, and Halle 1977).

One systematic empirical study has demonstrated that adults with mild to moderate intellectual impairments learned one-handed signs with greater ease, but only when the translucency (iconicity) of the signs was high (Doherty and Lloyd 1983). With signs of only moderate translucency, one- and two-handed signs were learned with equal ease or difficulty. Doherty (1985) suggested that final clarification of the effects of this feature must take into account not only handedness and symmetry but also possible developmental stage

differences among the handshapes used to produce the manual signs and the effects of crossing midline during sign formation.

Proximity, the presence or absence of contact between the hands or with the body, can be distinguished as involving the two hands (dyadic) or one hand and the body (spatial) and, within each of these two classes, as involving holding (pivoting vs. holding), continuous contact (sliding vs. rocking), and contact midway (grazing). (See Doherty, 1985, for a discussion of the theoretical development of these features.) For children with severe or profound intellectual impairments, the acquisition of manual sign production is facilitated when contact, either dyadic or spatial, is present (Kohl 1981; Stremel-Campbell, Cantrell, and Halle 1977). Thrasher (1985) found that, for adults with severe or profound intellectual impairments, there was an interaction between iconicity and contact such that proximity had no facilitative effect when iconicity was high but did facilitate acquisition when iconicity was low among the manual signs.

Doherty and Lloyd (1983) have reported that midpoint contact (grazing of one hand against the other in the middle of the sign production) may represent a special and more difficult type of contact. Error analysis of manual sign production by adults with mild or moderate intellectual impairment indicated that they converted midcontact to end-contact. Based on these results and on motor skill learning theory, Doherty (1985) has speculated that signs having a greater amount of continuous contact (rocking, holding, pivoting, and sliding contact) may be easier to learn than those providing less tactile feedback (beginning, ending, or double contact or grazing). However, this has not been verified through direct observation.

For the dimensions of repetition and visibility, observations during clinical or educational interventions suggest that repetitive movement (Stremel-Campbell, Cantrell, and Halle 1977) and visibility, especially with signs made in front at midline (Barrera, Lobato-Barrera, and Sulzer-Azaroff 1980; Stremel-Campbell, Cantrell, and Halle 1977), facilitate acquisition of sign production by learners with intellectual impairments. Doherty (1985) indicated that motor learning theory and data from deaf and hearing children generally support the use of repetition as a feature when selecting among signs for initial intervention. However, observations of early sign language development by children without intellectual impairments contradict the finding that the visibility of signs is a facilitative factor (Ibid.) and suggest that more systematic examination of this feature is needed.

In addition to these topographical dimensions, manual signs may also be characterized according to cheremic, or phonological, analysis. Chereme categories include those indicating location relative to the body, handshape or configuration, and movement. Differences in learning based on handshape configurations have been reported for children with severe intellectual impairments (Kiernan and Bowler 1980), and the suggestion has been made that such differences are related to the developmental difficulty of the required motor movements (Dennis, et al. 1982). Differences are hypothesized to be based on the developmental sequence of prehension and unilateral/bilateral movement patterns required to produce the signs, but with the acknowledgment that sufficient empirical data are lacking in this area (Ibid.).

More interesting for application to planning intervention for those with intellectual impairments is information concerning a developmental order of handshape difficulty that appears to exist among deaf children and hearing children of deaf parents (see Doherty, 1985, for a detailed review of these data). Handshapes are hypothesized to fall into one of four stages of acquisition (Boyes-Braem, cited in Doherty 1985, 1986): Stage 1—A, S, L, baby 0, 5, C, and G; Stage 2—B, F, and 0; Stage 3—I, D, Y, P, 3, V, H, and W; Stage 4—8, 7, X, R, T, M, N, and E. Doherty's

investigation (1986) of manual sign acquisition by four- and five-year-old children with normal hearing and intelligence suggested that (a) one-handed signs made with Stage 1 and 2 handshapes are more difficult to acquire than are signs made with Stage 3 and 4 handshapes, and (b) while two-handed signs do not appear to be learned according to the 4-stage model, those made with the Y, P, 8, F, C, and 5-dot handshapes are more difficult irrespective of stage level. Doherty suggested, in fact, that signs made with these handshapes be excluded from an initial lexicon.

Taking these various findings as a whole, Doherty (1985) has recommended certain strategies for selecting the manual signs to be used in initial communication intervention from a larger pool of items identified as being functionally relevant or motivating for the individual in question. For the first five to ten signs to be taught to an individual with intellectual impairment, the following strategies (grouped according to the extent of empirical support available) can be applied.

Group 1 Strategies. (derived directly from empirical research):
1. Select signs with contact over non-contact signs.
2. Select symmetric signs over asymmetric signs.
3. a. Select translucent one-handed signs over nontranslucent two-handed signs;
   b. Select highly translucent one-handed signs over highly translucent two-handed signs.

Doherty further suggested that this group of strategies can be applied to selection of the first ten signs for intervention by starting with highly translucent one-handed signs as the first two signs taught and including two-handed contact signs among the next signs taught.

Group 2 Strategies. (derived by inference from more basic research):
1. Select signs made with Stage 1 or 2

handshapes over those made with Stage 3 or 4 handshapes.

2. Select signs that maximize location differences in order to facilitate recall.

3. Pretest signers on motor abilities related to handshape and movement features in order to identify manual signs to be avoided or for which initial approximations will need to be accepted.

In aid of this last strategy, Bornstein and Jordan (1984) have provided empirical data on the comprehensibility of 330 manual signs when the signs had been "simplified." These signs had been identified by Fristoe and Lloyd (1979a) as appearing most frequently in manuals used with handicapped students throughout the United States. Simplification involved eliminating the handshape, movement, or location component of the manual sign. The resulting approximations were then shown to experienced readers of manual sign to determine the characteristics or features of the sign that may or may not need to be present for a reader to recognize the sign. Signs that can still be understood by at least 80 percent of experienced sign readers when a component is not present are considered to be *robust*. Thus, robust for handshape would describe all those signs that could be understood when handshape was not present. Such manual signs would be recommended when the individual demonstrated particular difficulty learning to form this component accurately. *Fragile* signs are those that 20 percent or fewer of the readers could recognize when a particular component is not present. Thus, fragile for movement, for example, are those signs that cannot be understood when the movement component has been eliminated.

Group 3 Strategies. (based on anecdotal reports or logical conjectures):

1. Select signs with repeated movement over those without repeated movement.

2. Select visible signs over those not visible to the signer.

3. Select signs made with single handshapes over those requiring multiple handshapes.

4. Select signs made with single movements over those requiring multiple movements.

Manual signs selected according to these criteria will have a high degree of representation and possess many of the facilitative motoric features. Examples of manual signs selected according to these strategies are BABY, BOOK, CAR, DRINK, EAT/FOOD, BREAK (BREAKTIME) and MILK. This information can also be used to decide whether to teach signs together within a learning set. For example, DRINK and EAT should not be taught together, as they are very similar in their motor characteristics and very similar conceptually. Conceptually and topographically similar signs have been observed to result in more confusion errors during acquisition (Stremel-Campbell, Cantrell, and Halle 1977). Some signs might be thought to have great functional value (e.g., TOILET/POTTY), but can be demonstrated to have low transparency (Karlan and Lloyd, 1988a), to not require contact, and to require only one hand for production. This suggests that unless TOILET is highly motivating to the individual with intellectual impairment, it will be a relatively difficult sign to acquire initially and might be better moved to a later position in the training order.

In summary, using the guidelines discussed earlier, an initial lexicon can be identified that includes a variety of potentially useful or functional items. Then, decisions concerning the relative order in which signs might be taught can be made using iconicity information and the presence of certain facilitative motor characteristics. It must be noted that the importance of iconicity and motor characteristics in the decision making process may be a function of the particular phase of intervention one is in. Transparent iconicity may have greater influence during teaching of the first five to ten signs when the perceptual features of the transparently iconic symbols are most useful. Translucent iconicity may have greater influence as the individual's conceptual and cognitive development become more sophisticated. Similarly, as more manual signs are learned by the individual, such motoric features as visibility, repetition, and symmetry may have less effect on the acquisition data.

INTERVENTION TECHNIQUES AND STRATEGIES FOR USE WITH MANUAL SIGNING

Techniques and strategies for interventions that use manual signing fall into two broad, and somewhat related, areas. The first comprises those procedures that are specific to the use of manual signs (i.e., the extent to which signs are paired with spoken words). The second is that more general area comprising intervention strategies and techniques for developing functional use of effective communication skills.

Procedures Specific to Manual Sign Intervention

For persons with severe communication deficits accompanied by intellectual impairment or autism, the use of manual signing as part of a program of communication intervention has come to be known as "simultaneous communication" or "Total Communication," indicating that the manual signs are presented by the teacher or parent at the same time as words are spoken (Bonvillian and Nelson 1978; Carr 1981; Creekmore 1982; Konstantareas, Oxman, and Webster 1978). In addition, the individuals being taught are encouraged, though not required, to vocalize while signing. While this has been the most widely used practice, there have been questions raised as to whether this is necessarily the best method, especially with autistic individuals (Schaeffer 1980a and b).

The concern is based on observed "stimulus overselectivity" (Lovaas and Schreibman 1971), or apparent perceptual disturbances, exhibited by autistic individuals (Bonvillian and Nelson 1978; Creekmore 1982). The argument has been made that, because these people have difficulty processing information in the auditory mode, presentation of simultaneous auditory and visual cues will prove to be confusing and beyond their capability. Schaeffer (1980) suggested that separate but concurrent training, in which the trainer presents either the manual sign alone or speech alone, be conducted prior to simultaneous, "signed speech" training.

This issue has not been pursued extensively, and those who have pursued it have not all addressed the question directly. Typical of this is a study by Carr and Dores (1981), who taught children diagnosed as autistic to comprehend sign plus speech presentations and then evaluated comprehension in each modality alone. They found that some autistic students had attended to only the manual signs during presentation while others, who had higher scores on a verbal imitation pretest, attended to both the visual and auditory information. This study and others like it (Carr, et al. 1978) present only one kind of training followed by an analysis of what was learned, and then suggest that simultaneous training does no better than sign training alone. This, however, is only indirect evidence. These researchers do not show directly that simultaneous training is less efficient or worse because of auditory "interference."

Those investigations that have directly compared training using simultaneous presentations with training using sign alone demonstrate that simultaneous training is actually better than sign-only training with autistic children (Brady and Smouse 1978; Barrera, Lobato-Barrera, and Sulzer-Azaroff 1980). As indicated by Carr and Dores, the problem of individual differences remains which suggests that Carr's (1981) advice to begin with simultaneous presentations for a period of time (e.g., eight weeks), and let individual student progress be a guide should be followed. If learning does not seem to be occurring, switch to sign only presentations for a period of time. Finally, little or no research exists that addresses this question for individuals with severe intellectual impairments rather than autism. Care must be used when generalizing these findings or recommendations to these other individuals.

Instructional Prompts and Time Delay. For teaching individuals with autism or intellectual impairments to produce manual signs for expressive communication, the most common instructional prompts include verbal prompts, modeling of the sign, and/or physical guidance in producing it. Where physical guidance is used, systematic decreasing of the amount provided by the instructor is used to transfer stimulus control from the instructor's guidance to the environmental cue or instructor's verbal prompt (Carr 1981). When, however, the individual has been taught using a system in which the instructor first uses a verbal prompt and then provides a model for the manual sign, it is sometimes difficult to get the individual to respond before the model is presented. In effect, he or she has learned to await the presentation of the model. In these cases, the use of a time-delay technique has been shown to facilitate transfer of responding from the model to the verbal prompt (Kleinert and Gast 1982; Smeets and Streifel 1976; Striefel, Bryan, and Aiken 1974).

In the time-delay procedure, pauses of systematically increasing length are inserted between the presentation of the task (or target stimulus) and the subsequent presentation of the controlling stimulus or prompt (Snell and Gast 1981). As used in expressive manual sign instruction, progressive time delay is initiated with a simultaneous, or zero-delay, trial. That is, the instructor presents the context cue (e.g., places a cup of juice on the table) and/or a verbal prompt (e.g., "what do you want?"), then immediately presents the model (e.g., the sign JUICE) without any intervening time between the first cue(s) and the model. During subsequent opportunities, delay trials are used in which a time delay starting at one second is inserted between the first cue or prompt and the model. With each correct response after the model the length of the delay is increased by one-second increments until the individual has made a specific number of correct responses before the model is presented (Gast and Isaac, cited in Kleinert and Gast 1982; Smeets and Streifel 1976). Kleinert and Gast have also shown with one individual with multiple handicaps that the use of a constant time delay (e.g., four seconds), rather than a progressive one, will also result in a transfer of control from the model to the target cue or prompt. In this procedure, however, the constant delay trials were preceded by a block of ten simultaneous (zero-delay) trials.

Manual Sign Instruction with Deaf-Blind Individuals. With individuals who are deaf-blind or, more accurately, auditorially and visually impaired, and who exhibit intellectual impairments, certain instructional variations should be considered (Pennington, Karlan, and Lloyd 1986). The first should be to emphasize the tactile channel by placing the individual's hands over those of the instructor to feel the sign and enhance feedback. The distance between the instructor and the learner should be based on the nature and extent of the individual's visual losses. Other considerations related to the manual signs themselves include

1. Modifying the formation of the sign to make it spatially more compact,
2. Slowing the production rate during teaching, and
3. Accepting less precise manual sign or gesture approximations from the individual.

Bornstein and Jordan's (1984) data for the comprehensibility of 330 reduced Signed

English signs could be used as a guide for selecting acceptable approximations. For individuals with less severe intellectual impairments, fingerspelling and palm writing (using the index finger to draw letters on the individual's palm) may also be used (Jensema 1979).

Developing Effective Use of Communication Skills

Hart and Rogers-Warren (1978) characterized communication intervention as having two levels of concern. At the first level, that of organized activities or the teaching environment, concern is with the initial acquisition of appropriate behaviors (e.g., an initial manual sign lexicon) needed to support communicative interaction. At the second level, the interventionist is concerned with functional use of these communicative behaviors in the natural, or "talking," environment. These two levels of concern overlap. As the individual begins to acquire linguistic forms (e.g., manual signs) there is an immediate need to ensure that these forms are used communicatively in everyday interactions. This is supported by an overwhelming emphasis, in the augmentative and alternative communication literature, on the need for assessment and intervention to occur in natural environments with a variety of trained communicative partners, if the ability to engage in functional, interactive, social communication is to be developed (Bottdorf and DePape 1982; Farrier, et al. 1985; Keough and Reichle 1985, Yorkston and Karlan 1986; Williams, et al. 1982).

The natural talking environment has certain characteristics that may or may not be of advantage to the communicatively impaired learner (Hart and Rogers-Warren 1978). The talking environment usually involves a number of people and contains multiple stimulus sources. The environment is unsystematic and variable. Language presented to the child is varied in form and purpose, including instructions, questions, and comments of a social or conversational type. It is often unclear whether a language response is required or even expected by the adult. Models for appropriate language occur to which the language learner may not be attending. Many models will be presented that, because the adult is unaware of the learner's precise skill level, may be too complex and therefore beyond his or her ability to imitate. These characteristics are typical of the communicatively "busy" setting in which adults are communicating with one another and with various students, language learners are engaged in nonlinguistic work or play, and the language learners may be attempting to communicate with one another (although for those with severe intellectual impairments, this may be the exception rather than the rule).

There may be some advantages to such a talking environment. Adults respond to all those instances that appropriately communicate a message or intent. Initially, adults are more likely to focus on precise forms only when the message is incomprehensible; otherwise, function is the chief concern. "Natural responsiveness to the social nature of language ensures that improvements in the child's language will receive appropriate feedback. . ." (Hart and Rogers-Warren 1978, 197). When less attention is paid to precise form or topography of responses, more reinforcement is given to higher rates of responding. Higher rates of approximate responses, in turn, provide higher probabilities that language will come under varied environmental control, which provides natural conditions for elaboration or refinement and generalization of communicative responding. But it is also true that these may be advantages only for the typical language learner. Much discussion over time has focused on the lack of generalization displayed by the severely communicatively impaired individual in transferring skills learned in the training environment to the natural environment. Such individuals have not all demonstrated generalization to spontaneous (self-initiated) usage and have not all generalized across settings or persons (Bryen and Joyce 1985). Hart and Rogers-Warren suggest that, rather than depending solely on teaching environments to both build communicative forms and foster their functional use, one must develop a setting that is intermediate between the teaching and talking environment.

The Milieu Language Teaching Model. An effective communication training model that has been successfully taught to teachers of speaking children with communication deficits and needs similar to those of individuals who use augmentative modes of communication, including manual signing, is the Milieu Language Teaching (MLT) model. The MLT model, which was designed to facilitate communication development and generalization in everyday situations, is used in natural environments by communicative partners and addresses many of the language delays and deficits often identified among users of augmentative communication. Some of these concerns include low frequency of communication (Hart and Risley 1975), limited communicative functions, with responses to others predominating (Warren, McQuarter, and Rogers-Warren 1984), preemption of student "turns" by adults (Halle, Baer, and Spradlin 1981), lack of generalization of communication skills from structured training situations to everyday environments (Blackstone 1986; Guess, Keogh, and Sailor 1978; Halle 1982, 1987; Miller and Allaire 1987; Rogers-Warren and Warren 1980; Rusch and Karlan 1983), and the need for teachers, parents, and others to become more skilled communication partners (Hart 1985).

MLT is a member of a family of teaching strategies that utilize natural environments to train and facilitate generalization of language through multiple exemplars with naturally occurring reinforcers (Kaiser, Alpert, and Warren 1987). All the environmental approaches not only address language acquisition, but also are sensitive to the need for skill generalization and maintenance.

> The common premises that connect these intervention techniques are (a) that language and communication skills should be taught in the child's natural environment, (b) in conversational contexts, (c) utilizing a dispersed trial training approach that (d) emphasizes following the child's attentional lead, and (e) using functional reinforcers indicated by child requests and attention. (Warren and Kaiser 1986, p. 291).

An important feature of this model is that it contains strategies that can be easily implemented by virtually any person who has frequent and regular contact with the communicatively impaired individual. Furthermore, this model can be employed without the use of specialized materials and does not require the communication trainer to substantially alter the daily routine. Using this model, desired communication behaviors are elicited within the existing context and routine of the environment.

The MLT model requires the completion of three general types of activity.
1. Arrangement of the environment to prompt the use of language.
2. Assessment of the individual's current skill level to select areas for teaching functional language.
3. Training of the adults in the environment so that the individual does work with language and the individual's language is effective.

In arranging the environment to support milieu teaching, three things are considered—what the individuals do, what they want to do, and what reinforces the teacher or other adults mediating for the individuals (Hart and Rogers-Warren 1978). A moderately high rate of engagement of the individual with materials is fundamental to this model's effectiveness. This means that a variety of materials and activities that are desirable to the individual must be available and accessible. After the environment has been organized so that those materials or activities that are preferred or desired by the individual are located within close proximity to an adult who can provide appropriate consequences, an incidental teaching episode can be conducted.

The first goal of milieu teaching is to build communicative rate; therefore, the first type of incidental teaching provides immediate and consistent consequences—both very positive attention and verbal feedback from the adult and desired materials and activities—for any functional communicative response, regardless of whether it is an approximation of language or nonlinguistic (e.g., pointing). As such responses become more frequent, a more structured milieu teaching format is used to facilitate the acquisition and use of more appropriate forms of communicative responding. At the point when the individual verbally or nonverbally initiates an interaction that indicates a desire for some reinforcers, be they people, materials, or activities, the teacher or adult makes a decision about whether to use this as a milieu teaching experience.

Various degrees of prompting by the teacher are used (see table 5), based on what is known of the individual's ability. In general, full prompts consist of requests for imitation accompanied by a fully modeled response. Medium-degree prompts consist of requests for partial imitation and a reduction of the adult model. Minimal-degree prompts are requests (mands) for the terminal language behavior ("You need to tell me what you want"). Zero-degree prompts are open adult questions ("What do you want?") and pauses (Halle 1982, 1987).

Mand-Model Procedure. The mand-model procedure is one of several techniques utilized in the MLT model. Systematized by Rogers-Warren and Warren (1980), it is based on observed normal patterns of interaction between mothers and their young children. Bruner (1978) and Moerk (1975) found that parents and ed-

ucators often pause, waiting for their children to communicate. Trainer-selected activities are arranged, with all necessary materials available to the learner. The trainer then pauses and waits for the learner to approach one of the materials and responds to that action with a prompt, or a mand, for communication, (e.g., What do you need?). If the desired response is produced, the learner is rewarded with praise and access to the material. If, after a reasonable pause, the learner gives a response that does not approximate the target behavior, the trainer may choose to provide a prompt of the desired behavior (e.g., Do you need soda or a sandwich?). If the response to the prompt is insufficient, the trainer then models the appropriate response and waits for an imitated production. The learner is reinforced for target responses with descriptive praise (e.g., Good, you asked for a sandwich) and the desired material.

The mand-model technique has been found to be beneficial in enhancing the communication skills of individuals with communication impairments. This procedure has been effective in increasing the frequency of low-rate communicative behaviors, partially due to the fact that the number of training opportunities is under the control of the facilitator. When combined with structured intervention, use of the mand-model procedure increases the frequency of verbalization, the responsiveness in obligatory speech situations, and generalization from structured training to the classroom, and results in the display of more complex language by severely language-delayed children (Rogers-Warren and Warren 1980). A subsequent replication by Warren, McQuarter, and Rogers-Warren (1984) demonstrated that the mand-model procedure also increased initiated (nonobligatory) speech and produced generalization within a second, nontreatment setting.

One study has been reported that used the mand-model procedure with three severely retarded individuals (Anderson, cited

Table 5. Cues and Prompts Used in Milieu Teaching (ordered from least to most assistance)

Prompt	When to Use It	How to Use It	Example
Focused attention) (pause ex- pectant pause)	Use it whenever a child initiates an interaction	Look at the child and remain silent for a few seconds. Wait for the child to respond	A child points to a toy truck on a shelf. The teacher pauses and looks expectantly at the child.
Open question	Use it when you believe the child knows the answer, because you have heard the child say it in the past, without prompts.	Ask a question starting with what, why, who, when, where, or how.	"What do you want?" "Where should I put it?"
Mand or request for verbalization	Use it when you believe the child knows what to say, but needs to be reminded to use language or to elaborate. (This is particularly helpful if a child whines to indicate a need, but is capable of talking.)	Tell the child that he needs to use language, or elaborate (for example, by using a complete sentence).	"Tell me what you want." "You need to ask me." "Use a whole sentence."
Partial prompt	Use it when you have heard the child say the answer in the past, but only a few times or with prompting.	Provide part of the answer by giving a hint or clue, asking a question that contains a choice, or modeling the first few letters or sounds of the answer.	"It's the same color as your shirt." "Do you want a red one or a blue one?" "Say B! . . . " "Say, I want . . . "
Full model	Use it when you have not heard the child say the answer in the past, or if the child has said the answer only after it was modeled.	Model the answer, and tell the child to repeat it.	"Say, blue." "Say, I want a blue truck."

Note. Adapted, by permission of the publisher, from C. C. Cavallaro, "Language Intervention in Natural Settings," *Teaching Exceptional Children* 16 (1983):65–70.

in Halle 1982). Teachers were instructed in the use of the mand-model procedure, and measures were taken of both the adults' and the severely intellectually impaired persons' behavior. Adult verbal behavior did not change in frequency, but the form of the communicative acts changed from predominantly rhetorical questions to a preponderance of mands and models. As a consequence of this change in adult verbal behavior, all three individuals dem-

onstrated increased rates of verbalization (two immediately) and an increased percentage of appropriate responses to teacher mands and models. There is no reason to suppose that similar results would not obtain if manual signing rather than vocalization were required (Oliver and Halle 1982).

A second treatment condition had an interesting negative impact. In this condition, adults were required to provide each individual with a specific number of interaction opportunities. This resulted in improvement in response rate and the individuals' responsivity, but two of the three severely retarded individuals demonstrated decreased rates of initiation. Halle (1982) has suggested that assigning a target number of interactions caused the adults to take over the situations and preempt initiations by the handicapped individual; adult cues, mands, and models were so frequent as to preclude opportunities for initiation.

Time Delay. In the MLT model, the time-delay procedure is also used. For example, an individual may see a desired object that is out of reach. Initially, the instructor verbally prompts communication as soon as it is apparent that the individual wants the object. As the individual becomes more proficient, the instructor may pause for about five seconds before delivering the verbal prompt to communicate. This technique is an excellent complement to the mand-model procedure, as it permits the learner to make use of more subtle cues for communication opportunities that are already present in the daily environment. This strategy has the additional advantage of eliciting target behaviors with low error rates.

Halle, Marshall, and Spradlin (1979) and Halle, Baer, and Spradlin (1981) were among the first to utilize the time-delay procedure in a standardized fashion. The first requirement for use of this strategy is establishing proximity between the instructor and the learner. The instructor then looks at the learner and assumes an interested and expectant posture. When the learner makes eye contact, the instructor pauses (for about fifteen seconds) to wait for a target response. If the response does not approximate the desired behavior, it is modeled by the instructor. (This prompt can be repeated twice, if necessary, allowing adequate pause time for the learner to respond.) Correct responses are reinforced with objects or events desired by the

learner. If the learner fails to provide the appropriate response after the target behavior has been modeled for the third time, the learner is still provided with the desired item. Time delay has been used with individuals with cognitive impairments to teach object labeling (Risley and Wolf 1967), receptive and expressive use of manual signs (Browder, Morris, and Snell 1981; Smeets and Striefel 1976; Snell and Gast 1981; Stremel-Campbell, Cantrell, and Halle 1977), following instructions (Striefel, Bryan, and Aiken 1974), verbal requesting (Halle, Marshall, and Spradlin 1979), and increasing verbal responding (Hall and Broden 1977).

Halle and his colleagues employed the time-delay strategy in an intervention program in which they successfully increased spoken initiations by children with severe and profound mental retardation who were residents of a large institution. Systematic delays of fifteen seconds were implemented prior to providing the children with their food trays at breakfast time. Five of the six subjects learned to initiate the request, "Tray, please," when the time-delay procedure was utilized. However, all the children required some initial modeling prompts of the desired behavior before they learned to initiate the behavior independently. More intensive massed-trial training was required to facilitate increased initiations in the sixth child. The increased initiations generalized across mealtimes, other food servers, and both mealtimes and food servers. Informal data indicated that some of the children attempted to utilize the newly learned linguistic form with other objects as well (e.g., "Popcorn, please"). However, their small noun vocabularies limited the extent to which this new form could be effectively used.

In another investigation, Halle, Baer, and Spradlin (1981) used this procedure to increase the spoken initiations of children with moderate mental retardation. These researchers taught teachers to delay offers of assistance to six children as they engaged in various activities. Use of the strategy effectively increased the children's spoken initiations. A second experiment by the same researchers systematically replicated the first study and validated the original findings. In addition, the latter investigation demonstrated that teachers generalized their implementation of the strategy to novel situations. This increase in the number of times the strategy was used resulted in substantial increases in initiation of spoken utterances by children.

The time-delay procedure was also used to teach manual sign skills to a nonspeaking, institutionalized adolescent with severe cognitive impairments (Browder, Morris, and Snell 1981). The boy had learned to produce two signs prior to the commencement of this investigation. However, extensive training was required to teach him those two signs. Prompts (a model of the target sign or a physical guidance cue) were delayed for up to eight seconds. The student successfully learned to produce five food signs within twenty-eight sessions via this method. While no formal generalization data were taken, informal probes indicated that this subject was able to transfer his new sign skills to a different setting. A retention probe, conducted seven months after training had ceased, revealed that he could produce two of the signs 100 percent of the time, two of the signs 75 percent of the time, and one sign 50 percent of the time when asked to label pictures of the food items.

An Integrative Model. Halle (1982) has provided an excellent comparative evaluation of the three major milieu teaching techniques (incidental teaching, mand-model, time delay), as applied to the problem of communication intervention with the severely handicapped. (See table 6 for a summary comparison of these procedures.) He assumed that, while none of the three techniques alone is capable of transforming moderately and severely handicapped children with very low rates of initiation and small expressive vocabu-

laries into fluent communicators (i.e., able to use elaborate vocal language as a means of controlling their environment), these procedures could be used together to shape age-appropriate language use.

While the mand-model procedure is dependent on adult cues or prompts, it is particularly appropriate (a) for increasing rate of language use, because the frequency of opportunity to communicate is partially controlled by the adult; or (b) as a transitional step from structured training to natural environments or contexts (Halle 1982). The delay procedure (pausing) can be used to prevent adult cue/prompt dependence by teaching child initiation (i.e., responding to natural environmental cues that can be verbal or contextual). Thus, the mand-model technique produces increased response rate, and the time-delay procedure facilitates the development of initiation by the communication learner. The time-delay strategy, however, lacks the means to foster the use of more elaborate language (complexity of form), although once consistent initiation has been demonstrated, incidental teaching becomes appropriate. Incidental teaching procedures begin at the point of the individual's initiation of an interaction and are designed to produce increasingly elaborate language. In this instance, "elaborate" refers to increased length of utterance (i.e., the number of elements sequenced together in a response).

There is some empirical support for the use of Halle's integrative model. Oliver and Halle (1982) taught initiated use of manual signs to a young, moderately handicapped child using a combination of time delay and a variation of the mand-model procedure within two settings (exercise/play and lunch). In the natural environment, the child used only primitive intentional communicative behaviors spontaneously, despite having acquired twenty expressive manual signs in structured training. Procedurally, a ten-second delay was used at the beginning of targeted opportunities to use the selected signs. If the correct sign

Table 6.   Comparison of Three Procedures Used in Milieu Teaching

	Mand-Model	Delay	Incidental Teaching
1. Arranging the environment	Yes Attractive toys and materials	Yes Predetermined situations	Yes Toys out of reach Play materials
2. Initiator of interaction	Adult or child	Adult first, child later	Child
3. Elaboration of language	Yes	No	Yes
4. Prompting procedure	Yes Models and mands Minimum necessary	Yes Models	Yes Gradient-model, partial-model, mand, question
5. Natural consequence programmed	Yes	Yes	Yes
6. Locale of training[a]	Natural environment free play	Natural environment any time	Natural environment free play
7. Purpose	To facilitate generalized effects of structured training by increasing language opportunities in the natural environment	To provide more reasons for talking by rearranging contingencies in the natural environment and to transfer control from adult language to environmental stimuli, including adult presence	To approximate age-appropriate language by continually demanding more elaborate and complex language

Note. Adapted, by permission of the publisher, from J. W. Halle, "Teaching Functional Language to the Handicapped: An Integrative Model of Natural Environment Teaching Techniques," *Journal of the Association for the Severely Handicapped* 7(1982).

[a] The locales described were those used in the experimental investigations; effective application of the procedures is not necessarily restricted to these situations.

was initiated during the pause, the teacher confirmed the accuracy of the response, offered a final model of the appropriate response, and fulfilled the request that occasioned the initial pause. If no response or an incorrect response occurred, the teacher presented a prompt sequence at the end of the delay interval. The prompt sequence consisted of the teacher's selecting a degree of prompt, appropriate to the child's current level based on prior responding, from among (a) full-degree prompt: model sign, physically guide response, then request child to imitate; (b) medium-degree prompt: model sign, then request imitation; or (c) minimal-degree prompt: mand (verbally request) sign production. Results indicated that, in both milieu teaching settings, student initiation of signing increased while adult prompts and incorrect sign production decreased. Generalization of self-initiated manual signing to other adults in the same setting and to use of the target manual signs (e.g., HELP, JUICE, PUSH) in novel contexts was also demonstrated.

SUMMARY

Communication training in natural context settings, such as the classroom, has a number of inherent advantages over training that occurs in more isolated and traditional settings, such as therapy rooms. There are, for example, many more meaningful opportunities to learn appropriate use of new communication forms and functions in natural settings than in contrived ones. This is a crucial advantage for the augmentative communicators, including those using manual signing, who require an extensive number of opportunities to develop and refine emerging communication skills. Furthermore, the quality of the communicative exchange in natural settings is frequently different in contrived ones. Communication that occurs in natural settings is generally more meaningful, having true purposes and consequences for the interactants. In contrived settings, the purposes of the communicative exchange are more often related to development of a particular skill rather than meeting a real need and, thus, have less meaning and importance to the augmentative communicator. Training that occurs in natural contexts also provides multiple opportunities for reinforcement, a factor that should encourage skill maintenance and generalization.

The MLT model has another feature that renders it suitable and appropriate for use with augmentative communicators, namely the essential role of the communication instructor or partner. This approach to training requires that the communication instructor (e.g., teacher, aide, or parent) make decisions regarding specific communicative objectives (i.e., the desired skill), as well as when and under what circumstances teaching will occur. Because the MLT model advocates communication training within the context of naturally occurring events and activities by persons typically present, there is an increased likelihood that opportunities to display and be reinforced for appropriate communication behaviors will continue to be presented by these persons even after the individual has mastered the new skill. Obviously, this would have a positive effect on the retention of the newly learned behavior. However, one must not forget that the MLT model, like other strategies that are implemented in naturalistic settings, is wholly dependent on the ability of the communication partners to set up the conditions necessary for the development of specific communication skills by nonspeaking individuals. Therefore, it is essential that the training received by communication partners effectively teach them how to employ milieu teaching strategies.

REFERENCES

Alpert, C. 1980. Procedures for determining the optimal nonspeech mode with the autistic child. In *Nonspeech language and communication: Analysis and intervention*, ed. R. L. Schiefelbusch, 389–420. Baltimore: University Park Press.

Anthony, D. 1971. *Seeing Essential English, Vols. 1 and 2,* Anaheim, CA: Educational Services Division, Anaheim Union School District.

Balick, S. Spiegel, D., and Green, G. 1976. Mime in language therapy and clinician training. *Archives of Physical Medicine and Rehabilitation* 57:35–38.

Barrera, R. D., Lobato-Barrera, D., and Sulzer-Azaroff, B. A. 1980. A simultaneous treatment comparison of three expressive language training programs with a mute autistic child. *Journal of Autism and Developmental Disabilities* 10:21–37.

Bates, E., Benigni, L., Bretherton, I., Camaioni, L., and Volterra, V. 1979. *The emergence of symbols: Communication and cognition in infancy.* New York: Academic Press.

Bellugi, U., and Klima, E. 1975. Aspects of sign language and its structure. In *The role of speech in language*, ed. J. K. Kavanaugh and J. E. Cutting. Cambridge, MA: MIT Press.

Beukelman, D., and Yorkston, K. 1982. Communication interaction of adult communication augmentation system use. *Topics in Language Disorders* 2(2):39–53.

Blackstone, S. 1986. Training strategies. In *Augmentative communication: An introduction*, ed. S. Blackstone. Rockville, MD: American Speech-Language-Hearing Association.

Bonvillian, J., and Nelson, K. E. 1978. Development of sign language in autistic children and other language-handicapped individuals. In *Understanding language through sign language research*, ed. P. Siple, 187–209. New York: Academic Press.

Bornstein, H., and Hamilton, L. 1978. Signed English. In *Ways and means*, ed. T. Tebbs. Houndmills, Basingstroke, Hampshire: Globe Education.

Bornstein, H., and Jordan, I. K. 1984. *Functional signs: A new approach from simple to complex.* Baltimore: University Park Press.

Bornstein, H., Saulnier, K. L., and Hamilton, L. 1983. *The comprehensive Signed English dictionary.* Washington, DC: Gallaudet University Press.

Bottdorf, L., and DePape, D. 1982. Initiating systems for severely speech impaired persons. *Topics in Language Disorders* 2:55–71.

Brady, E., and Smouse, A. A. 1978. A simultaneous comparison of three methods for language training with an autistic child: An experimental single case analysis. *Journal of Autism and Developmental Disabilities* 8:271–279.

Bricker, W. A., and Bricker, D. D. 1970. A program of language training for the severely language handicapped child. *Exceptional Children* 1:101–110.

Browder, D. M., Morris, W. W., and Snell, M. E. 1981. Using time delay to teach manual signs to a severely retarded student. *Education and Training of the Mentally Retarded* 7:252–258.

Brown, R. 1978. Why are signed languages easier to learn than spoken languages? Part 2. *Bulletin of the American Academy of Arts and Sciences* 32:25–44.

Bruner, J. S. 1977. Early social interaction and language acquisition. In *Studies in mother-infant interaction,* ed. H. R. Shaffer. New York: Academic Press.

———. 1978. Prelinguistic requisites of speech. In *Recent advances in the psychology of language: Language development and mother-child interaction,* ed. R. N. Campbell and P. T. Smith. New York: Plenum.

Bryen, D. N., and Joyce, D. G. 1985. Language intervention with the severely handicapped: A decade of research. *The Journal of Special Education* 19: 7–39.

Calculator, S., and Luchko, C. 1983. Evaluating the effectiveness of a communication board training program. *Journal of Speech and Hearing Disorders* 48:185–191.

Carlson, F. 1982. *Alternate methods of communication.* Danville, IL: Interstate Printers and Publishers.

Carr, E. G. 1979. Teaching autistic children to use sign language: Some research issues. *Journal of Autism and Developmental Disorders* 9:345–359.

———. 1981. Sign language. In *Teaching developmentally delayed children: The ME book,* ed. O. I. Lovaas, 153–161. Baltimore: University Park Press.

Carr, E. G., Binkoff, J. A., Kologinsky, E., and Eddy, M. 1978. Acquisition of sign language by autistic children I: Expressive labeling. *Journal of Applied Behavior Analysis* 11:489–501.

Carr, E. G., and Dores, P. A. 1981. Patterns of language acquisition following simultaneous communication with autistic children. *Analysis and Intervention in Developmental Disabilities* 1:347–361.

Cavallaro, C. C. 1983. Language intervention in nat-

ural settings. *Teaching Exceptional Children* 16(1): 65–70.

Chomsky, C. 1986. Analytic study of the Tadoma method: Language abilities of three deaf-blind subjects. *Journal of Speech and Hearing Research* 29: 332–347.

Cirrin, F. M., and Rowland, C. M. 1985. Communicative assessment of nonverbal youths with severe, profound mental retardation. *Mental Retardation* 23:52–62.

Cohen, M. 1981. Development of language behavior in an autistic child using total communication. *Exceptional Children* 27:379–381.

Creedon, M. 1973. *Language development in nonverbal autistic children using a simultaneous communication system.* Paper presented at the Society for Research in Child Development Annual Meeting, Philadelphia.

Creekmore, N. 1982. Use of sign alone and sign plus speech in language training of nonverbal autistic children. *Journal of the Association for Severely Handicapped* 6:45–55.

Daniloff, J., and Lloyd, L. L. 1983. Amer-Ind transparency. *Journal of Speech and Hearing Disorders* 48: 103–110.

Daniloff, J., and Shafer, A. 1981. A gestural communication program for severely and profoundly handicapped children. *Language Speech and Hearing Services in Schools* 12:258–267.

Daniloff, J., and Vergera, D. 1984. Comparison between the motoric constraints for Amer-Ind and ASL sign formation. *Journal of Speech and Hearing Research* 27:76–88.

Dennis, R., Reichle, J., Williams, W., and Vogelsberg, T. 1982. Motoric consideration involved in the selection of signs to teach handicapped learners. *Journal of the Association for the Severely Handicapped* 7:20–32.

Doherty, J. E. 1985. The effects of sign characteristics on sign acquisition and retention: An integrative review of the literature. *Augmentative and Alternative Communication* 1:108–121.

———. 1986. The effects of translucency and handshape difficulty on sign acquisition by preschool children. *Dissertation Abstracts International* 46:3317A.

Doherty, J. E., Karlan, G. R., and Lloyd, L. L. 1982. Establishing the transparency of two gestural systems. *ASHA* (Abstract) 24:834.

Doherty, J. E., and Lloyd, L. L. 1983. The effects of production mode, translucency and manuality on sign acquisition by retarded adults. Paper presented at the convention of the American Association on Mental Deficiency, Minneapolis.

Farrier, L. D., Yorkston, K. M., Marriner, N. A., and Buekelman, D. R. 1985. Conversational control in nonimpaired speakers using an augmentative communication system. *Augmentative and Alternative Communication* 1:65–73.

Fogel, A. 1982. Social play, positive affect, and coping skills in the first 6 months of life. *Topics in Early Childhood Special Education* 2:53–65.

Fristoe, M., and Lloyd, L. L. 1979a. Nonspeech communication. In *Handbook of mental deficiency: Psychological therapy and research*, ed. N. R. Ellis. New York: Lawrence Erlbaum Associates.

———. 1979b. Signs used in manual communication training with persons having severe communication impairment. *AAESPH Review* 4(4):364–373.

———. 1980. Planning an initial expressive sign lexicon for persons with severe communication impairment. *Journal of Speech and Hearing Disorders* 45(2):170–180.

Goossens', C. A. 1984. The relative iconicity and learnability of verb referents differentially represented by manual signs, Blissymbols, and Rebus symbols: An investigation with moderately retarded individuals. *Dissertation Abstracts International* 45:809A.

Griffith, P. L. 1980. The influence of iconicity and chronological similarity on sign learning in mentally retarded persons. *Dissertation Abstracts International* 40:5398A.

Griffith, P. L., and Robinson, J. H. 1981. A comparative and normative study of the iconicity of signs rated by three groups. *American Annals of the Deaf* 126:440–449.

Griffith, P. E., Robinson, J. H., and Panagos, J. H. 1983. Tactile iconicity: Signs rated for use with deaf-blind children. *Journal of the Association for the Severely Handicapped* 8:26–38.

Grinnel, M., Detamore, K., and Lippke, B. 1976. Sign it successful: Manual English encourages expressive communication. *Teaching Exceptional Children* 43:123–124.

Guess, D., Keogh, W., and Sailor, W. 1978. Generalization of speech and language behavior: Measurement and training tactics. In *Bases of language intervention*, ed. R. L. Schiefelbusch. Baltimore: University Park Press.

Guess, D., Sailor, W., and Baer, D. M. 1977. A behavioral-remedial approach to language training for the severely handicapped. In *Educational programming for the severely and profoundly handicapped*, eds. E. Sontag, J. Smith, and N. Certo. Reston, VA: Division on Mental Retardation, Council for Exceptional Children.

Gustason, G., Pfetzing, D., and Zawolkow, E. 1972. *Signing Exact English*. Rossmoor, CA: Modern Signs Press.

Hall, R. V., and Broden, M. 1977. Helping teachers and parents to modify the behavior of their retarded and behavior-disordered children. In *Research to practice in mental retardation: Education and*

training, Vol. II, ed. P. Mittler. International Association for the Study of Mental Deficiency.

Hall, S. M., and Talkington, L. 1970. Learning by doing: A unit approach for deaf-retarded. Austin, TX: Austin State School. *Mental Retardation Research Series*, No. 18.

Halle, J. W. 1982. Teaching functional language to the handicapped: An integrative model of natural environment teaching techniques. *Journal of the Association for the Severely Handicapped* 7(4):29–37.

———. 1987. Teaching language in the natural environment: An analysis of spontaneity. *Journal of the Association for Persons with Severe Handicaps* 12:28–37.

Halle, J. W., Baer, D. M., and Spradlin, J. E. 1981. Teachers' generalized use of delay as a stimulus control procedure to increase language use in handicapped children. *Journal of Applied Behavior Analysis* 14:389–409.

Halle, J. W., Marshall, A. M., and Spradlin, J. E. 1979. Time delay: A technique to increase language use and facilitate generalization in retarded children. *Journal of Applied Behavior Analysis* 12:431–439.

Hamre-Nietupski, S., Stoll, A., Holtz, K., Fullerton, P., Flottum-Ryan, M., and Brown, L. 1977. Curricular strategies for teaching selected nonverbal communication skills to verbal and nonverbal severely handicapped students. In *Curricular strategies for teaching functional object use, nonverbal communication and problem solving and mealtime skills to severely handicapped students*. Vol. VII, Part 1, eds. L. Brown, J. Nietupski, S. Lyon, S. Hamre-Nietupski, T. Crowner, and L. Gruenewals. Madison, WI: University of Wisconsin-Madison and Madison Metropolitan School District.

Hart, B. 1985. Naturalistic language training techniques. In *Teaching functional language; Generalization and maintenance of language skills*, eds. S. F. Warren and A. K. Rogers-Warren. Baltimore: University Park Press.

Hart, B., and Risley, T. R. 1975. Incidental teaching of language in the preschool. *Journal of Applied Behavior Analysis* 8:411–420.

Hart, B., and Rogers-Warren, A. 1978. A milieu approach to language teaching. In *Language intervention strategies*, ed. R. L. Schiefelbusch. Baltimore: University Park Press.

Hobson, P., and Duncan, P. 1979. Sign learning and profoundly retarded people. *Mental Retardation* 17:33–37.

Hoffmeister, R. J., and Farmer, A. 1972. Development of manual sign language in mentally retarded individuals. *Journal of Rehabilitation of the Deaf* 6:19–26.

Holland, A. 1975. Language therapy for children: Some thoughts on context and content. *Journal of Speech and Hearing Disorders* 40:514–523.

Jensema, C. K. 1981. A review of communication systems used by deaf-blind people, Part 1. *Deaf-Blind News*, October, 720–725.

Kaiser, A. P., Alpert, C. L., and Warren, S. F. 1987. Teaching functional language: Strategies for intervention. In *Systematic instruction of persons with severe handicaps, 3rd ed.*, ed. M. Snell, 247–272. Columbus, OH: Charles E. Merrill.

Karlan, G. R., and Fiocca, G. A. 1982. Generally understood gestures: An approach to communication for mentally retarded language impaired individuals. Unpublished manuscript, Purdue University, West Lafayette, IN.

Karlan, G. R., and Lloyd, L. L. 1983. Considerations in the planning of communication intervention: I. Selecting a lexicon. *Journal of the Association for the Severely Handicapped* 8:13–25.

———. 1988a. Considerations in the planning of communication intervention: II. Manual sign and gestural systems for representing the lexicon. Unpublished manuscript, Purdue University, West Lafayette, IN.

———. 1988b. Translucency of 910 Signed English signs. Unpublished manuscript, Purdue University, West Lafayette, IN.

Kaye, K. 1977. Toward the origin of dialogue. In *Studies in mother-infant interaction*, ed. H. R. Shaffer. New York: Academic Press.

Kazdin, A. E. 1977. Assessing the clinical or applied importance of behavior change through social validation. *Behavior Modification* 1:427–451.

Keough, W. J., and Reichle, J. 1985. Communication intervention for the "difficult-to-teach" severely handicapped. In *Teaching functional language*, eds. S. F. Warren and A. K. Rogers-Warren. Austin, TX: Pro-Ed.

Kiernan, C. 1977. Alternatives to speech: A review of research on manual and other forms of communication with the mentally handicapped and other noncommunicating populations. *British Journal of Mental Subnormality* 23:6–28.

Kiernan, C., and Bowler, D. M. 1980. *Factors affecting the acquisition of manual communication by the mentally handicapped*. Final report to the Medical Research Council, London, England.

Kleinert, H. L., and Gast, D. L. 1982. Teaching a multihandicapped adult manual signs using a constant time delay procedure. *Journal of the Association for the Severely Handicapped* 6(4):25–32.

Kohl, F. L. 1981. Effects of motoric requirements on the acquisition of manual sign responses by severely handicapped students. *American Journal of Mental Deficiency* 85:396–403.

Konstantareas, M. M., Oxman, J., and Webster, C. D. 1978. Iconicity: Effects on the acquisition of sign language by autistic and other severely dysfunctional children. In *Understanding language through sign language research*, ed. P. Siple, 213–235. New York: Academic Press.

Kopchick, G. A., and Lloyd, L. L. 1976. Total communication programming for the severely language impaired. In *Communication assessment and intervention strategies*, ed. L. Lloyd. Baltimore: University Park Press.

Kratt, A. W. 1985. *Communication interaction between aided and natural speakers: An IPCAS study report*. Toronto: Canadian Rehabilitation Council.

Kuczaj, S. A. 1988. The symbolic nature of words in young children. In *Language perspectives: Acquisition, retardation and intervention*, ed. R. L. Schiefelbusch and L. L. Lloyd, 23–33. Austin, TX: Pro-Ed.

Lahey, M., and Bloom, L. 1977. Planning a first lexicon: Which words to teach first. *Journal of Speech and Hearing Disorders* 42:340–349.

Layton, T. L., and Helmer, S. H. 1981. Initial language program for autistic and developmentally disordered children. Paper presented at the meeting of the American Association on Mental Deficiency, Detroit.

Leslie, C. M., Layton, T. L., and Helmer, S. H. 1982. A critical review pertaining to sign language acquisition in autistic children. Paper presented at the Fifteenth Annual Gatlinburg Conference on Research in Mental Retardation and Developmental Disabilities, Gatlinburg, TN.

Levett, L. M. 1969. A method of communication for nonspeaking severely subnormal children. *British Journal of Disorders of Communication* 4:64–66.

———. 1971. A method of communication for nonspeaking severely subnormal children—Trial results. *British Journal of Disorders of Communication* 6:125–128.

Light, J., Collier, B., and Parnes, P. 1985a. Communication interaction between young nonspeaking physically disabled children and their primary caregivers: Part I—Discourse patterns. *Augmentative and Alternative Communication* 1:74–83.

———. 1985b. Communication interaction between young nonspeaking physically disabled children and their primary caregivers: Part II—Communicative function. *Augmentative and Alternative Communication*, 1:98–107.

Lloyd, L. L., and Daniloff, J. 1983. Issues in using Amer-Ind code with retarded persons. In *Pragmatic assessment and intervention issues in language*, eds. T. M. Gallagher and C. A. Prutting. San Diego: College Hill Press.

Lloyd, L. L., and Fristoe, M. 1978. Iconicity of signs: Evidence in vocabularies used with severely impaired individuals in contrast with American Sign Language in general. Paper presented at the Eleventh Annual Gatlinburg Conference on Research in Mental Retardation, Gatlinburg, TN.

Lloyd, L. L., and Karlan, G. R. 1984. Nonspeech

communication symbols and systems: Where have we been and where are we going? *Journal of Mental Deficiency Research* 28:3–20.

Lobato, D., Barrera, R. A., and Feldman, R. S. 1981. Sensorimotor functioning and prelinguistic communication of severely and profoundly retarded individuals. *American Journal of Mental Deficiency* 85:489–496.

Lovaas, O. I., and Schreibman, L. 1971. Stimulus overselectivity of autistic children in a two-stimulus situation. *Behavior Research & Therapy* 9:305–310.

Luftig, R. L., Page, J. L., and Lloyd, L. L. 1983. Ratings of translucency in manual signs as a predictor of sign learnability. *Journal of Childhood Communication Disorders* 6:117–134.

McDade, H. L., Simpson, M. A., and Booth, C. 1980. The use of sign language with handicapped, normal-hearing infants. *Journal of Childhood Communication Disorders* 4:82–89.

Miller, J., and Allaire, J. 1987. Augmentative communication. In *Systematic instruction of persons with severe handicaps*, 3rd ed., ed. M. E. Snell. Columbus: Charles E. Merrill.

Moerk, E. 1975. Verbal interactions between children and their mothers during the preschool years. *Developmental Psychology* 11:788–795.

Nelson, K. 1973. Structure and strategy in learning to talk. *Monographs of the Society for Research in Child Development* 38:1–2, Serial No. 149.

Nietupski, J., and Hamre-Nietupski, S. 1979. Teaching auxiliary communication skills to severely handicapped students. *AAESPH Review* 4:107–124.

Oliver, C. B., and Halle, J. W. 1982. Language training in the everyday environment: Teaching functional sign use to a retarded child. *Journal of the Association for the Severely Handicapped* 8:50–63.

Page, J. L. 1985. Relative translucency of ASL signs representing three semantic classes. *Journal of Speech and Hearing Disorders* 50:241–247.

Pennington, G., Karlan, G. R., and Lloyd, L. L. 1986. Considerations in selection of sign systems and initial lexica. In *Sensory impairments in mentally handicapped people*, ed. D. Ellis, 383–407. San Diego: College Hill Press.

Reed, C. M., Durlach, N. I., and Braida, L. D. 1982. Research on tactile communication of speech: A review. *ASHA Monographs*, 20.

Reichle, J., Williams, W., and Ryan, S. 1981. Selecting signs for the formulation of an augmentative communicative modality. *Journal of the Association for the Severely Handicapped* 6:48–56.

Risley, T., and Wolf, M. 1967. Establishing functional speech in echolalic children. *Behavioral Research and Therapy* 5:73–88.

Rogers-Warren, A., and Warren, S. F. 1980. Mands for verbalization: Facilitating display of newly trained language in children. *Behavior Modification* 4:361–382.

Rusch, J. C., and Karlan, G. R. 1983. Nonspeech communication. In *Handbook of mental retardation*, eds. J. L. Matson and J. A. Mulick. New York: Pergamon Press.

Sameroff, A. J., and Harris-Fiese, B. 1988. The context of language development. In *Language perspectives: Acquisition, retardation and intervention*, eds. R. L. Schiefelbusch and L. L. Lloyd, 3–20. Austin, TX: Pro-Ed.

Sanders, D. A. 1976. A model for communication. In *Communication assessment and intervention strategies*, ed. L. L. Lloyd. Baltimore: University Park Press.

Schaeffer, B. 1980a. Spontaneous language through signed speech. In *Nonspeech language and communication: Analysis and intervention*, ed. R. L. Schiefelbusch. Baltimore: University Park Press.

Schaeffer, B. 1980b. Teaching signed speech to nonverbal children: Theory and method. *Sign Language Studies* 26:29–63.

Schiefelbusch, R. L. 1988. Introduction. In *Language perspectives: Acquisition, retardation and intervention*, eds. R. L. Schiefelbusch and L. L. Lloyd, xi–xviii. Austin, TX: Pro-Ed.

Skelly, M. 1979. *Amer-Ind gestural code: A simplified communication system based on Universal Hand Talk*. New York: Elsevier North Holland.

Skelly, M., Schinsky, L., Smith, R., Donaldson, R., and Griffin, J. 1975. American Indian Sign: A gestural communication system for the speechless. *Archives of Physical Medicine and Rehabilitation* 56:156–160.

Smeets, P., and Striefel, S. 1976. Acquisition and cross-modal generalization of receptive and expressive sign skills in a retarded deaf girl. *American Journal on Mental Deficiency* 20:197–205.

Snell, M. E., and Gast, D. L. 1981. Applying time delay procedure to the instruction of the severely handicapped. *Journal of the Association for the Severely Handicapped* 6:3–14.

Stremel-Campbell, K., Cantrell, D., and Halle, J. 1977. Manual signing as a language system and as a speech initiator for the nonverbal severely handicapped student. In *Exceptional programming for the severely and profoundly handicapped*, eds. E. Sontag, J. Smith, and N. Certo. Reston, VA: Division of Mental Retardation, Council for Exceptional Children.

Striefel, S., Bryan, K., and Aiken, D. 1974. Transfer of stimulus control from motor to verbal stimuli. *Journal of Applied Behavior Analysis* 7:123–135.

Thorley, B. J., Watkins, E., and Binepal, T. 1984. Teaching a severely intellectually retarded deaf-blind child to use Braille stimuli: A two-year project. Unpublished manuscript.

Thrasher, K. A. 1985. Effects of iconicity, taction, and

training modality on the initial acquisition of manual signs by the severely and profoundly mentally retarded. *Dissertation Abstracts International* 45:2344B.

Topper, S. T. 1975. Gesture language for a nonverbal severely retarded male. *Mental Retardation* 13: 30–31.

Vanderheiden, G. C., and Lloyd, L. L. 1986. Communication systems and their components. In *Augmentative communication: An introduction*, ed. S. Blackstone, 49–162. Rockville, MD: American Speech-Language-Hearing Association.

Vivian, R. 1966. The Tadoma method: A tactual approach to speech and speechreading. *Volta Review* 68:733–737.

Walker, M. 1973. An experimental evaluation of the success of a system of communication for the deaf mentally handicapped. Master's thesis, University of London, London, England.

Warren, S. F., and Kaiser, A. P. 1986. Incidental language teaching: A critical review. *Journal of Speech and Hearing Disorders* 51:291–299.

Warren, S. F., McQuarter, R. J., and Rogers-Warren, A. K. 1984. The effects of mand and models on the speech of unresponsive socially isolate children. *Journal of Speech and Hearing Disorders* 47: 42–52.

Wilber, R. B. 1976. The linguistics of manual sign systems. In *Communication assessment and intervention strategies*, ed. L. L. Lloyd. Baltimore: University Park Press.

Wilbur, R. B. 1979. *American Sign Language and sign systems*. Baltimore: University Park Press.

Williams, S. G., Lombardino, L. J., McDonald, J. D., and Owens, R. E. 1982. Total communication: Clinical report on a parent-based language training program. *Education and Training of the Mentally Retarded* 10:293–298.

Wolf, M. M. 1978. Social validity: The case for subjective measurement, or how applied behavior analysis is finding its heart. *Journal of Applied Behavior Analysis* 11:203–214.

Yoder, D. E. 1980. Communication systems for nonspeech children. *New Directions for Exceptional Children* 2:63–78.

Yorkston, K., and Karlan, G. R. 1986. Assessment. In *Augmentative communication: An introduction*, ed. S. Blackstone, 163–196. Rockville, MD: American Speech-Language-Hearing Association.

Some Afterwords

Harry Bornstein

As editor of this volume, I have refrained from imposing my point of view on any of its contributors. Now, however, I will take the liberty of briefly summing up the book's contents and offering some personal observations. Needless to say, some of my fellow contributors will not agree with me.

Stedt and Moores have thoroughly and, I think, brilliantly documented how opposing views of manual communication have persisted throughout the educational history of the deaf in the United States. Indeed, the fact that some current methodologies were formed apparently without awareness of historical precedent suggests that unmet needs and differing motives in this area are deep, persistent, and unlikely to go away.

Allen and Karchmer describe, in contemporary terms, other persistent, ongoing facts of deaf education. Deaf children are educated in a variety of settings. These are strikingly different communication environments. As one example, Allen and Karchmer show how moderate loss of hearing is associated with intelligible speech

and these, in turn, are associated with being integrated with hearing students. An integrated class is simply not the same communication environment as a residential class made up of students with mostly profound losses. However, as is virtually always the case in this field, teachers also report that some students who have profound losses also have very intelligible speech. Conversely, some students with moderate losses do not have intelligible speech. A fixed, unchanging communication method is not likely to be optimal for all students in almost any single setting. Still another point should be made about the different settings in which deaf children find themselves: These settings are not random or capricious. They reflect some amalgam of parental desires, geographic and social variation, and an economic allocation of resources for a very low-incidence group of children.

In an ideal world, parents would learn of their child's hearing impairment as soon as it exists. They then should be able to turn to completely knowledgeable and uninvested professionals, who would be able to describe all the known options and the chances of success associated with each of them. All the options should be equally available to the parents. The parents should then be able to choose the best course of action for their child and implement that course of action successfully. Unfortunately, reality is very, very different from this ideal picture. Some of the reasons are explained below.

The Need for Action

Parents must communicate with their child. The process cannot be put off. Ninety-one percent of deaf children lose their hearing by one year of age, 99 percent before they are of school age. Early on, parents must make choices about the form of communication they will use with their child. The communication choice they make may be (a) informed or uninformed, (b) conscious or unconscious, and/or (c) constant or changing. But communication must happen. By now it should be obvious that every communication technique currently available not only has its problems, but also yields a limited degree of success. Parenthetically, it is an interesting commentary that those who work with children who hear but have other severe learning problems are the ones who have, far and away, paid the most attention to the problems of initial vocabulary, sign learnability, and transfer to other settings.

Teachers also must communicate with their students. The technique may be determined and prescribed by the school or chosen by the teacher. When the technique is determined by the school, the prescribed procedures may be loosely or tightly described and monitored. The data presented in chapter 4 suggest that tight monitoring by school authorities may be the exception, rather than the rule, especially given the variety of sources from which teachers learn manual communication (see tables 17 and 18, chapter 3).

Finally, students must communicate with one another as well as with adults. There is probably not a school in the United States where the language that students use with one another does not vary in some systematic way from that used by the teacher in the classroom. That variation may be greater with deaf students. Children do not consciously model language for one another. Further, it is not likely that they will use those features of manual systems that provide redundant information but that, at the same time, increase their signing burden. It would be surprising indeed if some of the efficient features of ASL described by Hoffmeister were not included in children's communication (e.g., not using two signs to represent *two weeks* when one sign is equally clear). Woodward's notion of a PSE continuum certainly provides a valuable conceptual framework for understanding the myriad language forms found in these situations.

None of the communicators (i.e., parents, teachers, or children) in this situation can wait until educators determine which may be the most effective communicative technique to use in a given situation, nor can parents wait until a child reaches school age for the child to learn language from his or her peers. In my opinion, it is unlikely that many parents will allow intermediaries to communicate with their child in a language that they themselves cannot use, nor is it likely that they will defer speech and auditory training.

Emotional Investment in the Chosen Communication Technique

Communicating with a deaf child with any of the techniques described in this book requires sustained effort and practice, except for the approximately 3 percent of parents who may know and choose to use ASL. It is unlikely that most people will make such efforts unless they believe they are doing their best for their child. And parents almost must come to believe, at least for a time, that the way they communicate is best for them and their child. Similarly, I suspect that most teachers also must come to believe that their chosen or school-determined communication technique is most suitable for their students. Sometimes this is achieved by belittling alternative methods. It is one reason that controversy never seems to be absent in this field.

Some unfortunate by-products of emotional investment may follow results that do not live up to expectations. In some cases, parents may have an exaggerated view of their child's very limited language performance or competence in order to sustain their motivation and/or justify past communication choices and actions. The opposite may also happen. Significant accomplishment is denigrated and/or minimized because it falls short of expectations. The communication technique is thus deemed worthless and those who use it can be damned as frauds and incompetents. I do not know what percentage of parents react this way. It may be small, but it is a very painful experience for parents and professionals alike.

Power and Powerlessness

To be unable to communicate is to be almost powerless in contemporary society. Therefore, control over the communication technique is a way of gaining or maintaining power in institutions that serve deaf children and adults (e.g., schools and social service agencies). Thus, in schools that once used strictly oral techniques, the introduction of Total Communication, in effect, severely reduced the power of users of oral techniques. Similarly, the choice of ASL rather than Manual English would render Manual English users less powerful. Make no mistake. Power and the question of who will use it are very much a part of the controversy in this field.

I also believe that nowhere does power or the lack of it play a greater role than in the home. The dominant impression I have gained from visiting the homes of deaf children is that of the anxiety and frustration that parents experience when unable to communicate family attitudes, expectations, desires, feelings, desired conduct, etc., to their children. The ASL bilingual program proposed by Hoffmeister and others calls for parents to cease using their voices and depend on a newly learned language to communicate with their child. I do not think it likely that many parents will be willing and/or able to do this.

Demographics and the Nature of Deafness

About one child in 1,000 has a significant hearing impairment. Further, only 3 percent of these children have deaf parents. Children who are deaf, therefore, are born into a "hearing" world even though a sizable proportion of them will grow up to become a part of the Deaf community (a cultural minority in the United States). To further complicate the picture, those Deaf adults who identify with the Deaf community tend to live in a relatively small number of urban areas that provide them greater employment and social opportunities. I am aware of no other group quite like this, nor does it appear likely that this situation will change in the foreseeable future.

In effect, we can expect that a sizable group of deaf adolescents and adults will continue to communicate with others who share somewhat similar language, feelings, and outlooks on life. It is almost a certainty that there will be some who are likely to feel that the communication techniques adopted by their families and schools were less than optimal for them. And all of the evidence we have indicates that some will be right. Further, many Deaf adults view ASL as a source of pride and a mark of accomplishment, and they desire that it be shared by deaf children. Unfortunately, the parents of 97 percent of these children are part of a different culture and may have other desires for their children. I believe that the tension that arises from these circumstances is virtually inherent in the nature of deafness and never will disappear from this field. As an aside, I would guess that most Americans can find significant fault, real and/or imagined, with much of their own upbringing.

The Limited Effectiveness of the Education of Deaf Children

No communication technique yet devised or "naturally developed" has resulted in average academic achievement or English-language performance for deaf students that approximates the averages of hearing students (Moores 1987). Why have not the Total Communication practices adopted over the last fifteen to twenty years resulted in strikingly better achievement for deaf students? In part, because the recommended techniques are limited tools. However, the education of deaf children does not happen in a vacuum. It is possible that other occurrences in our society may have offset or limited the potential gains that could arise from the use of manual methods.

I believe that at least two aspects of contemporary life have had a negative impact on the effectiveness of manual communication in deaf education. First, mainstream practices arising from the concept of the least restrictive environment have resulted in the placement of deaf children in many settings where there are few, if any, experienced signers. As noted earlier, those Deaf adults who identify with the Deaf community are not evenly spread throughout the United States. Thus, families who avail themselves of local educational facilities, in a great many places, have still less opportunity to learn and use manual communication. This is suggested by the findings in chapter 3 of this volume.

The second problem may be even more serious. It centers on the economic circumstances and changing status of women in our society. Current labor statistics reveal that about half of today's mothers return to full-time employment by the time their child is one year old. This is a great change from the past. If this same proportion holds

for deaf children, the principal source of communication stimulation is largely removed for most of the work day. I doubt that most child care services, when available, are adequate substitutes. Regardless of the social justice of this situation, it probably has a devastating effect on the child's language development.

While I am discussing the family, I would like, once again, to bring to your attention that all the techniques discussed in this book almost surely will work best in a well-functioning, two-parent family unit. Parents need time, energy, motivation, and belief to learn and use the techniques described in this book. However, there isn't any reason to suppose that the families of deaf children differ radically from other American families in incidence of divorce, levels of economic success, education, intelligence, and social sophistication. We have painfully little to offer to many or most single parents, the economically disadvantaged, or those whose native spoken language is not English. As long as this situation obtains or worsens, it appears to me that there will continue to be widespread dissatisfaction with available communication and educational techniques. For the foreseeable future, I would expect continued calls for change. Each new methodology will be "the one" that will solve all the educational problems in this field. Rarely, if ever, will supporters of a new method provide a statement of limitations up front.

Social Behaviors and Technical Skills for Those Who Teach or Parent Deaf Children

In common with many others, I have suggested that teachers and parents of deaf children might profit from social interaction with Deaf adults who use manual communication. The reasoning is simple. This type of interaction should enable parents to broaden and improve their signing skills and to better appreciate the capabilities and attitudes of Deaf adults. Unfortunately, settings and demographics here, too, appear to limit these opportunities. At the highest contact level—in the residential school setting—some 39 percent of the teachers socialize a lot with Deaf adults. In other settings, only about 10 percent of the teachers report a lot of contact (see table 19 in chapter 3). I know of no data on the percentage of parents who socialize with Deaf adults, but I suspect that it is considerably lower than the lowest estimate for teachers. This suggests to me that this avenue of skill improvement is, at best, a very limited resource. Indeed, more than demographics may be involved. There are some who would perceive such suggestions as essentially using Deaf adults. It is hardly the most worthy and durable reason for associating with them. Finally, the array of skills that teachers of the deaf could master is staggering: ASL, Manual English, PSE, Cued Speech, oral and aural techniques, linguistics, audiology, subject matter content, and more.

What do these all add up to? They are all demands made on others. To me, they again signify the frustration that workers in this field feel, which, to be blunt, reflects hopes and expectations that cannot be completely fulfilled. Unfulfilled expectations get expressed as heightened demands.

Research

By now, if not much earlier, the reader must be wondering why these different manual techniques continue to be used to teach language to deaf children. Shouldn't one method be superior to the others? Why has there not been a definitive research study that would determine which is the most effective approach? These are fair questions that deserve straightforward answers, but this won't be a simple task.

Unfortunately, it is extremely difficult and expensive to do adequate research in this area. In more technical terms, the internal and external validity of the kind of research needed to settle this question has been and probably will continue to be exceedingly low. Hence, available evidence is simply unconvincing to most people in the field. Some people would say that even if the internal and external validity of research were high, most of the people in this field would remain unconvinced. In part, this is because different people have different goals. I shall return to this aspect of the problem later.

What I mean when I say that the internal validity of research in this area is low is essentially this: Almost everything that educators are interested in accomplishing with deaf children—better communication, better English, better speech, etc.—is multicaused. The specific manual technique developed or espoused by a given advocate is merely one aspect of an educational program designed to bring about a desired result. Take something seemingly as simple as the often noted superior achievement of those deaf children who have deaf parents. Is the language of the home the sole, or even the principal, reason for the observed difference? What about these other possibilities—Deaf parents probably are very much aware that they may have a deaf child; consequently, they may seek an earlier diagnosis; they may suffer much less emotional trauma; and they provide for a more effective communication environment both within and without the family much earlier than hearing parents. As yet, we do not know the effects, if any, of these factors. The same complications obtain in educational settings.

Obviously, the curriculum, the quality of the instructional staff, the home environment, and other resources all play a role in an educational program. In any given school, educational or language achievement is almost surely affected by all these factors. Therefore, an appropriate experimental design must control or account for these other variables in specific school settings. No current or completed study does so, because the cost is so high and the logistical controls required are extraordinarily difficult to achieve, as the following examples demonstrate.

1. Teachers or users of each communication technique should be equally proficient with their respective techniques.
2. Ideally, students should be randomly assigned to the different communication methods. Failing this, student groups should at least be matched on those variables that are related to the desired outcome.
3. Curriculum should be similar.
4. The attitudes and behaviors of family, friends, etc., all may have some effect on the results and hence should be described and perhaps statistically controlled.

Next, the results must be shown to obtain in other settings and with other children. This is called external validity. Frankly, it is not likely that any method is most effective with all children. The stubborn fact is that we are not able to control the variables so that all children with significant hearing loss will successfully learn the English language in its spoken and/or written form. Nor can we arrange the world so that others will share our values and behavioral patterns. For example, those parents of deaf children who value speech can be expected to be most concerned with that outcome.

There is a way, however, to obtain an objective, empirical description of the language performance of deaf children. It should be possible to design a communication database that, taking advantage of the personal computer, will allow the classroom teacher and others at any given school to monitor and better manage the language development of each child in the class or school. This database should be inclusive, covering all oral and manual communication techniques used in the classroom (e.g., speech, ASL, SEE I, SEE II, Signed English, PSE, Cued Speech, and locally devised systems).

Of equal importance, if possible, is that this information should be obtained for every deaf child in the United States and that it be routinely transmitted to a nonprofit organization for regular, systematic analysis as well as for hypothesis generation and verification. Thus, it would be possible for the first time to conduct longitudinal as well as cross-sectional analyses of language development of large, scientifically drawn samples of deaf children. This would vastly increase the quality and power of communication research in the United States.

The key to such an effort is the design of a language management tool so useful to the classroom teacher, counselor, and school administrator that they will come to use it routinely. It should allow the teacher to monitor and guide his or her language instruction. The information in the database should be formatted to fit the language approach used by the individual teacher. It should contain information on speech, speechreading, aided listening, and any or all forms of manual communication used with the child. The system would probably be menu driven and could provide developmental as well as current information about the student. Class, school, and national averages could also be supplied, if they make the management system more desirable to the teacher. Every effort should be made to make it user friendly and suited to the popular personal computers used in the United States. It must be emphasized again that it is essential that such a system impress both teachers and their schools as an important educational aid. Otherwise, the effort will surely fail.

The design effort should be a collaborative one. Programmers will need a statement of requirements for Cued Speech, SEE I, SEE II, Signed English, PSE, and ASL. A simple procedure for formatting local versions of manual systems must also be devised. Given this information, we can conduct interviews with teachers at a variety of schools to ascertain their perception of their needs. Initially, this information gathering will be iterative, that is, an exchanging and re-exchanging of information with the teachers. When our knowledge has matured, it would be desirable to develop questionnaires to be completed by a large sample of teachers. Subsequently, a series of tryouts of the language monitoring system would be made to see if the needs of both school personnel and national data gatherers were met. This process would be continued until all agreed that the program was what they wanted.

Obviously, it is not known if this proposal is truly feasible. However, it is worth a try. Otherwise, alternative methods of communication will never be compared in a scientifically acceptable manner.

Until information from such a database is available, this type of volume is all that is available. It has offered descriptions of a number of different ways to communicate with deaf students and others who may profit from the use of manual communication. At the very least, readers have been exposed to first-hand accounts of these methods, an historical account of past practices, and some objective descriptions of current ones. What this volume does not offer is a formula or method for choosing among techniques. At best, it may have alerted readers to the types of conditions and skills they may have to develop. Occasionally, the limitations of a given technique are described by the authors. More often than not, limitations will have to be inferred from the presentation of alternate techniques by other writers. We're good at finding the problems and limitations of other people's work.

Finally, this volume has also demonstrated that whatever gains have been achieved so far have been hard-earned. There is no reason to suppose that this will change in the future. However, there is also no reason to suppose that further gains will not continue to be made.

Index